CW01508853

A discouery and playne declaration of sundry subtill practises of the Holy Inquisition of Spayne Certaine speciall examples set aparte by them selues. Set forth in Latine, by Reginaldus Gonsaluius Montanus, and newly translated. (1569)

Vincent Skinner

A discouery and playne declaration of sundry subtill practises of the Holy Inquisition of Spayne
Certaine speciall examples set aparte by them selues
Sanctae Inquisitionis Hispanicae artes aliquot detectae, ac palam traductae.
González de Montes, R. 16th cent.
Skinner, Vincent, d. 1616.
Translation of: Sanctae Inquisitionis Hispanicae artes aliquot detectae, ac palam traductae.
Translator's dedication signed: V. Skinner.
With a final colophon leaf.
Running title reads: A discouery of the Spanish Inquisition.
The plate is captioned: The solemne procession of the triumphant Church of Rome, vsed at the execution of poore Christians.
[15], 99, [5] leaves, folded plate
Imprinted at London : By Iohn Day, dwelling ouer Aldersgate, beneath S. Martines. And are to be solde at his shop vnder the gate, 1569.
STC (2nd ed.) / 11997
English
Reproduction of the original in the Henry E. Huntington Library and Art Gallery

EARLY ENGLISH BOOKS ONLINE

EEBO
Editions

ProQuest

Early English Books Online (EEBO) Editions

Imagine holding history in your hands.

Now you can. Digitally preserved and previously accessible only through libraries as Early English Books Online, this rare material is now available in single print editions. Thousands of books written between 1475 and 1700 and ranging from religion to astronomy, medicine to music, can be delivered to your doorstep in individual volumes of high-quality historical reproductions.

We have been compiling these historic treasures for more than 70 years. Long before such a thing as "digital" even existed, ProQuest founder Eugene Power began the noble task of preserving the British Museum's collection on microfilm. He then sought out other rare and endangered titles, providing unparalleled access to these works and collaborating with the world's top academic institutions to make them widely available for the first time. This project furthers that original vision.

These texts have now made the full journey -- from their original printing-press versions available only in rare-book rooms to online library access to new single volumes made possible by the partnership between artifact preservation and modern printing technology. A portion of the proceeds from every book sold supports the libraries and institutions that made this collection possible, and that still work to preserve these invaluable treasures passed down through time.

This is history, traveling through time since the dawn of printing to your own personal library.

Initial Proquest EEBO Print Editions collections include:

Early Literature

This comprehensive collection begins with the famous Elizabethan Era that saw such literary giants as Chaucer, Shakespeare and Marlowe, as well as the introduction of the sonnet. Traveling through Jacobean and Restoration literature, the highlight of this series is the Pollard and Redgrave 1475-1640 selection of the rarest works from the English Renaissance.

Early Documents of World History

This collection combines early English perspectives on world history with documentation of Parliament records, royal decrees and military documents that reveal the delicate balance of Church and State in early English government. For social historians, almanacs and calendars offer insight into daily life of common citizens. This exhaustively complete series presents a thorough picture of history through the English Civil War.

Historical Almanacs

Historically, almanacs served a variety of purposes from the more practical, such as planting and harvesting crops and plotting nautical routes, to predicting the future through the movements of the stars. This collection provides a wide range of consecutive years of "almanacks" and calendars that depict a vast array of everyday life as it was several hundred years ago.

Early History of Astronomy & Space

Humankind has studied the skies for centuries, seeking to find our place in the universe. Some of the most important discoveries in the field of astronomy were made in these texts recorded by ancient stargazers, but almost as impactful were the perspectives of those who considered their discoveries to be heresy. Any independent astronomer will find this an invaluable collection of titles arguing the truth of the cosmic system.

Early History of Industry & Science

Acting as a kind of historical Wall Street, this collection of industry manuals and records explores the thriving industries of construction; textile, especially wool and linen; salt; livestock; and many more.

Early English Wit, Poetry & Satire

The power of literary device was never more in its prime than during this period of history, where a wide array of political and religious satire mocked the status quo and poetry called humankind to transcend the rigors of daily life through love, God or principle. This series comments on historical patterns of the human condition that are still visible today.

Early English Drama & Theatre

This collection needs no introduction, combining the works of some of the greatest canonical writers of all time, including many plays composed for royalty such as Queen Elizabeth I and King Edward VI. In addition, this series includes history and criticism of drama, as well as examinations of technique.

Early History of Travel & Geography

Offering a fascinating view into the perception of the world during the sixteenth and seventeenth centuries, this collection includes accounts of Columbus's discovery of the Americas and encompasses most of the Age of Discovery, during which Europeans and their descendants intensively explored and mapped the world. This series is a wealth of information from some the most groundbreaking explorers.

Early Fables & Fairy Tales

This series includes many translations, some illustrated, of some of the most well-known mythologies of today, including Aesop's Fables and English fairy tales, as well as many Greek, Latin and even Oriental parables and criticism and interpretation on the subject.

Early Documents of Language & Linguistics

The evolution of English and foreign languages is documented in these original texts studying and recording early philology from the study of a variety of languages including Greek, Latin and Chinese, as well as multilingual volumes, to current slang and obscure words. Translations from Latin, Hebrew and Aramaic, grammar treatises and even dictionaries and guides to translation make this collection rich in cultures from around the world.

Early History of the Law

With extensive collections of land tenure and business law "forms" in Great Britain, this is a comprehensive resource for all kinds of early English legal precedents from feudal to constitutional law, Jewish and Jesuit law, laws about public finance to food supply and forestry, and even "immoral conditions." An abundance of law dictionaries, philosophy and history and criticism completes this series.

Early History of Kings, Queens and Royalty

This collection includes debates on the divine right of kings, royal statutes and proclamations, and political ballads and songs as related to a number of English kings and queens, with notable concentrations on foreign rulers King Louis IX and King Louis XIV of France, and King Philip II of Spain. Writings on ancient rulers and royal tradition focus on Scottish and Roman kings, Cleopatra and the Biblical kings Nebuchadnezzar and Solomon.

Early History of Love, Marriage & Sex

Human relationships intrigued and baffled thinkers and writers well before the postmodern age of psychology and self-help. Now readers can access the insights and intricacies of Anglo-Saxon interactions in sex and love, marriage and politics, and the truth that lies somewhere in between action and thought.

Early History of Medicine, Health & Disease

This series includes fascinating studies on the human brain from as early as the 16th century, as well as early studies on the physiological effects of tobacco use. Anatomy texts, medical treatises and wound treatment are also discussed, revealing the exponential development of medical theory and practice over more than two hundred years.

Early History of Logic, Science and Math

The "hard sciences" developed exponentially during the 16th and 17th centuries, both relying upon centuries of tradition and adding to the foundation of modern application, as is evidenced by this extensive collection. This is a rich collection of practical mathematics as applied to business, carpentry and geography as well as explorations of mathematical instruments and arithmetic; logic and logicians such as Aristotle and Socrates; and a number of scientific disciplines from natural history to physics.

Early History of Military, War and Weaponry

Any professional or amateur student of war will thrill at the untold riches in this collection of war theory and practice in the early Western World. The Age of Discovery and Enlightenment was also a time of great political and religious unrest, revealed in accounts of conflicts such as the Wars of the Roses.

Early History of Food

This collection combines the commercial aspects of food handling, preservation and supply to the more specific aspects of canning and preserving, meat carving, brewing beer and even candy-making with fruits and flowers, with a large resource of cookery and recipe books. Not to be forgotten is a "the great eater of Kent," a study in food habits.

Early History of Religion

From the beginning of recorded history we have looked to the heavens for inspiration and guidance. In these early religious documents, sermons, and pamphlets, we see the spiritual impact on the lives of both royalty and the commoner. We also get insights into a clergy that was growing ever more powerful as a political force. This is one of the world's largest collections of religious works of this type, revealing much about our interpretation of the modern church and spirituality.

Early Social Customs

Social customs, human interaction and leisure are the driving force of any culture. These unique and quirky works give us a glimpse of interesting aspects of day-to-day life as it existed in an earlier time. With books on games, sports, traditions, festivals, and hobbies it is one of the most fascinating collections in the series.

The BiblioLife Network

This project was made possible in part by the BiblioLife Network (BLN), a project aimed at addressing some of the huge challenges facing book preservationists around the world. The BLN includes libraries, library networks, archives, subject matter experts, online communities and library service providers. We believe every book ever published should be available as a high-quality print reproduction; printed on-demand anywhere in the world. This insures the ongoing accessibility of the content and helps generate sustainable revenue for the libraries and organizations that work to preserve these important materials.

The following book is in the "public domain" and represents an authentic reproduction of the text as printed by the original publisher. While we have attempted to accurately maintain the integrity of the original work, there are sometimes problems with the original work or the micro-film from which the books were digitized. This can result in minor errors in reproduction. Possible imperfections include missing and blurred pages, poor pictures, markings and other reproduction issues beyond our control. Because this work is culturally important, we have made it available as part of our commitment to protecting, preserving, and promoting the world's literature.

GUIDE TO FOLD-OUTS MAPS and OVERSIZED IMAGES

The book you are reading was digitized from microfilm captured over the past thirty to forty years. Years after the creation of the original microfilm, the book was converted to digital files and made available in an online database.

In an online database, page images do not need to conform to the size restrictions found in a printed book. When converting these images back into a printed bound book, the page sizes are standardized in ways that maintain the detail of the original. For large images, such as fold-out maps, the original page image is split into two or more pages

Guidelines used to determine how to split the page image follows:

• Some images are split vertically; large images require vertical and horizontal splits.
• For horizontal splits, the content is split left to right.
• For vertical splits, the content is split from top to bottom.
• For both vertical and horizontal splits, the image is processed from top left to bottom right.

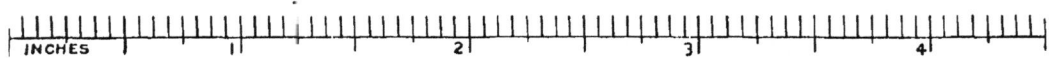

INCHES 1 2 3 4

A DISCOVERY

and playne Declaration of
sundry subtill practises of the
HOLY INQVISITION
of Spayne.

¶ Certaine speciall examples set aparte by
them selues, besides other that are here
and there dispersed in their most conuenient places, wherein a man may see the for-
said practises of the *Inquisition*, as they be
practised and exercised, very liuely described. Set forth in Latine, by *Re-
ginaldus Gonsaluius Montanus*,
and lately Tran-
slated.

Psalm.74.
Arise O Lord, and iudge thine owne cause.

Imprinted at London by

Iohn Day, dwelling ouer Aldersgate,
beneath S. Martines.
And are to be solde at his shop
vnder the gate.
1569.

¶ To the most re-
uerend father in God Mathew
Archbyshop of Caunterbury, Pri-
mate of all England and Metro-
politane.

T the first
impreßiō of
thys Booke
of the Spa-
nish Inqui
sitiō, I was
of opinion
that nei-
ther the re-
port could be neclected, conteining matter
of so great importaūce & feareful conse-
quence, nor the matter be doubted of, being so notorious, not onely by common and
conſtāt fame, but also witneſſed by so many pore & miserable brethrē which haue
choſen rather to abyde the loſſe of their

A.ij.

goods

goods and conntrey, then the fight of fo
horrible executions. But fince vnderftan-
ding that fome malicioufly bent againft
the truth, redier to couer the fhame of
their Idoll (a ftraunge vnnaturall tyraunt) then to prouide and helpe to the
defence and fafety of their owne naturall
Countrey, did not onely at the firft feeke to
fuppreſſe it, but others alfo haue of like
malice bene as impudent to difcredit the
report, as their confederates are cruell in
other partes with difplaied banners to
maintaine and practife the deede, I haue
thought it conuenient at this fecond im-
preſſion to dedicate the fame booke of the
Spaniſhe Inquifition to your grace as
chiefe of a contrary commiſsion. That
confidering the argument and fubiecte
thereof is fuch as not onely appertaineth to
vs of cōmon charity in refpect of our poore
neighbours, but alfo concerneth and tou-
cheth

cheth vs more nerely, the lyke crueltyes
being threatned to all the profeſſours of
the ſame religion, it might, vnder the authority & name of your grace, the rather
be recommended to the reading & conſideration of many, and haue the more credit agaynſt the malicious practiſes of the
aduerſaries. Beſides, that the multitude
of the ignoraunt people in ſo great a per-
plexity and doubt of two religions, and of
the authoryties, and officers, and proce-
dinges in ſetting forwarde the ſame (ſo
contrary the one to the other as is light
and darckenes, cruelty and mercy, warre
and peace) might thereby be occaſioned,
by conference of the one with the other to
diſcerne, who ſeeke their profitable inſtruction, and who ſeeke their owne profit
with the deſtruction of others: who ſeke to
feede their ſoules, and who ſeeke to ſucke
their bloud and to feede themſelues with

the

the loſſe of innocents ſoules: who call them to true liberty, and who would driue them to a ſlauery worſe then Egiptes bondage: and ſo they might chuſe to ply their necks vnder the eaſie yoke of Chriſt, that wheras they might with preſeruation of their goods, and liberty, and liues, by milde diſcipline haue bene brouht into the fold by their true ſheepeherds, they be not by the iuſt iudgement of God, for their ſtifneckednes and reſtiuenes againſt the truth, geuen ouer to moſt cruell and rauenyng Wolues, and ſo by outragious rackinges and moſt horrible tormēts with the ſpoile of their goods, liberty, and liues, be compelled to embrace lies for truth, and be throwne for euer out of the folde of Chriſt into errour and falſe religion to their vtter deſtruction. A thing very lamentable if it ſhould happen and yet very lykely for our vnthankefulnes both ſhortly and ſuddenly

denly to happen, if we repent not, and if it
be not spedely foresene. And therefore the
daunger beyng the greatest that may be,
that they may the better beleue it, and
more carefully prouide for it, it is fit that
the warning and notice thereof proceede
from and vnder the authority & name of
your grace who are placed of God in the
toppe of the tower a chiefe watchman for
these purposes. And thus trusting your
grace for these respectes will pardon
my boldnes J take my leaue with
my harty prayer to God for the
good directiõ of all your coun-
sells and procedings to his
honour and glory.

At Lincolnes Inne the 7. of February.

Your graces to commaund

V. Skinner.

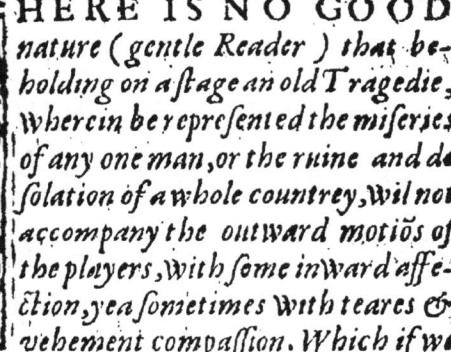HERE IS NO GOOD
nature (*gentle Reader*) that be-
holding on a stage an old Tragedie,
wherein be represented the miseries
of any one man, or the ruine and de
solation of a whole countrey, wil not
accompany the outward motiōs of
the players, with some inward affection, yea sometimes with teares &
vehement compassion. Which if we
doe in a play wherof the matter is many times but inuented, &
howsoeuer it be true, yet happened in Countreys farre of and long
agoe, the parties neither touching vs in kindred, nor the matter in
example: surely the dangerous practises and most horrible executions of the Spanishe Inquisition, declared in this boke, which
now is brought with fire and sword into the low Countreis, the sodaine imprisonment of honest men without processe of lawe, the
pitifull wandring in exile and pouertie of personages sometime
rich and welthy, the wiues hanging on their husbands shoulders,
and the pore banished infants on the mothers brests, the monstru-
ous racking of mē without order of law, the villanous and shameles tormenting of women naked beyond all humanitie, their miserable death without pity or mercy, the most reprochefull triumphing of the popish Sinagoge ouer Christians as ouer Painimes
and Ethnickes, the conquering of subiectes as though they were
enemies, the vnsatiable spoyling of mens goodes to fill the side
paunches of ambitious idle shauelings, the slender quarels piked
against kingdoms and nations, and all this only to hoise vp a pield
polling priest aboue all power and authoritie that is on earth: these
things ought surely much more to moue vs to compassion. Being
no stage play, but a matter fit for any Poet to make a Tragedie
of hereafter, either for that it will be an argument most lamentable, or most incredible to them which shall not haue seene it. The
persons

perſons which ſuffer being our neighbours by their habitation &
dwelling place, our acquaintaunce by entercourſe, our friendes by
long acquaintaunce, of the ſame houſholde of faith, and our very
brethren in Chriſt : And if we weepe when we ſee cruelties ſet
forth in playes, becauſe the like either hath happened to vs hereto-
fore, or herafter may betide vs, then haue we not onely good
cauſe in theſe calamities of our pore brethren to bewayle that is
happened to them, but alſo to feare what will follow vpon vs. For
if we that not .x. yeares ſince felt but a taſte of this yron whippe,
and ſince haue enioyed quietnes and leiſure to ſerue God, thinke
our ſelues ſure and the ſtorme paſſed, and that we be but hearers
and ſeers and haue no partes in this Tragedie, beſides that we
are vncharitable in ſo lightly eſteeming the griefes of other, we
doe alſo fooliſhly and daungerouſly abuſe our ſelues. For who is ſo
ignoraunt of the ſtate of theſe times, that knoweth not or hath
not heard tell of the holy Complote & Conſpiracie agreed on by
the Pope and his Champions for the execution of the counſell of
Trent, and the generall eſtabliſhing of this Inquiſition ? Be-
holde the attempts in Scotland, the procedings in Fraunce, the ex-
ecutions in Flaunders, and if we Engliſhmen haue one of the laſt
partes, let vs be ſure as in Tragedies the laſt partes and Actes be
moſt dolefull, ſo we neuer knew yet what perſecution ment in cõ-
pariſon, to that is ment and threatned vs now. If the Deuils holi-
nes, and his lieuetenaunt generall the Popes maieſtie were a little
moued thẽ, they be now (doubt ye not)enraged, and trãſubſtan-
tiat into furour and horne woodnes, to ſee their reuenues de-
cay, their monaſteries and ſinagoges defaced, their villanies de-
tected, their noble champions ſlaine. And therefore you muſt ſet
before your eyes the Deuil in perſone, and the Pope his chap-
laine and confeſſour gotten vp into the toppe of ſome highe
mountaine, and from thence ſhewing the kingdomes of the earth
to ſuche Princes as will them ſelues fall downe and worſhip, and
therto driue the worlde. Which is ſo farre of from any figuratiue
ſpeche, as it is knowne to be the very Platfourme and foundation
of all theſe broyles and troubles. Be not deceiued (good Reader)
vnderſtande the world, theſe men ſeeke no religion. For how can

¶.j.   *they*

The translatour to the Reader.

they seeke Religion, that thinke there is no God? They seeke the honoure and wealth of the world. If the Gospell would allow ambition, pleasure, profite, the Pope wold haue long since bene a protestāt. If Popery had allowed preaching of the truth, reformation of life, pouertie: popery had bene esteemed (as it is.) heresie, and so persecuted. But the Pope would be thought most holy, and be in deede most mighty, the world is fallen from him: he hath spent all: nought comes in to supply: he hath a great sorte to entertaine, a great sort to rewarde, a great pompe and state to maintaine. Trowe ye these things will be raised of the spoyle of poore protestantes? Nay, be thou sure of it, Papist or Protestant, if thou be riche and hast any fleece, it will be all one. Thy land will vndoe thee: thy goodes will condemne thee. Euen as the

Plut. Sylla. good Citizen of Rome, Q. Aurelius in Syllas time, that was neither of the one side nor the other, but lamented the spoile and misery of his countrey, when as he came into the market place, and heard his name redde among them that were proscribed to death, cried out, O vnhappy man that I am: my house at Alba is the cause of my death, and by and by was openly slaine. If euer there were time like to Syllas, it is now in our dayes, in which hungry neede and vnsatiable couetousnes armed with cruelty will spare nothing: The seruaunt will betray his maister: the friend his friend and acquaintaunce: the bro-

Plut. Sylla. ther shall murther his brother. As in the same time L. Catilina, he that after would haue set fire on the Citie, slew his owne brother, and after prayed Sylla that he might be proscribed. The which being graunted him, he recompenced with killing another, M. Marius one of the contrary faction, and bringing his heade the bloude running along his armes, presented it in the market place to Sylla, and ran to the holy water pot of Apollos temple which was hard by, to wash his hands, a very fit vse of suche holy water. The which story I the rather recite, sparing an infinite sorte of our times, because ye may vnderstande by the way, that Idols and holy water, be anciēt things, such as were before Christes comming, and will be continued by his enemies till

he.

he come againe, and that knowing the Papiſtes religion to be no
better thē thoſe hetheniſh peoples was, their couetouſnes greater,
their nede more, their cruelty farre paſſing not onely all preſent
example, but alſo all written hiſtory, you may duely loke for worſe
then Syllas time if they ouercome : hauing on the other ſide
no fierce or cruell Marius to withſtand them, nor to quarel with
them for the gouernemēt, but a poore flocke of ſeely ſhepe behinde
their ſhepheard afraid of the wolues, halfe yealding, halfe defending their liues : and on their ſides thouſands of deſperate Cati-
lines, that to repaire their decayed ſtates, will not ſpare neyther
to kill their owne brethren, nor to fire their countrey : and hauing at all times, but ſpecially now ſuche a Sylla, vnder whoſe
bāner they fight, as the old Sylla may in reſpeſt of this, be both
forgeuē & forgottē. Take heede, we haue now to our holy Father
a Frier, no ſecular prieſt, but a reguler Helhound, who though he
think it no robbery nor ſhame to be equall in pompe with his pre-
deceſſours, and in malice with the deuill his father : yet hath he
vouched ſafe to take vpon him the ſhape of a mã, and goeth (they
ſay) on foote, and maketh his tenauntes the ſtewes keepe in like
good huſwiues, (which is no ſmall reformation), and doeth good
deedes at home, and worketh wonders (forſoth) whiles he vndo-
eth all abrode, and openeth ſuche a gappe for the great Seigneure
the Turke, as neuer was yet made. But what will not theſe fellowes doe to reuenge their fall? And what ought not we rather to
endure, then to admit theſe ſpirituall tyrants? who would not rather be conquered of a mighty prince and honorable (in compariſon) then of a villaine bankrupt prieſt? who hath for theſe. viij.
or. ix. hundreth yeares occupied the whole world of œrvlite, and
now he ſhould come to accompt, killeth his creditours. A miſerable choice, but yet a ready choice. For the Turke contenteth him
ſelfe with honour and tribute permitting religion: The Pope, no
honour will ſatiſſie him, no riches ſuffice him, no bloude aſſwage
him: neither the deathe of the liuing, nor the ſoules of the deade
will content him. Whoſe very name ſhould not be ſpoken of without Surreuerence and great cōtempt, for the baſenes and vile-

nes of his counterfait ſtate, were he not ſo iuſtly to be hated and abhorred as the great abuſer and very vndoubted Antichriſte of the world, and ſworne enemy of God and man. The cruell and tyrannicall outrages of whoſe Inquiſitoures founded and eſtabliſhed by the Deuill and this Antichriſt, if we conferre with the milde procedings and diſcipline of Commiſſioners appoynted by God and his annoynted, we ſhal thereby ſee euidently by the heauenly iudgement and ſentence of wiſe Salomon, to which mother the liue childe appertaineth. To the Romiſh whore, who (in deſpite that ſhe can not poſſeſſe the pore infants that belong not to her, to ſmother them ſleping with the huge and filthy body of her traditions and ceremonies) ſeketh by al meanes poſſible to deuide and mangle them : or to the naturall and pitifull mother the true Church of the faithfull, whoſe fathers and miniſters (knowing of whoſe ſpirite they are) ſeeke with al gentlenes to call home the loſt ones, and watchfully to noriſh them. Whoſe prince imitating the peaceable raigne of Salomon, hath not ſo much as executed the falſe Prophets, not killed the wolues, not deſtroyed the foxes. Onely they are tied vp ſhort, which though it be no ſuche ſurety for the little ones as worldly wiſdome doth require, and neceſſitie, long ſince hath cried out for, yet is it to them no ſmall griefe to ſee the Lambes feede before their eyes, and the poreſt ſhepherds leaſt whelpe baying at them: whileſt they in the middeſt of their gluttony and dronkennes, houle for hunger of their brethrens fleſhe, and thirſtines of their bloude, and pine for very enuy of the proceding of Gods word. If the pore ignoraunt people, will but compare the impriſonmentes of the perſecuted proteſtantes, with the reſtraintes of the brideled Papiſts, their famine with theſe mens fatnes, their tonges fettered with Iron torments, with the libertie of railing that our men haue and vſe, ſeditiouſly againſt their prince, and blaſphemouſly againſt God, their moſt miſerable and ſtraunge kindes of deathes, with our mennes liuing and liking, they ſhall eaſely knowe the tree and the perſonnes by the fruite. Wherfore (good Reader) hauing ſo euident markes of their wolniſhe and rauening natures, and ſo good notice of their bloudy cõſpiracie,

The translatour to the Reader.

ſpiracy and ſo waying the very true cauſe of al theſe troubles and
warres that be in Chriſtendome, and therto conferring the preſent executions and ſlaughters, euen in our neighbours houſe, the
fire whereof may ſone imbrace our owne, let vs be ſtirred vppe to
pray for their deliueraunce, and that it wold pleaſe God, to turne
from vs the ſame iuſtly deſerued plague for our vnthankefulnes.
Let vs be ſtrong in faith, and couragious in deede, to repell theſe
common enemies from our countrey when ſo euer they ſhall offer
that they haue ſo long determined. For my part my meaning in
this my trauayle hath bene onely to make thee ſpedely vnderſtand
of ſo great and ſo imminent a perill: referring thee for the
reſidue of the outrages and crueltias not declared in
this booke to that good worke the booke of Martyrs, wherein thou mayſt haue a moſt plentifull and notable Hiſtory of the like
matter and argu-
ment.

(※)

❧ The speciall matters contayned
in this treatise, placed orderly in such
wise as the Inquisitours proceede in
their Courte.

1. THe ordinary maner and forme commonly vsed of the Inquisitours, as wel in citing as apprehending such persons, as are accused in their Consistory.

2. The Sequestration of their goodes, commonly called the *Sequester*.

3. The seuerall dayes of hearing.

4. The *publication* of the witnesses, as they terme it.

5. The Confutation of the same.

6. The iudgementes and condemnations to the rack, and the maner of execution thereof.

7. Other practises of the Inquisition.

8. Certaine other more secrete then the rest.

9. How the prisoners be entreated concerning the whole maner of their diet.

10. The visitation of the prisons.

11. The Acte contayning the *Publication* of the sentences.

Whereunto are annexed certaine other discourses vpon diuers Christian Martyrs, who taking their deathes like constant Christians, for the profession of fayth, the Inquisitors notwithstanding, practised to slaunder them with *apostacie* and recanting.

A Regester of such as haue bene either condemned to the fire or otherwise to perpetuall imprisonment, with confiscation of their goods, in Siuil and in Vallolet. Anno. 1559. 60. and 63.

The first originall of the Inquisition, with diuers other matters worthy of vnderstanding, the Reader may see in the Preface.

The maner of the Inquisitours proceding to execution with the great pompe and solemnitie vsed thereat in maner of Triumph, as also their sundry kinds of torments described in the booke more at large, is very liuely represented in a table hereunto annexed.

IN so great a hurly burly of ciuil diffensiõs, wherin so many people and natiõs bend their force against their own cõpanions & fellow citizens, & furiously rush their swordes & weapons into the very bowels of their owne natural countrey, and for none other cause in very dede but for the Inquifition, it would make a wife man doubt in this cafe whether of them were madde : the one fide, which maintaine the Inquifition, as a thing moft holy and wholefome for the common wealth, or the other, which feeke not to auoyd any godly Inquifition and reformation of religion, but to defend themfelues like men worthie of libertie wherin they were borne and bred, from a ftraunge, vnworthie, and intollerable flauerie. For though they be both a like readie armed, yet differing afmuch in their opiniõs and iudgementes, as they do in their mindes and affe&ions, it cannot be that right and equitie fhoulde be on both partes: fo that, if the one haue iuftly taken weapon in hande, the other (no doubt) haue done it vniuftly. And to paffe ouer the great nomber of inferiour eftates, it is not likely that the chiefe Soueraignes of the world, who are perfuaded that they ought by all meanes poffible to maintaine the fame, and haue vowed the defence thereof with great deuotion and folemne oth renued frõ yeare to yeare, fhould erre from the truth, or do any thing againft right or confcience : fpecially being neither the firft authors thereof, nor maintaining it as a thing newly deuifed, or without any certaine original, but as that, which being receiued from their forefathers and reuerenced both for the opinion of holines and countenance of antiquitie, hath by a power greater then is the power of man, bene eftemed here among men as a heauenly thing. Befides thefe glorious titles, there be alfo thereunto annexed other finguler commodities, to witte : a diligent endeuour to remoue the infe&ion that might grow afwell of the Iewifh and Mahometicall herefies that daily do arife, befides the reuenues of the Efchequer encreafed hereby, and the foddeine and meruelous enriching of diuers priuate perfons, which though they be great matters in worldly refpe&, yet are they not fo greatly to be accompted of in this caufe. But forafmuch as by Chriftes owne faying, and by naturall reafon, a man cannot haue a more eafy or perfe& iudgement of the qualitie of a tree, whether it be good or bad, then by

the fruite thereof, I may without offending of any man in the
triall of this matter, which is no lesse profitable then hard & dif-
ficult to do, obserue the same order: since the mischief is now already so farre detected & men growne to be so curious, that they
feare not to call into question such thinges, as they haue hetherto by great errour and doltishnes worshipped and held for most
holy and sacred. Now if the *Inquisition* be a good tree, or as they
delight to terme it a *Holy*, I doubt not but it will be content to
shew the fruites opély, by the goodnes or holines wherof, it may
without fraud or enuie be estemed, how good or holy the stocke
it selfe is. For light loueth the light, and he that dealeth truly and
vprightly, is willing to come into the light, in despight of the deuill and all other darkenes, that his woorkes done in the feare of
God, may come to light. But he that worketh the thinges that be
euel, hateth the light, and hauing power and authority, brideleth
mens tongues, couering his faultes with forced silence, least that
the light shold discouer them, and shew them to be reprouable.
Wherefore let all Christendome now behold these fruites of the
Holy Inquisition, which being otherwise very plentifull, by the
onely meanes of Gods goodnes, we haue here and there plucked
for a say and tast of the tree, and by these let them iudge (as easely
they may) whether this Holy Tree be worthy to stand still, or to
be turned vpside downe. For herein resteth all and some, concerning these matters : whether the reports that I shall make in this
treatise of the *Holy Inquisition* be true or no . Secondarily, how I
came to the knowledge thereof , for no man will doubt but that
this tree doth worthely deserue to be hewed downe, if there be
sufficient proof that it buddeth forth such pestilent blossomes, &
beareth like fruites as these be. Againe it were a daungerous and
inconuenient matter, if we heretickes that detest the *Inquisition*
as a sharpe and iust plague of God, & therfore worthy to be holden suspected, should haue any credite geuen vs herein. Wherefore I haue thought it a thing woorthy the trauaile , to shew the
briefest and most certaine way, wherby the truth thereof myght
without any great trouble be vnderstoode. That is to say, if the
king whose office it is, specially to see to the administration of iustice in his owne dominion, woulde first be broughte to beleue,
that both he might of his absolute authority, and of duety ought
to call the holy Court of *Inquisition* to accomptes, and that no
lawes or decrees of their making, no Priueleges, no Bulles, no
Pardon

The Preface.

Pardons or difpenfations, finally no Othe, ought to let or hinder him from the doing of his duety herein. Secondarily, if after he had appointed fuch a fpeciall Commiffion to examine the *Inquifition*, he would feeke meanes to be enformed of fuch matters by men of grauity & good confciences, who calling vnto thé others fuch as might be thought to haue the moft knowledge and beft experience in thefe matters, might learne out a truth, as the beft cuftome is in all other courtes and confiftories as they call them. For the which purpofes thofe that either prefently are, or haue bene heretofore fettered in the Inquifitours prifons, were firft to be fent for & examined but vnbrideled in any cafe, hauing thofe worfe then iron bittes, taken from their tongues, with the which the *Inquifition* hath hetherto kept her tyrany clofe: that is to fay, their folemne fwearing of them to be filent while they liue, inhibiting them the vttering of any thing by any meanes, that they either knew, or faw, or had experience of themfelues touching the *Holy Inquifition*, or their whole manner of proceding againft them in Court or otherwife. But that they fhould rather repute themfelues as dead perfons for that time concerning the knowledge or fence of any fuch matters. And as though theyr othe (forfooth) were not a matter of force enough, they annexe therunto terrible threatnings. By meanes wherof all the tricks of the *Inquifition* haue hetherto bene fecret and hidden, and paffed vnder couert to and fro, with a cloke and fhadow of a zeale of godlines, & yet not fo obfcurely or fecretly, but that the whole world (though confufedly and as it were a farre of,) hath at the length efpied and found out their outragious tyranny.

And this is the onely caufe that maketh all men keepe their tongues, leaft it might be their happes likewife to haue experiéce therof in théfelues. This bridle I fay muft firft be remoued & taken away fró thé of whom thefe queftions fhould be afked, & libertie muft be giuen to fpeake boldly and without dauuger, if a man wold haue thefe fecrecies come to lyght, that haue ben kept clofe fo long to the great decay and hinderaunce of the common wealth. Wherfore if fmall credite fhalbe giuen to vs in this treatife, or none at all, bicaufe we be as it were a partye, and therfore iuftly to be fufpected, feing for our owne partes we defire no credite, but referre the matter wholy to diligent and orderly triall, there is no caufe why any fhould thinke better or worfe of it for vs, but iudge of it indifferently by it felfe as it is.

¶B.ij.   More-

Moreouer, it is as greatly pertinent to our purpose, to shew how we came to the knowledge hereof: Wherin, allbeit we take God to recorde and our conscience that all this is true, yet notwithstanding we craue no suche credite to be aided therby: neither shall any haue iust cause to lay that to our charge, that we haue gone from the triall of the matter, and vsed this as a shift.

But to passe the kings treasorie, and the enriching of other priuate persons, how so euer they came by their wealth, bicause we would not be thought to enuie their prosperitie, of many other and so great commodities as we haue before rehearsed, (wherof the fauourers and maintainers of the *Inquisition* do comonly make their bragges) that there is nothing that maketh for them, but rather for the contrary parte it is easie for any man to perceiue, that wil consider with vs but thus much, that of so many thousandes of people either Turkes or Iewes, or true christians or heretikes (as they terme them) and reuolters from the Romishe faith, as haue come within the Inquisitours iurisdiction from the very first beginning of the *Inquisition* till this daye, there are to be seene many thousandes of *Sambenites*, as monuments of some that were burned, some whome besides the perpetuall and vnrecouerable infamie that hath redounded thereby both to themselues, and to their whole poster(tye, they haue depriued of al their substance. To be short, that so many spoyles of pore soules do remaine to be sene as haue suffred at their hands for very trifles: but of any whom they haue instructed and amēded or withdrawne from their errors, not so much as one example, nor any one memoriall.

Now as concerning the originall of the Inquisition, the cōtinuaunce, and the glorious title that bleareth and blindeth mens eyes now a dayes (for what mā is he that would not bow down and worship these sacred names and titles: *The holy Inquisition. The fathers of the faith: The Inquisitors of lewd heresies and apostacie?*)I will speake somewhat to the intent men may vnderstād by what right they claime and holde the same.

After the warres were ended wherin *Ferdinando* and *Isabella* of famous memory expelled the Turkes out of the territorie and Citie of *Granata*, and other places in *Spaine*, which had vsurped there by the space of. 778. yeres, from the time of *Roderic* the last king of *Spaine* that was of the race and line of the *Gothes*, hauing restored their countrey into the ancient estate that it was in before.

fore, and gotten to them selues perpetuall fame and renowme, they fell from those continuall troubles and tumults of warre to reforming and purging of religion. The occasion whereof came as wel by the *Mores*, that being conquered, had libertie to remain in *spaine*, and to enioy all their goods with condicion that they shold receiue the christiã faith: as by the Iewes that were in nũber as many as the other, who were permitted to cõtinue stil vnder the same condition, that the *Mores* did, cõmaundemẽt being giuẽ to al that were not contẽt to admit this cõdition, that they should immediately departe *Spaine*, passing ouer the straites of *Marrocke* and retyre into their owne countrey. For the *Iewes* (as their most auncient Chronicles doe reporte, did inhabite *Spaine* from the time that *Titus* Emperour of *Rome* destroyed *Ierusalem*. Who caused them to be transported thither there to remaine in misery and thraldome, being notwithstanding in good case for one thing, in that they were not compelled by any to alter their religion till the time of *Ferdinando*. Wherupon, the kings of *Spain* considering that those people were but only Christians by name and for fashion sake, submitting themselues for feare and awe, and for safegarde of their richesse rather than any loue or zeale which they bare to christianitie, deuised to make prouision, and to take some order for their better instruction. A godly purpose surely, and mete for christian princes, if euell coũsellours had not maliciously peruerted their good intents. For ther were alwayes about the King, certaine Friers of the order of S. *Dominike*, to whome diuers well disposed Princes gaue very great care and credite, specially in matters of religion and cõscience, which being a proud & an ambitious sect, that toke vpon them great skil, and outwardly professed much holines most arrogantly and impudently, by meanes therof had more free accesse to Princes priuy chambers, and thereupon growing to be of their priuie counsell, and obtaining such credite, that kings were content to be ordred and directed by them in these and such like good purposes, wheras they shold haue prouided godly instructors, pastours and teachers, to win and allure the counterfait christians (as it becomed them) by charitie and gentlenes, labouring with al diligence to withdraw them from their errours to embrace true christianitie sincerely and without dissimulation, they erected a new kind of Consistorie of an *Inquisition*, wherein the poore wretches, insteade of better instructions, wherewith there was some hope to

Moreouer, it is as greatly pertinent to our purpose, to shew how we came to the knowledge hereof: Wherin, allbeit we take God to recorde and our conscience that all this is true, yet notwithstanding we craue no suche credite to be aided therby: neither shall any haue iust cause to lay that to our charge, that we haue gone from the triall of the matter, and vsed this as a shift.

But to passe the kings treasorie, and the enriching of other priuate persons, how so euer they came by their wealth, bicause we would not be thought to enuie their prosperitie, of many other and so great commodities as we haue before rehearsed, (wherof the fauourers and maintainers of the *Inquisition* do comonly make their bragges) that there is nothing that maketh for them, but rather for the contrary parte it is easie for any man to perceiue, that wil consider with vs but thus much, that of so many thousandes of people either Turkes or Iewes, or true christians or heretikes (as they terme them) and reuolters from the Romishe faith, as haue come within the Inquisitours iurisdiction from the very first beginning of the *Inquisition* till this daye, there are to be seene many thousandes of *Sambenites,* as monuments of some that were burned, some whome besides the perpetuall and vnrecouerable infamie that hath redounded thereby both to themselues, and to their whole posterítye, they haue depriued of al their substance. To be short, that so many spoyles of pore soules do remaine to be sene as haue suffred at their hands for very trifles: but of any whom they haue instructed and amēded or withdrawne from their errors, not so much as one example, nor any one memoriall.

Now as concerning the originall of the Inquisition, the cōtinuaunce, and the glorious title that bleareth and blindeth mens eyes now a dayes (for what mā is he that would not bow down and worship these sacred names and titles: *The holy Inquisition. The fathers of the faith: The Inquisitors of lewd heresies and apostacie?*) I will speake somewhat to the intent men may vnderstād by what right they claime and holde the same.

After the warres were ended wherin *Ferdinando* and *Isabella* of famous memory expelled the Turkes out of the territorie and Citie of *Granata,* and other places in *Spaine,* which had vsurped there by the space of.778.yeres, from the time of *Roderic* the last king of *Spaine* that was of the race and line of the *Gothes,* hauing restored their countrey into the ancient estate that it was in before

fore , and gotten to them felues perpetuall fame and renowme, they fell from thofe continuall troubles and tumults of warre to reforming and purging of religion . The occafion whereof came as wel by the *Mores*,that being conquered, had libertie to remain in *fpaine*, and to enioy all their goods with condicion that they fhold receiue the chriftiã faith : as by the Iewes that were in nũber as many as the other, who were permitted to cõtinue ftil vnder the fame condition, that the *Mores* did, cõmaundemēt being giuē to al that were not contēt to admit this cõdition, that they fhould immediately departe *Spaine* , pailing ouer the ftraites of *Marrocke* and retyre into their owne countrey. For the *Iewes* (as their moft auncient Chronicles doe reporte, did inhabite *Spaine* from the time that *Titus* Emperour of *Rome* deftroyed *Ierufalem*. Who caufed them to be tranfported thither there to remaine in mifery and thraldome, being notwithftanding in good cafe for one thing, in that they were not compelled by any to alter their religion till the time of *Ferdinando*. Wherupon,the kings of *Spain* confidering that thofe people were but only Chriftians by name and for fafhion fake , fubmitting themfelues for feare and awe, and for fafegarde of their richeffe rather than any loue or zeale which they bare to chriftianitie,deuifed to make prouifion, and to take fome order for their better inftruction. A godly purpofe furely,and mete for chriftian princes,if euell coũfellours had not malicioufly peruerted their good intents. For ther were alwayes about the King , certaine Friers of the order of S.*Dominike*,to whome diuers well difpofed Princes gaue very great eare and credite,fpecially in matters of religion and cõfcience, which being a proud & an ambitious fect, that toke vpon them great fkil, andoutwardly profeffed much holines moft arrogantly and impudently, by meanes therof had more free acceffe to Princes priuy chambers,and thereupon growing to be of their priuie counfell,and obtaining fuch credite,that kings were content to be ordred and directed by them in thefe and fuch like good purpofes, wheras they fhold haue prouided godly inftructors,paftours and teachers,to win and allure the counterfait chriftians (as it becomed them)by charitie and gentlenes,labouring with al diligence to withdraw them from their errours to embrace true chriftianitie fincerely and without diffimulation, they erected a new kind of Confiftorie of an *Inquifition*, wherein the poore wretches, infteade of better inftructions, wherewith there was fome hope to win them, fhould be robbed and fpoiled of all their goodes and poffefsions, and either put to moft cruell death, or fuffer moft in tollerable tormentes by whippe or otherwife, leading the reft o their life in perpetuall obloquie and ignominie, and fuftayning extreme pouerty by loffe of landes and goodes. Neither was this executed only vpon fuche, as had moft fhamefully blafphemed Chrift but the leaft and mofte triffling ceremonie of the *Iewifh* or *Morifh* law, or the fmalleft errour in chriftian religion, whereo they did neuer teache them fo muche as their articles, had bene matter fufficient to condemne them. To the furtheraunce of thi new deuife *Sixtus* the .4. of that name Pope of Rome, put his helping hand by adding his confirmation, fo that at the length it became of fuch force, being ratified and eftablifhed by the king auctoritie and the Popes, that were it not for that the hugeneffe therof is fuch, that is not able to fuftaine it felfe, being a thing fo burdenous to the worlde and fo importable, a man might very well thinke it to be impregnable. See I pray you how well thef godly paftoures prouided for the new increafe of Chriftes flock whom they ought to haue had greater regard to fede then they owne bellies, and fhould not in milking them, haue drawen the very bloud to deuoure it, nor befides the hauing of their fleec flain them alfo moft cruelly to couer thefelues with the fkinnes nether ought to haue killed the fatlings, but to cherifh the weak lings, to binde the broken, to feke the ftrayfhepe, and bring then home to the folde like good and carefull fhepheards, without v fing fuche force and violence, or claiming any iurifdiction or fu perioritie ouer them, to whom they fhould rather fubmit ther felues and become feruaunts, confidering that they are the fold of Chrift. But as for feking, they fought in deede and daily do, in quiring with great diligence after the wandring fheepe pantin and fainting, but it is to flay the, not to faue the. But to procede As the *Dominicanes* were the firft authours rherof, fo for the au ctoritie and eftimation that they were in with princes, they ob tained the execution of this tyranny vnder the pretence of tea ching the true chriftian faith, wherof they had of long time ben accompted the patrones. But afterwardes by meanes of their vnfa tiable couetoufnes and ambition, (for the which two vices the are already difcredited among the common people,) as alfo fo their cruelty and tyranny which they practifed, being exalted that high eftate and dignitie, they became fo intollerable, th

the

him after as a Saint . For it is very certainely reported that the bloud issuing out of his body , being newly slaine, sprang out in such aboundāce, that it spirted vp to the altare . By the which miracle (say they) God declared both the innocency of the person, and the goodnes of the quarel wherin he was slain. Notwithstāding al this, and that diuers other miracles are sundry times sene vpon his tombe to confirme the same opinion and fansie of the common people (suche is the folly of men, and the power of the deuill (as *S. Pawle* saith) to deceiue men which haue reiected tho loue and zeale of the truthe) he could neuer yet attaine to be canonized a Saint, and called *Saint Aepila:* forasmuche as enterprising a iust quarell , he was not only found to haue a shirt of male on at the time of his death, (which thing notwithstanding they say, he might wel inough haue enioyed the holy name of a Saint) but he had also vnder his other garmentes a short hanger by his side, and that (forsothe) only hindred his absolute honour.

This Inquisition you will say was not brought in, to the ende that any should thereby be instructed in the principles of true religion, but onely that heresie by meanes hereof might be abolished. Mary so much we yeld vnto them in dede. For it appeareth plainly by the zeale that was in those good princes, that they had a better meaning with them at the first, then that which through their wicked counsellours afterwarde, was put in execution. The *Inquisition* being thus established for the same ends and purposes which I haue before mencioned (as some affirme) before the battaile at *Granata,* which maketh nothing against me if it be so, the charge of instructing the people in the principles of religion, was first referred to Vicares and Curates, and from them translated to the Wardens of the Church, and afterward to the Clarkes in euery towne and parish, who taught the simple abused people their *Aue Maria, Pater noster,* their *Credo,* with *Salue regina,* in Latin shall I say , nay in a barbarous kinde of Latin , and that with sporting them selues, and mocking the pore sely soules, without any deuotion or zeale , not without rewarde neither , but very dearly and at a high price , many times besides their cōmon wages, they were payd with the goodwiues honesty, or the daughters virginitie. For the other.v.commaūdements of holy church which they said were necessary to saluation : that is to say , the hearing of Masse on holy dayes and sondayes. The going toshrift and holy confession, The receiuing of holy bread, the due obser-

B.j.   uing

uing of faſtes enioyned by the churche : and the true paying of
their tithes and church dueties,theſe things I warrant you were
beaten into their heads in plaine words and mother tongue . By
which kinde of diſcipline , what other thing I pray you coulde
ſeeme to be ſought,then to bring men into a heape of perpetuall
errours . And the court of Inquiſitiō being erected on the other
parte for reformation of erroures , they might be ſure like good
hunters to lodge the Deare,and take their ſtand,and ſo to obtain
a continuall pray.But to procede,let vs graunt them thus much,
that the Inquiſition was ordained to none other ende , and that
they be two ſeueral and diſtinct offices,to teach the fayth,and to
roote out hereſies,yet were it the part & duety of good and diſ-
crete counſellours, to prouide that the authority committed to
biſhops by the holy ſcripture of God, ſhould not thereby be taken from them : neither ſhould any other perſuaſion enter into
their heads that there were any other fire or ſword to roote out
hereſies,but only the ſworde of Gods worde : bothe the which
things the holy Apoſtle did moſt euidently teache in the Epiſtle
to *Titus*, where among other qualities required in a Biſhop , he
would haue him embrace the worde of God fit for inſtruction,
that he may be able to exhort by wholeſome doctrine , and to
conuince the gainſayers and aduerſaries.For ſurely as a true and
iuſtifying faith can not be forced(the nature thereof is ſuche)no
more can hereſie be deſtroyed by the heretikes deathe . But the
worde ofGod is moſt apt and fit for bothe purpoſes.For thereby
faith is not only engendred,but increaſed and multiplied meruelouſly, and whatſoeuer is not agreable to true faith,if it be examined and tried by the light of this word, ſhall ſone be bewray-
ed . Wherfore they ought firſt to haue reſorted to the ſcriptures,
and taken coūſel of them,whether they had limited any puniſhment,for ſuch as ſhould ſhew theſelues wilfull and obſtinate a-
gainſt the truthe,or the moſt cruel execution that can be by fire.
For as concerning the confiſcation of goods,what cā be thought
more wretched and couetous, or more vniuſt and ſhameleſſe,or
furder from the profeſſiō of a chriſtian mā?And to let paſſe their
open infamy,the ſtaine wherof wil hardly be ſpunged out again,
who can worthely ſpeake inough againſt them,that vſe the ſame
kinde of puniſhment euen againſt thoſe poore wretches,whome
they haue perſuaded to recant their errours.Paule in the place a-
boue mentioned,apointed no penaltie, foraſmuch as it may wel

be

the Princes them selues, who lately before had aduaunced them to those estates, were enforced to displace them, pretending diuers reasonable causes and allegations, and so committed it vnto the clergy. Wherof the ancient churches of the *Dominicans* hong round about with Ancients and Ensignes of victory, ouer such as they conquered during the time that they were in auctoritye, is profe sufficient.

Ne from hir heart the causes olde, of wrath and sore disdaine
Was slaked yet, but in hir brest high spite did still remaine :
How Paris Venus beautie praised, and hers estemed at naught,
She abhors the stocke of Ganimede, whome Ioue to heaue had raught.

Æn
Virg

How be it they retaine till this day the title and name of Inquisitoures still with toth & naile, & wil one day no doubt, haue a cast at the office againe, and claime their right. So that we may thanke these wicked counsellours and none other for the *Inquisition* at this day, most diuelishly peruerting the godly purposes of Princes, which tended to the weale of the church, and conerting them wholy to the aduauncement of their owne commoditie and estimation. Or else, wherto I beseche you appertayned it, that they which would be accompted diligent and faithfull sowers of the seede of christianitie, and the zealous furtherers of the same, should erecte a newe kinde of *Consistory* so rare and strange to the whole world, which is not set vp to informe the ignorant, or to conuince the obstinate, and bring them to the knowledge of true religion, either by persuasion of learning, or by charitable dealing the onely meanes that Christ wold haue his ministers to worke by, but to compell them by force & might, by rigoure & extremitie, by commissions and auctoritie, *by Rackes and Torments, Chaines, Halters, Barnacles, Sambenites* by *Fire* and by *Fagots,* which holy *Consistorie* of theirs, is not assisted with men of godly conuersation, or knowne to be learned in the misteryes of holy scripture, suche as would laboure painefully in the Lordes vineyard, and set forward his haruest : but is garded with *Sherifs, Treasorers, Notaries, Somners, Iaylers, Proctors, Promoters or Familiers* (as they call them) a foule and an infinite company. And who would not iudge thinke ye, that all these things were deuised rather to lay newe taxes and impositions vpon the people, and to eucrease the reuenues of the Eschequer, then for the furtheraunce

¶B.iiij.

theraunce of religion . As for the purpose, if a man would chuse
out a cunning huntesman with all his furniture, hauing his artil-
lery about him, his snares, grinnes, heyes, dogges. &c. and sende
him thus arayed to preache the Gospell, and publish Christes religion , what man I pray you that were well aduised, and should
behold suche a man, hauing his handes daily imbrued with the
chaunge of prayes and spoyles, would not accompt him a better
hunter then a preacher? For (doubtles) the commission and authoritie of preaching was giuen to good and godly bishops and
pastours (if any suche there were) both by the lawes of God and
constitutions of man, that they should teach and instruct, as well
the yong nouices as the elder schollers, to tread the path of true
godlines. But these men being so blind, or so carelesse, or bothe,
that either they could not, or would not see to their office & du
ty in this behalf, there was neuer a mã of thẽ all, eyther bishop or
diuine, but he thought that a great part of his duty touching his
function was abridged and dispensed withal, by meanes of erecting the court of Inquisition , all good & godly lawes concerning
christianity, are so cleane raced out of the tables of their heartes.

And this *Inquisition* being erected in this wise at the first, and
ratified afterwards by the greatest authoritie in the worlde, that
is to say the Kings and the Popes , though it had the opinion of
holines to countenaunce it, so that it should seme to deserue the
approbation of most men, yet was it neuer generally receiued of
all . For at what time king *Ferdinando* went about to establishe it
in *Arragon*, which was his owne inheritaunce discended frõ his
father, the Nobles of the realme did first make humble supplication that it might not be established. Afterwardes, being by violence forced vpon them , they did also with force and violence
withstand it, alleaging that it tended rather to the impechement
of the liberty of their countrey, then to the reformation of religion . In so muche that it was not receiued (if a man may say it
were receiued at all that was forced vpon them against their
wils) till the setling therof had cost many a manhis life. And besides the hatred which the Nobles and commons of that Realme
beare against this their holy Inquisition at this day, it doeth well
appeare by the death of *Seignor Aepila*, who being sent thither by
the king with large commissions to execute the same, was slaine
of the noble men at *Sarragossa* in the Cathedrall churche . The
which caused many of the folish superstitious people to worship
him

be that the party condemned, may in time be reclaimed, and ther
fore mercy ought rather to be practised of euery good shepheard
with all gentlenesse and loue, then any such extremity. But let vs
enter further, and see what Paule apointed for such as are obstinate persones. Auoide the company of an heretike (saith he) after
one or two admonitions. First he would haue him charitably ad-
monished of his error twise or thrise, and that by the bishop, not
cited into the court, not put to the torments, or otherwise punished for his erronious opinions with such extremity, and so con
tinually. Then if gentle admonition will reclaime him, there is
good cause why both the bishop and the whole congregatiō may
reioyce of the winning of a brother, to be a meber of Christ. But
if suche admonitions will not preuaile, he counselleth vs to procede to excommunicatiō: that is to say, to cut him of & exclude
him the copany and felowship of the Christians: the which not-
withstading must not be executed in way of reuege of his error,
but ministred as a medicine for his amendment. And this iudgement of the disciple agreeth with the rule of his master. *If he will
not geue eare to thee, nor other* (sayth he) that is to say, thē that haue
giuen him admonition the seconde time, *Let hym be thenceforthe
accompted of, as an Ethnicke or Publicane* . Which is as much in
vnderstanding, as if he had neuer receiued the faith . In this de-
gree of seueritie, which being duely considered, is sharp inough,
Christes discipline stayeth and procedeth no further. And this is
the Court, these be the lawes therof, and the whole maner of
proceding, wherewith a true Christian man (if there had bene a-
ny suche among them) should haue contented him selfe in proceding against his brother being beside the right way, or against
any heresies, of what sort or condition so euer they be, because
Christ hath thought them to be sufficient, and prouided these re
medies which the church hath alwayes vsed from time to time
to great profite in the roting vp of all heresies that at any time
grewe therin . As concerning the putting of heretikes to death,
surely it is like altogither as if a Phisitian to the intent to rid the
patient of his disease, shold for the nonce rid him also of his life.
Moreouer they that doe pretend most of all now adayes the roo-
ting vp of heresies by such meanes, do not only not attaine therunto (for as yet the world is blinded, to take falshode for truthe)
but if it were so, thē by taking away his life, they cut him of from
all those meanes & possibilities wherby he might attain his own

salua-

ſaluation. For it might very well come to paſſe in time foraſmuch as Gods iudgementes are deepe and incomprehenſible , that the partie continuing aliue might be broughte into ſome better caſe. But it is to be feared(wil ſome ſay)leaſt he infect other. True it is and for that conſideration, both Chriſt and his Apoſtle commaũdeth vs to eſchue him , and to cut him of from the body of the church. But if they would needes procede farther, and vpon other reaſonable conſiderations puniſh ſuch obſtinate perſons more ſeuerely, were not the ordinary magiſtrate ſufficient to execute the ſame. Doubtleſſe their anſwere wil be this, that the knowledge of hereſies, can in no caſe appertaine to the ſeculare magiſtrates, bicauſe they for the moſt part are ignorãt in the holy ſcriptures and Eccleſiaſticall affaires : For this is a common ſaying with theſe fathers that are ſo farre ſeene in Gods ſecretes , that neither the knowledge nor determination of matters in religion doe appertaine to the *Seculare* magiſtrate as they terme him in deſpite and reproche. But I pray you in what reſpect are they themſelues choſen to ſupply thoſe places, and to be Inquiſitors to determine maters of faith , whereof they are termed the Fathers, or to diſcuſſe hereſies, wherof they are ſaid to rid the world, being neither learned in ſcriptures, nor able to teach the belief? For they ar thought men good inough for that office if they be doctors in the ciuil and canõ lawes. As for their diuines(and yet a ſely diuinitie god wot) truely ſince the time that the *Dominicanes* were diſplaced thence, (whereof I made mention before) we haue not ſene any of them execute any ſuch office. Yea, what if ſince that time ther hath bene an order taken by the Inquiſitors , and entred into their bookes, that no diuine thenceforth ſhould occupy any ſuch place. Now as concerning the ciuil law, ſurely the Inquiſitours do not excell the ſeculare Magiſtrate, and as for the Canon, if a man were neuer ſo well ſeene in it, they cannot deny, but it ſerueth as little to the deciding of matters in religion, as the ciuil . How then is it poſſible to be otherwiſe, but that when ſuch ignorant men be admitted to determine matters of Religion, as haue no manner of knowledge in the holy Scriptures, ſaue only a little poore ſkill in the conſtitutions of mannes braine, they muſt needes turne ſwete into ſoure, and ſoure into ſwete: call light darknes, and darknes light? That is to ſay in profeſſing them ſelues to be the Patrones of faith, roote out all faith, and maintaine monſtruous errours: ſlea the children of God, and cheriſh the children of the deuil: kil the ſeruaunts of

Chriſt,

Chriſt, foſter, maintain, and encreaſe the ſeruaunts of Antichriſt.

Here they wil aunſwer vs, that albeit they them ſelues can no more iudge of matters touching faith, than a blinde man can of colours, yet they take into counſell and commiſſion with them to debate ſuch matters diuers diuines, whoſe preſcript rule and order they put in execution, ſpecially *Dominicanes*, who haue nothing now to do with the high authoritie and commiſſion of Inquiſition, ſaue only that they are admitted to côſultations, and to the *Qualifications of doctrine*, as they terme it.

And here though we examine not narowly with what quantitie of Diuinitie, they come furniſhed to this office, yet we may eaſely geſſe, that being remoued for the cauſes aforeſayde, and thought vnfit for the place, they are not ſince grown much more apt : ſpecially ſeing beſides their olde infirmities, they are greuouſly ſick of their auncient ſhame, daily renewed by beholding from a low place, the lofty Tribunall ſeat from whence they are diſmoûted, and are in a perpetual headache and woodnes of iealous men, to ſee their aduerſaries enioy the honour which they haue loſt. Wherin we report vs to the Inquiſitours them ſelues, for no man knoweth better then they, what tokens the pore *Dominicanes* giue outwardly of the great bile within their breſt full of malitious matter, as oft as they are called to thoſe graue and waighty deliberations : in ſo much that it hath perhappes bene thought on, to ſhut them quite out of the Inquiſitoures doores. But goe to, they are peraduenture amended ſince . Why might not thê the ordinary magiſtrate cal the ſame diuines to the ſame conſultatiôs ? Now to appoint any man iudge of matters which he vnderſtandeth not, wherby he muſt nedes hang altogether of other mennes opinions & ſentences what ſo euer they be , what an iniquitie is this? What a peruerting of al law and iuſtice? Who therfore can meruail, if when we ſee the *Holy Inquiſition* ſit in her heauenly Tribunal ſeat, we ſay with *Salomon* . *I haue ſeene vngodlines ſit in the ſeate of iudgement, and iniquitie in the place of iuſtice.* And yet notwithſtanding all this , what libertie and prerogatiue they will alow them ſelues, in the very ſame matters which they puniſh in others, as the higheſt points of hereſie, you may behold in the example following.

It happened a fewe yeares paſſed in *Barchinon* a very famous City in the territorie of *Cathalonia*, that when they ſhold marche forewarde in their proceſſion on *Corpus Chriſti* day to cary the

Maſſe breade about, and all things were ready requiſite to ſo ſolemne a ſhew, euen as the prieſt that had daunced the Tragicall
high Maſſe, ſhould couche the bleſſed hoſt in the golden pixe, as
the Deuill would haue it, it was to great a compaſſe to be put in
the boxe. All men were amaſed: the whole ſhewe ſtayed; there
was not a mã in that great and notable aſſembly that knew what
to do, in a caſe ſo ſtraunge and ſo vnloked for: Now ſurely it was
a ſport alone, and a ieſt worthy ſo great a company.

Some (perhaps of the wiſer ſort) ſawe no way but one to helpe
at a pinche: namely, to begin a new Maſſe in Goddes name, and
with better lucke, and to ſhape a cake fitte for the boxe. But
that was to late: for the proceſſion had farre to goe, and it was
toto much paines to defer it any longer. And beſides, perchance
there was neuer a ſir Ihon there but had broke his faſt well, the
better to take paines in ſo great a ſolemnitie. And though the di
uines were of opiniõ that he that ſang the high Maſſe might diſ-
patche another in caſe of neceſſitie, yet he good ſoule loking for
nothing leſſe then ſuch a chaunce, had already ſupt vp the rinſing
of the chalice, as his duety was to doe, Well ſir, there was one of
the Inquiſitours, a man of *Aragon*, whoſe name was *Molonio*. This
gentleman being as haſty by nature, as bold by authoritie, made
no more a doe, but toke a paire of ſciſſoures, and pared his maker
where he was ouergrowne, and ſo by a little paring, put bothe
him in the boxe, and the people out of doubt. Some perhaps wil
praiſe this mannes preſent wit in ſo great a difficultie: other will
abhorre and deteſt his godleſſe and raſh boldnes: others wil be-
waile and lament the harde fortune of their God ſo to be pared
and circumciſed by the curſed hands of a cruel Inquiſitoure. But
good Lord, if any other had bene ſo ſaucie but an Inquiſitor, ſpe
cially if he had had any Iewes bloud in him, how woulde they
haue handled him trow you. In deede *Molonio* was put out of office: but he taryed not manye dayes ere he was ſent to be Inquiſitour at *Siuil*, for they might not loſe ſo ſtout a ſouldior of the
Inquiſition for a trifle. What ſhould we here talke of the Popes
authoritie? they extoll and abaſe him: they adore him and contemne him: they reuenge his wrong and doe him wrong, euen
as he ſerueth or hindreth their holy office. We purpoſe not to
proſecute theſe matters any further, meaning only to touch thẽ
in way of Preface, to declare by what beginnings and occaſions
the *Inquiſition* is growne: what antiquitie & holines it caryeth:

and

and what profite it hath brought to the worlde vnder the title of reforming religion . Thefe things being as we haue declared them, fo true in deede and fuche in qualitie , as no honeft
man can either plainly deny them, or iuftly excufe them, no man
ought to meruaile if the people, which haue otherwife hetherto
bene moft duetifully obedient to their magiftrates , to driue fo
horrible a peftilence from their countrey , haue betaken themfelues to their weapons and defence of armes, as hauing none o-
ther more reafonable meanes to helpe them felues.

They proteft that they feeke not to auoyde the reformation of
religion which they hartely wifhe for, fo that it be fuch a one as
is worthy fo good a name, and be directed by the prefcript word
of God, which ought to be the onely rule of religion , to all that
loue true religion. And in that behalfe, what cã they hope for of
the Inquifition, befides that it hath already yelded. They proteft
further that they owe to their lawfull gouernoures , and that by
the expreffe worde of God, obedience, honoure and tribute, the
which they are moft ready fo perfourme with their accuftomed
chearefulnes and hearty good wil . Only they humbly pray and
befeche that it may be taken of them without the difhonoure
of God, and the moft miferable captiuitie and thraldom of their
confciences , the which ought to be more recommended and
deare to good and godly men, then their very liues. They proteft
befides, that they will not any maner of wayes fhake of the yoke
of iuft obedience to their Magiftrates, but they complayne (and
that not without great caufe) that befides the eafie and gentle
yoke , which they haue hitherto korne with that meekeneffe of
heart that became them , they are fcourged with the Iron whips
of the *Inquifition*, which feeketh nothing but the flaughter of innocent Citizens, and the confifcation and fpoile of their goodes.
They might haue in times paft with fome coloure blamed the
men of *Arragon*, which receiued not the Inquifition without tu-
mult and bloudfhed , for it was then couered with that goodly
and frefhe name and fhew of holines: neither as yet had it raged
againft al indifferently, but only againft the *Iewes* and *Mores*, and
that alfo for very plaufible and apparaunt caufes. But nowe fince
it hath not ceafed to bring forth fuch fruites, as we haue rehear-
fed for thefe three fcore & fiftene yeares: I thincke they fhal not
feeme to be madde, that feeke by all meanes to them poffible, to
driue it frõ their borders. Nay, they might rather be truely iud-

ged to be madde men, if in steade of their faithfull fathers and
good shepheardes and preachers of true religion, they wold wittingly and willingly receiue into their houses the very enemies,
and most cruell destroyers of all faith and religion. And if there
be any that knowe them not to be suche as we terme them, let
them read but parte of their sleights and manner of procedings discouered in this booke (for we could not
learne them all) and let them wel way
and consider them, and
then iudge.

(∵)

A discouery and plaine declaration
of sondry subtill practises of the
Spanish Inquisition.

¶ The ordinary manner and forme, commonly vsed as well in citing, as apprehending such persons as are accused.

Whensoeuer any denuntiation (as they terme it) or rather information is geuen against any person, be it onely for matters of no great importance (as nothing commeth into thys courte so small or so simple, but the parties accused are very greatly endamaged therby) the Inquisitors accustomably vse this kind of practise. Firste, they suborne some one out of a nomber, such as haue lerned their lessons for the nonce (commonly called familiars, who of purpose shall The inquisitors familiars. cast himselfe to meete one, & being prouided aforehand what to say, shall greete him on this wise. Sir, Yesterday it was my chaunce to be with my Lordes the Inquisitors, and as they happened to haue speech of you, they sayd they had to talke with you about certaine of their affaires, and therfore gaue me in charge to summon you to appeare before them to morrow at such an houre. Now may not the party being once warned, ether refuse or differ to come, but at hys very great perill. Wherupon, the next day he repayreth to the place where the Commissioners sitte, and requireth the porter to signify vnto the Lords, that he is come. Wherof as soone as they haue intelligence, al three if they be present (for they are commonly so many in commission), or at the least two of them meete in a Counsell chamber, where the court The court and person of the Inquisition. is commonly kept, as at Siuil, in the castle Triana, or such like places elswhere in other cities abroade, and calling the partie in before them, they demaund of hym what his sute is. Who answereth, that yesterday he was warned vnder their precept to come and speake with them. Then inquire

they

they his name, and that known, what he would: for as for vs
(say they,) we wot not whether you be the same man that
we commaunded to be here with vs, yea or no . Mary now
sithens you are come, if you haue any thing to enforme vs of
in this holy Court, either of your selfe or of any other, in discharge of your conscience (man) let vs heare it . Wherunto the partie either answereth that he hath no such matters to enforme them of(as in dede to stand vpon that point
to the end with them, who seke nothing els but his vndoing
and such as he shall appeach, is the wisest and safest way
that may be taken) or els of mere simplicitie, not knowing
how he entangleth himselfe, rashly and vnaduisedly vtte-
reth some thing of himself or of some other. Then my Lords
the Inquisitors glad that they haue caught him, to the intent
the more easly to feare & amase him, that thus foolishly hath
made himselfe so fitte a morsell for them to pray vpon, cast
lokes one at an other, & reioycing as though they had smel-
led the ratte, all at once fixe their eyes vpon him and behold
him earnestly, & whispering together a little whyle, (I wot
not whether they say ought or nought) at the last either a-
warde the partie to prison, if the matter that he discloseth of
himself seme any thing waighty, or if he chaunce to confesse
nothing at all, they will him to depart, pretending that they
knowe not without better information, whether he be the
same party whom they commaunded to come before them or
no . Whilst the partie is thus in examination, prouision is
made that the promoter, who gaue information against him, is
secretly hidd behind some tapistry where he cannot be sene,
yet so as he may see the parties face, & know if it be the same
man, or no, if happely the Inquisitors know him not. Then
licence they him to depart, being assured that it is he whych
shall minister matter for this tragedy, and perhaps call him
not before them of ii. or iii. monethes after, specially if he be
there inhabitante, for if he be a forrener, they lightly geue
him not so great respite. The next time when their pleasure

is to send for him, they exhort him againe, that if he know or haue heard any thing that concerneth their holy Court, to disclose it vnto them. For we know right well (say they) that you haue dealt with certaine persons suspected in religion, which if you will confesse of your owne accorde, assure your selfe you shall receiue no harme: therefore we rede you take héede and looke well to your selfe. Our opinion is of you, that like a good christian man you wil cal to your remembraunce such things as are bypast: for in déede a mannes memorye is weake (we wot well) and may faile him, and therfore it may be you haue forgotten, and faine woulde tell all you know, if you could call it to mind. By these and such like subtelties they abuse many séely soules, or els dismisse them for that time: yet so, as they shall not thinke themselues clearely discharged: but to kepe them continually occupied and vnquieted in their minds, and to make them stand in daily feare and awe of them, tel them it may be that they shal haue further matter against them, and occasion to call them againe. Yet sometime it happeneth that they beare with some person, and winke at him many dayes, and wyth some whole yeares, ere they cause him to be apprehended, alwayes prouided that he shall haue one or other of these iolly mates to kéepe him company wheresoeuer he goe, and wait vpon him at an inche to créepe into his bosome & grope his conscience: who vnder the colour of frendship & familiarity, very craftely and sublity, whilst he (good man) thinkes no harme, shall daily come and visite him, and haue an eye to all his doings, and marke with whome he conferreth, where he vseth to resort, what he doth there, and as nigh as may be, whereabouts he goeth, and what he entendeth: in so much that without the speciall ayde of Gods holy prouidence, it is not possible for a man to escape their snares. Now if any of the Inquisitors chaunce to méete any such persons so dismissed, they salute him very curteously, & shew him a good countenance, promising to stand his good frend. All which curteous kind of entertainment tendeth to none other ende but to make the man moze careles of his estate, and so to vndoe him ere he be aware. But what good (I pzay you) can they gette by these detestable and abominable sleightes, excepte perhaps they vse them foz their recreation, and take like pleasure in them as doth the fouler in his pastime when he playeth and dallieth with his game : oz the fisher, who after he hath striken the fish, suffreth her to play with the line, & to spozt her self foz a time, that will scarsely last the turning of her taile: oz as the catte that playeth with the mouse, after she hath geuē him some pziuy pinch, leauing him at large, and hunting him afresh, by and by teareth him with her teeth, and eateth vp euery mozsel. Wherin it may be that some secret mistery be hid, which all the wozld barketh not at, not altogether without gaine to these holy Officers. Howbeit this kinde of dalying with their pzay, they vse not with euery body a like, in such sozt as is befoze declared. Foz they haue very great respect of persons, & causes in this behalf. Which is a plaine token that they deale not in this sozt either with such strangers oz towne dwellers, as they thinke are like to escape from them by this libertie, neyther yet with such as are charged with great matters, whom they thinke needefull to be sene vnto betimes, specially if there be any hope that by their confession they shall haue intelligence of any other. But first, when they are determined to appzehend any person that is accused, they vse to send foz the bishops de-

Ozdinarie. puty of that dioces oz Ozdinary (as they call him), and making him pziuy to the depositions of the witnesses against the party accused(which they cal an infozmation)after a litle consultation had with hym of the matter, they all subscribe to a wziting, which is a warrant directed from them to attach him: which kind of dealing semeth to haue a shew of good equity. Forsoth they wil not be thought to touch any of an other mans flocke without thaduise and consent of his own Pastour; who being full ignozant and vnskilfull (God knowes)

knowes) in the dutty of a pastor, (as commonly all of that
coate vnder papacy are)is soone brought to geue his consent
that the sheepe ouer whom he hath a speciall charge, shall
first be fleeced and afterward miserably slaine, & bereft both
of goods and life. For as yet there hath neuer any breach
bene heard of about these matters betwixt the Inquisitors
& the Ordinary,for defending any of his flock that hath bene
by them sent to execution. Yet may a man see oftentimes,
yea daily almost, great nombers die in prison, some hunger-
sterued, some extremely racked and dismembred in euery
ioynt of their bodyes, some euen in the middest of theyr torments, yelding vp the Ghost betwixt the tormentors hands
(as I will not faile hereafter to declare,when I shalbe occasioned to treat thereof more conueniently), in so much that
the Inquisitors will say themselues of some of them, that they
were as harmeles men, and as innocent, and put to death
as wrongfully as any men could be. Wherby it is euident,
that this sending for the Ordinary to confer withall, about
the apprehending of some vnder his cure, is a very vayne
thing, and rather a foolish ceremony, then a matter seri-
ous, or done of any iustice. And to tell the plaine truth,
theyr manner is to bidde the Ordinary to a banquette, to Banquet.
quaffe his parte of the bloude of hys owne sheepe, that the
wolues may continue the faster frends. Our Lord CHRIST
the great shepeherd of the sheepe come whe he seeth his time,
and render to ech of them according to their owne desertes.
Yet sometimes it happeneth that they call not the Ordinary to counsell,before the party be both accused and apprehe-
ded. For being well assured that he will not gainsay them,
nor controle any of theyr doinges, they thinke it enough
when the partie is faste and forthcomming, then to declare
to the Ordinary, the occasion & maner of their procedings:
who hearing it read vnto him,liketh very wel therof,aswel
that they haue already done, as is also content wyth whatsoeuer els they can deuise to do. Now if any that is accused,

do chaunce to make an escape, either before he be apprehended or after, then vse they al deuises that may be to find him
and fetch him againe: neither is it sufficiente that they geue
the serchers certayne common signes and tokens to know
him by, as to describe his apparell, his countenance, age, &c.

Counterfaites. But they draw his counterfaite as liuely as may be in sundry paternes, and distribute them amonge the searchers, to
know the party the more easely by, whom perhaps they neuer saw in all their liues: whereof I will here report you a
true tale for example.

Not long agone they apprehended a certaine Italian at
Siuil, who had wounded one of the Paratours on a time being at Rome, commonly called the Inquisitours Alguazil.
And albeit the Familiars that were sent to seeke him, had
**The Alguazil is in
manner of
Shriefe.** his counterfait about them, as they vse to haue: yet notwithstanding happening vnto him at Siuil, and halfe in doubte
whether it were he or no, because he had altered his apparel,
and of purpose chaunged his name, they pursued him a good
while, onely of a bare suspition which they had by his countenaunce, that it should be he. Therefore one day, as he was
walking and talking with diuers in the Cathedrall church
at Siuil, they found out this new deuise to attempt him with
all, séemely for such Famillars. Two or thrée of them came
somewhat nigh about him, and as he happened to turne in
his walke, his backe being towards them, on a sodayne one
of them calleth him by his old name. The partie being in ernest talke, and mistrusting nothing, sodenly looked behinde
him, and made aunswere: whereupon the catchpoles forthwith laid handes on him, and were cléerely resolued that he
was the selfe same man. This fellowe laye in yrons a good
season, and after long imprisonment, was whipped about
the towne, and condemned to the gally perpetually, & thus
was serued for hurting the Alguazil, partlye throughe hys
owne folly and negligence for want of a little héede taking.
The which deuises albeit they be very subtil, and such as no
mans

mans wisedome can auoid, yet shall it not be greatly amisse
to shewe one other speciall example, howe God oftentimes
maketh thē starke foles, and gardeth his with a holy kind
of policy, that they may be able to go an ace beyonde them.
This last yeare there was a certayne man of the low coun-
treyes that had escaped out of the Inquisitors prisō at Valladolit, who was apprehended for the profession of the Gospell and had bene a longe season in prison. There went out
to seeke him (as the custome is) diuers of these hunting Familiars, who within a fewe leagues of, ouertoke him in the   The Fiscal
high way and stayed him. The party tolde thē flatly he was
not the man they toke him for, and yet would not these good
felowes leaue him, but by force & strong hand wēt about to
bind & bring him backe agayne, still contrarying him, affirming him to be the selfe same man whom they toke him to
be, & therupon demaunded of him, not doubtingly, but as
though ý matter were very cleare. Are not you he (Sir) that
escaped out of the Inquisitours prisō at Valladolit, about 8.
dayes since? Not I (Sirs) sayth he setting a good face on the
matter, & therefore biew me better. I am no such man, but
am newly come from Leon, where I haue wrought in
mine occupation a great while: and because you shall the
better credit my wordes and know it to be so, here is my testimoniall which I cary for my pasport, take and reade it:
and forthwith toke out a certayne writing which he had a-
bout him and offred it them to read. Which, after they had
read, they gaue credit vnto, and let hym go with shame
inough that they had bene so childishely deceaued in taking
one man for an other, as to their thinking they had done.
And as touching the testimoniall that stode him in so good
stede, this is the trouth of it. After his departure out of prison, making as much spede in his iorney as possibly he
coulde, he chaunced to mete with a countreyman of hys be
the way, one of his old acquaintance, newly come frō Leon,
and to helpe himselfe withal in this distresse, found meanes

Paſporte. to obtayne his paſport, which beyond both their expectations, as God would haue it, (a thing ſo appointed by his ſecrete prouidence) did ſerue this mans turne, and ſaued hym from ſo great a pearill. For the other was departed from him but two dayes before, and lett his teſtimoniall behind him in this mans hands to kæpe: whereby he was in good tyme preſerued, and they colted like knaues very pretely. Yet haue theſe Familiars an other fetch beyõd al this, to retriue thẽ that are eſcaped & fled away. As ſome of them ſhall trace him by his footing if they can finde his footeſteps: other ſhall purſue him that way, whether they thinke in their own iudgemẽts he is moſt like to be gone: an other crew of them ſhall lye in wayte for him by night, becauſe they are ſure he will trauaile by night rather then by day. For I tell you they are moe then a good ſort that are appointed for theſe purpoſes, in ſo much that a flee cannot eſcape the Inquiſitors fingers, but ther ſhalbe enow at hãd ready to fetch her againe. But God againſt all their deuiſes and narowe ſearching diligence, ſhal arme and ſafegard him, whom his good will and pleaſure is to deliuer. And thus much concerning the apprehending. Now to tel how they entreat them after they be arreſted and committed to ward.

¶*The Sequeſtration of their goodes commonly called the* Sequeſter.

Immediatly after euery arreſt done by the Alguazil, or complaint made to the court of any perſon, by any of the Familiars, they ſtraight way take from about him all the keyes of his cheſtes or lockes whatſoeuer, if he haue any, and forthwith ſend a Notarie, and certayn catchpoles with the Alguazil himſelfe, to take an inuentory of all ſuch goods as are in his houſe whatſoeuer they be. Which being done very exactly, ſuch as they finde they leaue in the cuſtody of ſome rich man dwelling therabout, who vndertaketh to be accomptable therefore, and to redeliuer them duly and truly, whenſoeuer they ſhall be demaunded. But in this Sequeſter

quester(as they terme it) ȳ owners of such goods had néede
to looke well about them and alwayes haue an eye to their
fingers which are at the sequestratiō and are the doers, specially when they come to rifling of money and iewels either
gold or siluer,or any other thing els that is of any price and
light for conueiaunce,or wil be couched in a narow rowme.
For they are commōly lime fingered,and will lightly make
some thing sticke by them,if they be not narrowly sene vn-
to.And in déede the greater part of this rable of Familiars
are bauds,thieues,shifters, and the vilest sort of people that
liue only by filching,which cannot, nor will not holde their
hands if they should hang for it. Besides that, they are perswaded in conscience,that they should not in such cases for-
beare other mens goodes, although they haue no manner of
right thereto.

   Now to tell you briefly wherto this sequestration ten-
deth.Forsooth,that if it happen the party be condemned, so
that his goodes or any parte thereof be confiscate, this holy
house I warrāt you will not loose so much as a dodkin of thē.
for who knoweth not thus much that the pray and spoyles
of such séely soules is all that they séeke for: els what should
these holy fathers that respect nothing but vertue and godlines do with their goods(I pray you) whome they beare vs
in hand they would so faine bring home againe to the right
way?Or who is so madde to thinke that misbelief can be a-
mended by losse of lands or goods? Yet it may very well be-
séeme Christian men to be spoyled of all their substaunce,
yea and of their clothes from their backs also, by their enemies,seing their head whose members they are, and whose
truth they professe was so serued : for whose garmentes in
likewise not much woorth, perhaps halfe thréede bare wyth
wearing, after they had put him self most cruelly to death,
they determined also to cast lottes. And this kinde of sacri-
ledge is now so ratified and confirmed by the common consent of their diuines that is to say,the Monkes and the rest

                C.j.   due

due of the clergie that they shame not to preach and teach
openly, that whatsoeuer is not iumpe with the Pope, or dis-
senteth from him in the least iote, is bound in conscience,
in all hast (say they) to bring in all his goods into the kinges
Eschequer, and that he hath no more right vnto them then
if he had robbed the king of them before, alledging this reason, that for so much as he is reuolted from the churche of
Rome, he is no longer any right owner thereof, but the
king, to whom the Pope hath adiudged them. Wherfore a
man is bound (say they) to restore them vnto him although
the Inquisitours neuer heard so much as one worde of him.
And thus these subtill Foxes by this one pollicie, are both
greatly gracious with Princes, and therwithall do inueigle
the consciences and pycke the purses of the sæly foolish people dæming them as Gods. But to returne to our purpose.
As sone as the prisoner is entred within the first gate of
the prison, the keper hauing with him a Notary, asketh him
if he haue any knife about him, or money, or ringes or any
other iewels. And if it be a woman that hath a sheath of
small kniues at her girdle, ringes, litle cheynes, bracelets,
ouches, or any other ornaments, such as womē weare, they
stripe them of all these, and commonly they be his fees that
findeth them. This is done to this ende, that the prisoners
during the time of their imprisonment shall haue nothyng
to succour themselues withall any wayes. They search thē
also least they bring in priuily about them any writing, or
booke, or any other such like thing. But after they be once
entred into prison, they are shutte vp in a close cabbaine,
where they haue scarcely good elbowroume, for cleanlines
and lightsomnes not much vnlike to Little ease. And some
are close prisoners all alone for vij. or xv. dayes, some by the
space of ij. or iij. monthes, and other some al their liues long:
Some againe, haue fellowes and companions from the very first day of their imprisonment, as the Lordes Inquisitours will, and as they thinke most conuenient to bring
their matters about.   After

¶ The seuerall dayes of hearing.

Fter they haue thus cōtinued in prison about a wéeke
or two, the Inquisitors priuily pack with the Iayler to
be in hand with the prisoner as though it came from himselfe, & to aduise him to sue that he may come to his answer
and pray to haue a day of hearing. Wherin, it is not to be
thought the contrary, but that there is some mistery ment
therby, that the prisoner must first beginne to sturre in his
owne cause. The keper therfore either at dinner tyme, or
some other most conuenient to bring his matters about,
resorteth to his prisoner, and among other talke, at the last
falleth to question with him how it happeneth that he sueth not to come to his aunswer that his matters may be
more spedely ended, and aduiseth him to labour it with as
much spéede as may be, making him beleue, the sooner the
better, and that it will much further his cause so to do, and
at the légth bring his sute to some good effect: Adding moreouer, that for the acquaintaunce which he hath with hym,
in the way of frendship he is moued to geue him the best
councell he can, and such as is méetest for his behoofe, promising to do and deale for him therin to his power, like a
faythfull and trusty frende. Yet surely it may be thought
with good reason, that if any thing may do the poore wretch
good being in case redy for to be deuoured by these rauenous
beastes, it will fall out in the end to be better for him if he
refuse to pray a day of hearing and tary till the Commissioners do call for him. But if there be none other good to be
done, he may chaunce to get this by his tarying, in driuyng
them to beginne with him, to take care for nothing but only to make aunswer to their obiections. But sith it is so secret a mistery, I wil let it go & leaue it to the iudgementes
and considerations of the wiser sort to scanne and iudge
vpon. The poore prisoner knowing none of these subtelties,
for the most part is ruled by his kéeper, thinking that he
hath geué him good and wholesome aduise, and prayeth him

C.ii.   there

therfore to be a meane for him, and in his behalfe to craue a day of hearing, whose sute is easely heard of the Inquisitour, and graunted at the first I warrant you. Wherupon the party is brought into the Consistory, where the Inquisitour, as though he were altogether ignorant of the matter, beginneth to talke with him much after this sorte. Syrha, your keper came and told vs that you were desirous to come to your aunswer. Now say on, what is your sute? the prisoner aunswereth, that he would be very glad to haue his matter heard. And vnlesse he loke well about him & be circumspect in his dealing, very lothsomnes of his imprisonment, and feare of afterclaps driueth him to confesse somewhat wherof he suspecteth himself to be accused. The which thing doth the fathers god at their hartes, because they are accustomed at this and sundry other seasons, to graunt the prisoners dayes of hearing, and to call them often into the Court before they shall know their whole accusation, and all that is deposed against them (which by order and common course of law should haue bene the first acte that should haue bene done against them) and all is to this onely ende, to make the party vtter somewhat of himselfe rashly & vnawares that they as yet know not of. They aduise him moreouer to let it come frō himselfe, promising that if he wil acknowledge his faultes voluntarily, he shalbe forthwith sent home again to his own house, and be dispatched with all expedition, & dealt withall as gently as may be. But if for all these vayne and flattering promises he holde them hard and stand mute (as in dede it is best for him) they charge him earnestly to disburden his owne conscience: & when he hath bethought himself and is disposed to confesse any thing, that thē he should sue to come to his aunswer, saying that in the meane time, they wil consider of his case & so they remaund him to prison. Then after vj. or viij. dayes or moe, as they thinke god, they call for him againe, and aske him if as yet e be determined to confesse ought. The prisoner aunswe-

reth

reth either that he hath nothing to say, but that he is innocent, oz perhaps confesseth somewhat. But whatsoeuer his
aunswer be, they are sure still harping on their old string,
vrging him to discharge his conscience, & perswading him
that they go about no other thing but to do him good, and to
procure his safetie, of very loue and mere compassion which
they take vppon him. Which gentlenes of theirs and well
meaning towards him, if he refuse now and set light by, he
shall finde them sharpe iusticers henceforth if the Fiscal informe against him, and so send him agayne to prison. The
Fiscal is an officer which taketh all such accusations as the
Promoters bring vnto him, and by office is the onely plea-
der, during the whole time that the causes be hanging, as it
were ye kinges Attorney, hauing his name no doubt a Fisco
that is to say, the Eschequer for whose aduauntage he is altogether, and from whence he is aunswered his fee.

At the third day of Audience (for so we call the law dayes
by knowne and vsuall termes) the party is called for againe,
& demaunded, if yet he be resolued what to do, with earnest request after their accustomed maner, to confes a troth
of his owne accord: if not, they threaten to vse extremity towardes him, and what they can do by law. And here they
vnderstand by this word law, extreme tormenting & mang-
ling of men, yea such as their owne lawes do proue very
innocentes, saying he may well assure himselfe, ye no man
shall sustaine any iniury within their holy Office, and that
their fashion is not to trouble any man but vppon good and
sufficient information against him, with such lyke talke.
Howbeit if the party happen to disclose any thing: nay (say
they) yet ar we not satisfied, we haue not al you can say, we
suspect you kepe somthing in of purpose, & so send him to prison, putting him to further payne, and calling him coram
day by day, as they perceaue ye by these meanes they wring
more and more out of him, though it be but by litle and litle
But if he stand stoutly in the matter, geuing them directe

C.i.

aunſwer that he hath nought to ſay in that place, by a ſhiſt of deſcāt (as it wer) they try him an other way, exacting an othe of him, ꝛ to ẏ intent to proue his zeal, they hold him an Idoll repreſentyng the crucifixe, couered with a blacke lawne, and certayne other Iools, I wot not what. They do alſo lay before him a Maſſebooke or a Miſſall, and ſome time the bare image of the croſſe. For ſuch deuiſes and fooliſh toyes as theſe be, they haue alwayes in a redines to vſe as occaſion ſerueth, and as they think moſt requiſite, reſpecting the party whom they are to deale withall. Here is the chriſtian man driuen into a narrow ſtrayght, ſo that he muſt nedes vtter himſelfe, and plainly ſhew what he is in conſcience and in belief. For if he be a faithfull man in dede, and one that from the bottome of his hart abhorreth Idolatry, hauing before his eyes the feare of God moſt mighty ꝛ ielous, which in his moſt holy law hath reſerued this glory to himſelfe, that we ſhould ſweare by him alone, he will beware that in no wiſe he geue part therof to ſuch vile Idols of wood or mettall, which reſembling the higheſt in ſhape and proportiō, are ſo much the more abhominable in ẏ ſight of god and of his congregation. Therfore a godly man will take hæde of ſuch a wicked and vngodly othe, yea though he were to be torne in pieces preſētly, ſeing they be very Idols ꝛ not god, to whom alone that honor belongeth, as ẏ Inquiſitours thēſelues cānot ſay to the contrary. After they haue thus put him to his othe, they begin to examine him vpon theſe interrogatories. What countreiman he is, and vnder whoſe allegeance. Of what prouince or dioces. In what city town or village he dwelleth. Who were his anceſtours and what their names were. What brethren or ſiſters he hath. What his father and mother were, and what were their names: how they liued, and by what trade and occupation. If he or any of his kindred at any time haue bene conuented before the Inquiſitours, and vppon what occaſions. Moreouer, many other things they inquire of him, as of his

age

age and trade of life, where and with what maner of men
he hath bene most conuersant: and thus is he forced to geue
a straight accompt of his whole life, where he hath passed
his time yearely, and made his most abode, answering to e-
uery point seuerally & particularly. For out of ech of these
questions they fetch no small argumentes wherwith they
charge the poore soule afterward to to pitifully. When he
hath answered to all these by questions, then fall they a fresh
to their old exhortation, sometyme by faire meanes, and
somtime by foule, aduising him to tell the truth frankely,
assuring himselfe that they neuer cause any to be arrested
without iust cause why, or without sufficient witnesses, so
that whether he confesse or no, away he goeth to prison a-
gayne.

And in these iij. first times of hearing, a great sorte are
either allured with their faire speaches and promises that
they shalbe sent home to their owne houses as soone as
they will confesse that that is demaunded of them, or els
of very awe and feare of their euill and menacing wordes,
vtter many things wherof the Inquisitours knew not one
iote before, because none had informed them therof, but them
selues only suspected, least they had bene accused by some,
with whom they had dealt heretofore in such affairs. Thus
betraying themselues like fooles, they bring other men into
as euill case as themselues, which perhappes neither feared
any such matter at all, nor the Inquisitours had euer heard
any thing of them before. But most of all, when they perceaue that these most holy fathers, who hunt after nothing
so much, as daily to haue chaunge of spoyles, will take it
thankefully at their hands, then labour they by all meanes
possible to curry fauour with them, to get themselues rid
out of misery and to be set at liberty: So that it commeth
oftentymes to passe that the parties being at the first arrested
for very trifling matters, undoo both themselues and many
other mo, by geuing ouer much credite to the faire promi-

ses and godly gloses, of these false & faithles Inquisitours
through want of skill how to behaue themselues in theyr
owne affaires, being much lesse able to iudge and discerne
what opinion they should haue of these fathers, that is to say,
not to be fathers(as they glory to be called in derision of all
humanitie, pietie, and fatherlines)but their most cruel and
deadly enemies, which by craft, subtiltie, and lying: and by
all kind of knaueries, priuily go about to get that they gape
for, both life and goodes of the guilty and of the guiltlesse.
Against all which snares of theirs there is one onely way
of auoydaunce, to wit, that he whose desteny it is (I meane
by Gods ordinaunce and appoyntement) to fall into theyr
hands, beleue neuer a word they say, promise they neuer so
faire, nor be afraid of them threat or thunder they neuer so
terribly, hauing alwaies before his eies the loue and dread
of him, who after he hath killed the body hath power also o-
uer the soule to send it to hell fire, and hauing numbred the
very heares of our head to the vttermost, will not suffer the
least of them to perish or fall to the ground without his good
pleasure and prouidence. The next lesson to kepe his tong
for lyfe, and speake not one word till the time that he hath
heard his accusation, with the depositions, wherunto he is
bound by order of law to make aunswer.

A generall
Caueat.

Furthermore, at the fourth day of hearing they tender
him an othe, vehemently exhorting him to shriue himselfe
voluntarily: otherwise they will deale with him as hardly
as the law will permitte them, if the Fiscal once commence
his sute against him. And if he do yet perseuer constantly,
affirming that he hath no more to say, then reade they vnto
him a long inditement, and charge him with many great
matters falsely forged and deuised against him, such as neither the party did euer so much as thinke vppon, nor any
had accused him of to them. For it is a point of conning forsoth in this their crafty faculty, for the fathers to make
these great matters and huge offeces on their fingers endes
for

foz these speciall causes. First, by thus loding the pooze man
and laying to his charge many great and made matters, to
bzing him into such a maſe, that being ſcarcely his owne
man he ſhall not well know where he is, noz which way
to turne him, noz what aunſwer to make. Secondarily, to
pzoue if happely he wil admit any of theſe miſdemeanours
that are layd againſt him, oz at the leaſt, if by argument a⸗
boute any of them they can trippe him in his tale, and ſo
maſh him in their net. Is this then their following of gods
iudgementes, whoſe cauſe theſe fathers of the faith bzagge
and beaſt ſo much, and beare the ſœly ignozaunt people in
hand, that they take vpon them to maintaine, in the very
firſt ſteppe of the ſtage wheron they are ready bent to do
execution of a ſozt of innocents, thus ſhamefully and moc⸗
kingly to cry. Ariſe (O Lord) & iudge thine own cauſe Do *Pſal.*74
theſe policies pzocœde of faith (trowe ye) wherof they terme
themſelues the Patrones? Did euer any true Patrones of
faith either teach them to other, oz els vſe the themſelues?
Are theſe the moſt directe meanes to bzyng hym into the
right way that of mere ignozance and ſimplicity hath gone
aſtray frō the truth and wozd of God, oz to teach the vnlear
ned, oz to cozrect and amend him, who hath erred and fallen
of common infirmity? Oz are they not rather moze likely
to be the ſnares of Sathan pzactiſed from time to tyme by
contentious and diuiliſh people, pziuily layd to ſupplante
a pooze man withall, and very ſtumbling blockes craftely
and maliciouſly caſt foz the nonce, to make him bzeake not
alonely his ſhinnes, but his necke alſo, that playnely and
ſimply ſhall paſſe therby & lœkes not warely to his fœting?
And who would haue thought (I pzay you) that theſe holy
fathers would haue buſied thēſelues in making ſuch mouſe
trappes and ſetting ſuch pitfals? But how many gœd chzi⸗
ſtians haue fallen into theſe ſnares, to the greate peryll
both of their bodies and ſoules, onely by the deteſtable
meanes of theſe peſtilent and pernicious Tyzants. Chziſt
D.i.
the

the sercher of secretes & chiefe Inquisitour ouer al at his generall dome sitting in his seat of maiesty wil one day make manifest.

As touching their accusations, the great and principall matters wherwith they burden euery one that commeth within their iurisdiction, be these: First, for ȳ he being baptized and vnder the obedience of the church of Rome, forsaking her profession and doctrine, is become one of Luthers disciples by admittyng and harbouring his heresies in hys harte, and yet not content therwithall to be an heretike himself, hath prouoked and poysoned other by teaching and preaching the same heresies vnto thē. And to this effect wel neare they vse many bigge woordes to make the simple folke afraid withall. Next to this they charge them also with other matters sometime of moze importaunce, sometyme of lesse: Prouided alwayes, that the matter wherof the party is accused, be brought in, either in the beginning or ending, or els some other thing that some man hath him halfe in a ielousie for. The which thing they lay to his charge not as a matter surmised or of likehoode, but most constantly affirmed and testified by witnesses. For in this holy Consistory they may do what they list, and what they thinke expedient. Then is the party, accused put to aunswer vnto euery article that is laid against him, seuerally & directly, either yea or no, as he thinketh good, hauing alwayes a clarke by him to record euery woord that he speaketh. After this examination and confession thus had and done Ex tempore, without either order or any great aduisement, they strayghtway geue him penne, inke, and paper to put in his aunswer in wrytyng if he will, pretending hereby, that they worke for him all the meanes and helpes that may be to try himselfe an honest man. And thus is this crafty Inquisition cloked with this goodly pretence of equity and iustice, where in very deede this is their fetch, that hearing him first make one confession by woord of mouth sodenly and without aduise

The Inquisitours generall obiection.

tifement,and after that an other with moze deliberatiō in wziting, they may eafely finde fome ods betwixt the one & the other,hauing neither any copy of his fozmer confeſſiō to lay befoze him,noz being able foz very feare & trouble of mind to remēber euery wozd that hath efcaped him.But if there chaunce to be no contrarietie,yet happly ſhal there be fomwhat either moze oz leſſe in the one then in the other. Mozeouer it ſtādeth them vpon to be able to chop Loogicke with them, and to find out fuch contradictions as the other looke foz,becaufe his latter confeſſion penned with fome diligence,alwayes miniſtreth fome matter of new cauillatiōs.Which fetch of theirs who fo will wifely and warely auoyde , muſt take hæde hæ play mumme and fpeake not one wozde but pzemeditate and deuife vppon afozehande : and being mute in all other matters, craue onely this one thing at their handes, and that in as few and apte wozdes as he can poſſibly, to haue a copy of his accufation, with paper,inke,and fufficient time graunted him, that he may by leyfure and with fome good deliberation make aunfwer to fuch matters as are layd to his charge. But fozafmuch as they(no doubt)will not hold themfelues contented with one aunfwer, but wil ſæke to haue it both by mouth & by wziting foz the caufes befoze alleadged, the party muſt in any cafe fæ to himfelfe and fæke to wipe their nofes by ſhaping them a ſhozt aunfwer: yea be they neuer fo full of their queſtions and flozifhes, oz how frowaro oz vntoward fo euer they be,let thē not get within him in any wife, but holde them of alœfe, and be as bziefe with them as he can. Foz albeit thefe raueners be very grædy of that aunfwer that was foodenly made and without any ſtudy, yet fet they moſt ſtoze by that,that was of his owne penning,fpecially, if it be done by one that is learned, whom by common and dayly experiēce they know to be of that nature foz the moſt part,that whiles they labour to auoide matters of fo great impoztance by fome nice conſtruction, they fall into diuers other abfurdities,oz at the leaſt by vttering a little of their

poore skill they minister much matter for captious fellowes
to quarell and cauil vpon. By meanes wherof, many times
such learned clarkes, who at the first fell into their fingers
onely for trifles, were afterward burdened with so many
matters and so weighty, that they could neuer rid themselues thence, till either they went to the stake, or els endu-
ring some other punishment, led the rest of their life in perpetuall shame and ignominy. Wherof I could shew you
sundry examples but that I would be loth to fal from descri-
bing the subtill practises of the Inquisition, to discourse in
maner of a whole history. Wherfore, I hold him wise which
can obserue in that place, vpon a litle study to make a briefe
and a resolute aunswer Christianlike, so as he neither hurt
his conscience by suppressing or shadowing a truth, nor by his
long processe geue his aduersary any thing to take hold v-
pon, or haue any aduantage against him, which (doubtles) is
the onely marke they shoote at, in putting him to aunswer
it by writing. It is also very good for him, that so ofte as he
can, he make sure his side by some of their Canonistes and

Scholemē
and Cano=
nistes.

schoolemen (as they call them) for so shall neither the truth
be obscured, nor they so easely make a quarell to his answer
being ratified and confirmed with his aduersaries argumentes. But whensoeuer any either by writing or word of
mouth confesseth any thing openly before them that is here
ticall, they vse this order commonly, out of that one saying
to draw and deriue diuers other by hooke or by crooke, and to
charge him with ech of them seuerally, as if he had spoken
and affirmed them all precisely, though the party neuer
spake them, nor then will graunt them, nor greatly vnder-
standeth them, or wel knoweth what to make of thē. As for
example I wil report a thing that happened at Siuil ij or iij.
yeares ago: neither néede I to coyne any examples in a case
so common as this is, that is almost in experience daily in
that holy Court of theirs, to the great losse and vtter vndoing of many séely and simple soules.

There

There was a certain man cited before the Inquisitors at Siuil for saying in presence of his familiar frends and acquaintance, that he knew none other purgatory but one, & that was the bloud of Christ, which daily washeth and purgeth our sinnes. The partie who sayd it was but a simple man, brought vp in the countrey all the dayes of his life, hauing no sparck of good ciuilitie in him or of any good education, and by chaunce hearing this on a tyme among certaine of his companions, lyked thereof very well, but now, comming before the fathers for the same matter, told them plainly how hee was of the same minde once, mary sith it mislyketh their worships, he is very well content to forsake it. But what did it auaile (thou foole) to make so rashe and so sodaine a recantation? By confessing the matter, thou settest them a gogge. By kæping thy tounge thou haddest græued them to their very galles. By making thy purgation, thou couldest but haue lost thy labour. Yet this did not content the Commissioners, but there must nædes be some other quarrell picked to hym. The Inquisitours Organs (forsooth) went hard for want of exercise, and therfore they must necessarily haue some body to play vpon them and kæpe them from rusting. Ergo say they, and conclude of this antecedēt against this poore ploughmā, the church of Rome which in tyme past hath determined the contrary by lawe doth erre, and the Councell erreth also, and iustification commeth by fayth onely wherin a man is made frée and absolued a pœna & culpa. To be short, out of these they fetch a rable of opinions & assertions, which they call heresies, and charge the poore man with euery of them, as if he had affirmed them all in plaine terme, say he nay neuer so stoutly that he knoweth nothyng of any such matters, nor so much as once euer thought vppon them. Now who séeth not that this kind of proceding in this holy office is packed full of subtill pollicies and all the diuelish practises and deuises that may be? Yet herein is the mighty prouidence of

God

god toward his elect, specially to be had in admiration, that these men wanting the meanes of calling & teaching which other men haue to induce them by, in a place so quite contrary to these meanes as is fire to water, are both called & taught by God, hauing their eies opened by him and their vnderstanding lightened. For the Inquisitours themselues who seeke vtterly to destroy and roote vp all faith and truth, they (I say) by such meanes as I haue before declared, are the very preachers, teachers, and furtherers of ỹ same, as it is euident and manifest by many notable examples of sundry persons that haue fallen into their hands only for prating rashly and folishly, rather then of purpose or aduisedly, that there is no purgatory, and that it is but a dreame and no such thing in deede, where as they haue bene at their first comming in, ignorant in most of the pointes concerning saluation, by their only questionings, collections, illations, brought either in forme or out of forme, haue departed thēce very wel instructed: wherof this rude fellow of ỹ country, of whom I last made mencion, may be a sufficient testimony.

Moreouer if the party chaunce to confesse ought, they vse to haue an other hooke ready bayted sharpe and perilous enough, I warraunt you: to wit, they inquire of him what soeuer it be, of whom he learned or heard it, or if he haue happely read it in some booke, or if he haue had any conference with any other about the same matter, or he himselfe haue bene an instructour to others, or by any meanes haue mencioned it in the presence of any : in what place he did so, and who they were that stoode by ? For whosoeuer was present, whether they liked his talk or no, yea though it were his owne father, or nigher him, if nigher could be, they are sure to buy it full dearly : the Inquisitours will haue a glyke at them, because they came not forthwith and made complaint therof vnto them. All which things it behoues a man greatly to be cunning in, that if it be Gods will that he fall into their handes, he may learne before hand out of

his

his holy word & wil how to preuent the,and prouide an answer to such demaundes, lest he vndoe both himselfe and o-
thers through his owne folly & necligéce. At ý last, when his
accusatiö is read, if the party be an infant (as we terme one
win age) they prouide him a Patrone whom they cal a Tutor. A very godly way (no doubt) if such a man were apointed to that place as would play his part stoutly and as it becommeth him in respect of his office. Howbeit he is no such
maner of man as the infant would and should haue for the
better bringing of his matters about,but one of their owne
choyse,which either is a very wolfe to ioyne with them a-
gainst the simple Lambe, or at the most, to stand like a ci-
phar in Algorisme and do nothing but fill vp a place,and for
fashion sake & order stand in steede of a Tutor to performe
the ceremonies and circumstaunces of the law. For most
commöly the Porter of their holy house serueth that turne
or in his absence some other of the Porters lodge, and in
deede but onely that he beareth the bare name and title of a
Tutor,dealing in nothing that appertaineth to the office,
my Lordes muleter may easely be Tutor in such sort to the
whole company of the prisoners all at once.By reasö wherof,the porter cannot alwayes be redy to aunswer euery body that knocketh at the gate. And on this sort do these holy
Fathers fulfil the commaundements of God and the lawes
of man touching poore infantes and Orphanes,who as wel
by the law of God as of nature, are recömended so specially
to the consideration and regard of all men,but most chiefly
to iudges.

The Tutor

Neither rest they here,contenting themselues to mocke
the law in this point alone, but in an other of more importaunce,whereas the law prouideth that euery defendaunt
shall haue his Aduocate, some man experte in the lawe to
pleade his cause,and order it discretly according to law and
conscience,and to defend their right,if any they haue, or at
the least to temper the rigour of the law,that it be not con-

The Ad-
uocate.

D.iiij.   Crue▪

strued and ministred with extremity, in this so waighty a matter and the onely succour that these seely soules haue to helpe themselues withall, they deale with them in like sort as they do in the former, for appointing them a Tutor, and so shift it of with a mere shadow and a bare ceremony: onely, because it is a very waighty matter, therfore they would seeme full of curtesy and humanity, and would fayne cloke their wicked contempt of lawes with some goodly pretece. For they name vnto the party 3. or 4. of the most famous men toward the lawes to chuse out of them some one to plead his cause, and besides all this their gentlenes (of fatherly affection I dare say) they aduise him to take such a man who in their iudgementes is the best learned. And what would a man desire more? Yet whosoeuer is chosen to be his Aduocate, wil be sure that he tell not his Clyent any point of law that may doo him ease any way. For he knoweth right well, that if the Inquisitours haue intelligence therof, he shall not escape scotfree, seeyng their meaning is nothing lesse the to prouide him an Aduocate to defend his cause, but only to bleare the common peoples eyes withall, and make them beleue that they proceede by order of law like good conscionable fathers, where in very deede they compasse their matters both against Gods law and mans. For the Aduocate & his Clyent may not so much as haue a word together secretly of any matter, but in presece and hearyng of the Inquisitours or of some Notary. And what doth the Aduocate then would a man thinke? Forsooth he receiueth his Clyents aunswer to the accusation rude and rough hewen, as it were, and that doth he smooth and set together in forme of law (yet ilfauouredly framed full oft, God wots) and all this while taketh vpon him the name of an Aduocate, only to delude the law withal. But forward to our purpose,

Within 2. or 3. dayes after the party hath had the copy of his accusation he is called into the court, where his Aduocate

uocate standeth, like one that would stoutly defende his Clyentes cause, and salue al such matters as should seeme to make against him. Then the Inquisitour, as though he had done the party an high pleasure, and discharged hys conscience wholy for that part of the lawe, pointeth out ý Client his Aduocate with his finger, and straight way falleth to his old note, exhorting him to vtter the truth and take heede to his conscience, and if he haue any more to say, to say it at once. All which time the Aduocate sitteth or standeth mute, and if he haue ought to say, yet dare he not let it come out before he haue made the Inquisitours of his counsell. For the Aduocate all the while that he is telling his tale so eyeth the Inquisitours, that one of their eyes is neuer of from the other: the Inquisitour is so much afrayd lest the prating Aduocate vtter somethyng rashly and vnawares, wherin the Clyent might espy somwhat for his aduantage in lawe, and so auoyd the daunger of their secret and hidde snares. The Aduocate on the other side is as much afrayd and quaketh euery part of him, least any word chaunce to slippe him suddenly that the Inquisitours happly shall not well like of, and therefore dare say nothing for his Clyent, but onely geue him a few wordes of comfort and bid him be of good chere, and tel the truth in any case, saying that, that is ý only way to preuaile in this Court: and as for me (sayth he) I wilbe ready to do for you the best that I can. Thé commeth the Inquisitour in with his part, singing the same note, and so is the prisoner sent to his prison agayne.

After this day of hearing, the party beginneth to be of better courage, hoping that his matter draweth nigh to an ende: but (God knoweth) it is far otherwise. For many of them are forgotten, some for a yeare, or halfe a yeare, or perhaps for three or fower yeares, as it pleaseth these good Fathers to deale with them, and there they lye in prison, lyke a pece of lether that lyeth steeping in the

C.i. tanners

tanners fatte. During all which tyme, they neither are called any moze, noz one woed mencioned foz their deliue-raunce. Then, if any foz very lothsomnes and intolerable filth by reason of their long imprisonmēt, do craue to come to their aunswere, some perhaps obtayne it, and some go without it: but in the end both their luckes is a like. For they that after lōg sute get a graunt therof, are cōmaunded into a Parler where they haue such countenaunces made them, and such speach vsed towards them, that it is easie to be espied that they haue no maner of regard vnto them at all: and there (forsooth) they put them a question a greate deale meeter to be asked of men in a farre better case then they are in. As foz the purpose: what their sute is? oz what they woulde haue? Whereunto eche aunswereth that he would be glad to haue some ende and determinati-on of his trouble. Mary and thereaboutes we go (say they) as carefully as we can, and assure your selfe we will not forget you. But if he be earnest to haue it determined, they bidde him bethinke himselfe then and say the truth, asking him why he no moze regardeth his cōsciēce? &c. At ŷ lēgth, laying the faulte of his long imprisonmente to hymselfe (whereas he poze man woulde haue bene contente, if he myght haue had his choyce to come foeth to the stake, ra-ther then to continue there so long) they send him to prisō agayne. And albeit they afterward do graunt him diuers other dayes of hearing: yet as he continueth his sute, so kæpe they him of with their accustomed delayes, till they thinke it be time to communicate vnto him the depositions made againsst him, which they terme the publication of the witnesses.

The publication of the witnesses.

AFter a long & lothsome time of imprisonment, in such sort as mans nature is not able to endure it any lon-ger, when the poze soule in their iudgementes is bzought

so low that he could be content to be deliuered with all his
harte, though it cost him his life, and therefore likely to tell
al and more too, yea euen as much as they them selues can
demaund or desire: they call him yet agayne before them,
& in a speach framed as it were meane betwixte a sharpe
rebuking and a gentle admonition, do aske him how it hap
peneth that he hath slept his owne matters so long: & now
at the length would haue him come in & tell the truth. Up-
pon which poynt they stand very long in perswading him, &
the either in this or the next day of hearing, the Fiscall entreth
his action against him, praying that publication may be
made of the witnesses: which being graunted, forthwith the
depositiõs are deliuered to the party, but yet without any
names subscribed. The order and pening wherof is a sufficient declaration what greate zeale this holy Court hath
to bring the truth to light. For all thinges are so difficult-
ly reported and so abruptly, so wrested & wrong, with such
doubtfull termes of double sense and vnderstanding, that a
man would iudge him (sure) neuer well in his wittes that
vttered them. And this is a peece of the Legeir demaine of
that holy house, purposely conueighed to driue the party alwayes into a doubt, euë of those poynts which he knoweth
are already deposed against him. Secondarily, that so nigh
as may be, he should haue no maner of knowledge of the wit
nesses, who they were that did depose against him, lest hap
ly he might take some exceptiõ against thë. Finally, that if
he haue conferred with any other then his accusers cõcer-
ning those matters wherof he is accused, and knowing not
who where his accusers, but labouring to find them out,
might perhappes reckë vp all, and so by that meanes bring
a great sort of mo fishes into the Inquisitours holy Angle.

And here would I be glad to know of these Fathers of
the faith seing they are so wel learned in the lawes (if they
would be so good as to tell vs how it commeth about) that
whereas the Publication of witnesses is ordayned of com-

C.ii.   men

mon right to be vsed sincerely and playnly, yet in this holy
Court it hath no place nether is allowed for law, by reaso̅
that the names of the witnesses are suppressed, and so the
one halfe of the lawe, yea the better halfe of it, is curtalled and quartered, and the residue nether vprightly hādled,
nor faithfully, but most craftely and falsly abused, as I will
make relatio̅ hereafter. And if an exceptio̅ wil lye against
witnesses, not onely by order of law, but in other respectes
vpon very good & necessary consideratio̅s, bicause knaues &
vilaines should not any way trouble nor molest honest me̅
that are guiltles & innocent, why is there no place in this
most holy court for such exceptio̅s? For in ciuil causes but
of small importaunce, they wil not admitte a mās enemy
nor a lyer, nor a defamed person, nor an Idiot, nor a Bedlem, nor a drōkard, nor a Iew, nor a villaine, nor any such
kind of people to be swor̅ne as witnesses: & who the̅(I pray
you)hath enabled al this route of Rakehels, in matters of
religion & the waightiest causes that can be, to be accepted
and admitted for witnesses, & that their testimony shalbe
receaued and reputed of in matters touching life & death,
seing they are dishabled by all lawes to condemne any mā
in the least trifles that may come in questiō betwirt man
and man? But here perchaunce they wil say they deny not
but the party hath very good liberty of chalēge against the
witnesses if he could learne by any meanes or coniecture
who they be that deposed agaynste him. Therefore if he
chaunce at any time to gesse him right that hath thus testi
fied against him, so that the Court iudge him insufficient
and doth therfore refuse him, they haue done notable iniury to both partes, or to one of them at the least. First of all
to the witnes, by refusing him now, if they did right before
in suppressing his name, bicause y party should not know
him: nexte, to the party him selfe, being now at the length
content to admit his exceptions, so he can gesse or by some
other meanes learne his name, and haue sufficient matter
to charge him withall, and such as may be thought good
cause

(marginal note:) Witnesses admitted in their holy Inquisitio̅.

cause of challenge, which surely in all indifferēt mēs iudge
mentes that haue any consciences at all, is an horrible &
most detestable kinde of iniury. But to returne to theyr
practises. The depositiōs of y witnesses therefore is an euident proofe, aswell by their order and maner of examination, as also by theyr forme of speach therein vsed, whether y
Inquisitours haue kept the euen strete, or gone by crooked
lane. For this is most sure, that they are not commōly read
to the party in such sort as the witnesses haue deposed, but
if any thing be vttered besides by the witnesses that might
make for the prisoner or be construed on his side, they reiecte all that as needelesse and superfluous, admitting only
that which maketh most against him, and clappe on all y
on their owne biace side. For the further proofe and declaration whereof it wilbe worthy the noting vnto you, to
shew what their common vsage is in registring of such depositions. As for example.

　　N. a witnesse (suppressing his name) sworne & allowed, &c. saith, that he the sayd N. heard in such a place, and
such a yeare, & such a day of such a moneth (if he cā so precisely remember the times) such a man reporte, that the a
foresaid, that is to say the party accused, said thus and thus,
&c And in their Records which they call their Originall
processe they haue all those circumstances at large, which
they exacte of the witnesses for a further truth and trial of
the matter, but in y exemplified copie which they deliuer
to the party himselfe, very subtilly they suppresse all y circumstances of time and persons present, whereby the partie might haue any incling of his accuser or witnes, suppli-
ing those places with these or such like wordes. A certaine
person: an other man: and a third person. In which kind
of depositions there be certaine priuie points and nice con-
ceites diligently to be obserued, that is to wit: When soeuer they say that he heard it of a certayne person whome
he hath named, it is to be vnderstode that y witnes heard

the party himselfe spake, & by the crafty conuesauce of the
Inquisitours it is so brought about, that in ÿ counterfeate
copy which they deliuer to the parties handes, it semeth as
though he had heard it of some other mans mouth because
he shall not gesse who it was that gaue euidence agaynste
him: but hauing côferred therin with diuers others, as wel
as with this man that deposed against him, should no moȝe
know who hurt him, thê he that plaieth at blind man buffe
can gesse who gaue him the blowe. And in this behalfe, if
the prisoner chaunce to mention any such persons as the
Court hath not yet bene enformed of, they are incôtinêtly
outlawed & reputed as fauourers of hereticks foȝ suffering
an heretick to sow such pestilêt sædes among thê without
making complaynt thereof foȝthwith to the Inquisitours,

But if the depositions be one this wise, that he heard
it of an other certayne person whom he hath named &c.
it is to be vnderstode that the witnes heard it by a meane,
and therfoȝe wil not serue to ioyne with an other witnes,
though he be a man good enough foȝ them, and fitte to fæde
their suspicious humoȝes. The differêce betwixt both these
depositions is no moȝe but this, that in the one this woȝde
other is vsed, that is not put in the foȝmer, which is onely
thus, that he heard it of a certayne person &c. This geare,
I tell you, is taken out of their Sancta Sanctorum. Thus
by these subtill and captious quiddities, the Inquisitours
begile many a chȝistiã soule that knoweth not their sleigh-
tie dealings, but thinketh him selfe safe enough because he
fæleth his conscience fræ from vttering any vntruth. And
truely it is greatly to be lamêted, that such poȝe wretches
being giltles (god knoweth) a great soȝt of them should be
so hemmed in of these crafty catchpoles, so farre beyond all
humanity, foȝ want of a little skill in these their subtill
and sleightfull deuises. Wherein this counsell of ours (per
haps) may do them some maner of pleasure, foȝ the moȝe
easy espying and auoyding of these their pollicies. The de-

tendant therefore must take hede that he speake not one word at this day of hearing, tending to the confutation of that which the witnesses affirme, yea though it be as false as God is true, and he himselfe neuer so well able in hys owne iudgement to answere it presently, lest the Inquisitours by their importunity happen to wring out somwhat from him on a suddayne, as they vse to deale with diuers. Onely let him this doo, that is to say, craue a Copy of the depositions, and licence to answere them in writing by leasure and with deliberation, against the next Court day, or so soone as he can conueniently. In which answere let him see in any case that he obserue those things, whereof in the accusation made by the Fiscall, I haue geue him instructions before. Secondarily, after he hath obtained the Copy diligently to marke of himselfe, who be witnesses with the witnesses, and who not, and whether theyr testimony be able & sufficeint to condemne him in these matters wherin they beare witnes with y other or no. As for his Aduocate, he is but only for fashion sake, and it were as good for him to haue one of clouts, for any helpe y he is like to haue at his hand, much lesse (may he thinke) at y Inquisitours.

But as concerning the witnesses, two y heard it of report are in this lawles Court as good as one y heard it of his own mouth: so y two such witnesses of heresay, and one that heard it of the parties own mouth, are enough to condemne him. Moreouer it is to be noted that the keper of the Inquisitours prison whome they commouly call Alcaidium, is as good as two of the best witnesses. And therfore for such matters as he hath sene and obserued in the prison, his onely testimony is sufficient to condemne any whome he him selfe accuseth. Yea, and in some cases one only witnes, though he haue nothing but by heresay, yet is he sufficient to put y party in ieoperdy of the rack, if he haus not some iust cause of challege against him. But if there were any respect at all or regard of iustice in this Court so farre

The nomber and qualitie of theyr witnesses.

C.iij.   from

from all conscience it were enough in all godly & indiffe-
rent mens iudgemēts, either for the parties deliueraūce,
or at the least for his purgation, to auoyde that quidditie in
the depositions which I mentioned before, by faire and flat
deniall of that, which the witnesse sayd onely of heresay.
were this word other there or no. Wherwith the Inquisitours seeke to salue the matter and to saue them selues, being in dede but a very false and a friuolous cauill, onely to
colour a lye. For so should it fall out in the ende, that he
who deposed nothing but of heresay, should (as right and
reasō is) be refused as insufficient: and the other that spake
of his own precise knowledge, be likewise reiected, if there
were iust cause of exception: so that both theyr secrete practises should be auoyded, and the Inquisitours enforced to
lay away all this theyr double dealing, & to tel him plainly that the witnes heard it of his own mouth, and so driue
the party to auoyd it more substancially. But what shifts
should a man make in such a case? For, hauing the law in
theyr own hands like Lords, nay, like most cruel Tirants
rather, when they know the witnes had it at the first hād,
yet will they make as though they were content to admit
the exceptiō of the party who tooke the witnes to be none
other then such as had it by reporte, and wil afterward order the matter as it pleaseth them, whiles the party suppo-
seth that he hath sufficiently auoyded that witnes, & thinketh himselfe sure inough for him. Let him therefore well
and warely cast with himselfe aforehand, or rather pray
vnto God to reueale vnto him, what is to bee done in thys
perplexitie.

The Pro-
moters ser-
uing their
holy Inqui-
sition. Furthermore in this holy Court euery Iohn a Vale may
be a promoter, and euery frantike Bedlem that is besides
himselfe, euery verlet or villaine (& so forth euery one of
the 24. orders) be he a persō neuer so much disabled in law
to be a witnes. For a hungry hunter and one that is gredy
of his game, will be glad of euery curtalled curre that will

do him ſeruice to bring home his pray And if ꝑ Promoter
in his information chaunce to wante wordes of weight, or
to miſplace them, or haue forgotten the very wordes which
he heard the partie ſay, ſo he can hit of the matter and remember the ſubſtance, the Inquiſitours by vertue of theyr
office(forſooth)inſtruct him, & bring it into his remembraunce
again: In ſo much, that oftētimes the Promoter wil tel ſuch
a tale, as neither he heard, nor euer ment to tell, but euen
as they themſelues haue prompted him woord by woord,
whiche a man may well thinke is not all of the beſt ſorte.
Yet God hath ſometimes ſo blinded theyr ſenſes and vnder-
ſtandinges, that they haue quite forgotten both themſelues
and all theyr own practiſes and deuiſes. As it came to paſſe
on a time in the yere of our Lord God. 1555. at Siuill, that a
certaine frantike woman, in the abſence of her keper chan-
cing to breake loſe,& to vndoe her boltes and irons wherein
ſhe was fettered in a certaine godly mans houſe, came to the
Inquiſitours to ꝑ caſtle Triana, & there had almoſt diſcoue-
red vnto thē the whole aſſembly of the congreation, which
in that great citie here & there met in corners. The which
(no doubt) had bene a pray alone for them, but that God
marueloully defended that good flocke of his, being at that
time very ſmall (in compariſon) and farre vnable to abyde
the puniſhmentes which ſince that time they haue for the
profeſſion of Chriſt endured moſt conſtantly. This woman
before ſhe fell madde was one of the chiefe in the congregation: I meane for freuencie of zeale & ſkill in holy ſcripture,
farre aboue that, which a man would looke for at a womãs
hand. By meanes wherof, ſhe was very well acquainted w̄
all thoſe, who in this perillous time profeſſed the Goſpell
of Chriſt, but in the heat of her phrenſie all her former loue
& zeale that ſhe bare toward the congregation being turned
into an extreme & a deadly hatred, ſhe raged ſo vehemētly a-
gainſt ꝑ aſſembly of godly perſons, ꝑ in al her madding time
ſhe had nothing els in her mouth, but cryed vpō the Inquiſi-

F.i. tours

toures on this fort: fire & fagots, fire &burne them, poſſeſſed (no doubt) of ſome euill ſprite labozing quite to ouerthzow that good Chziſtian congregation by the meanes of that madde woman. Therefoze ſo ſoone as euer ſhe was gotte looſe, ſhe went ſtraight way with all ſpæede to the Caſtle where the Inquiſitours lay,and there knocked at the gate, which were opened vnto her by and by, as commonly they are not ſtraite kept vpon any that can infozme that ho-ly Court agaynſt a ſozt of pooze innocents. Whereupon at her firſte entraunce within the gate, ſhe required that in all haſt ſhe might come to the ſpeach of the Inquiſitours. Who ſtraight way aſſembled al together in their Parler as it were to conſult about ſome waighty affaires, and ſent foz the womā befoze thē to heare what ſhe could ſay.Which immediatly declared vnto them that ſhe had bzought them a Bedzol of Lutherans that ſwarmed abzoad in the Citie, whiles they that ſhould diligently ſæe to ſuch thinges, ſatte idell within and ſlepte theyz matters: and ſo beganne to recken them, and if ſhe had pzoceded, ſhe had appeached to the number of 300 and aboue, that were very earneſt pzo-feſſozs of the Goſpell but that the Inquiſitours aſtonyed at this ſuddayne ſight, and meruailing at the firſt what thys ſhould meane (foz till that time there had bene little talke oz none of any Lutherans) beſides,eſpying many madde toyes which ſhe vſed in the telling of her tale (which was a truth in dæde as ſhe repozted it) cauſed her to ceaſſe her pzatyng in good tyme. Yet becauſe they would not bee thought negligent in doing theyz duty, though the matter were but of ſmall impoztaunce, they kept the woman ſtill, and ſent foz the good man in whoſe houſe ſhe was kept, whom ſhe ment to haue made fozeman in her bill, becauſe he had entreated her ſomwhat roughly at ſuch tymes as her fittes were vpon her, to the end to make her leaue her ra-uing. The mans name was Franciſco a Cafra, the parſon of Saint Vincentes church; who afterwardes was impzi-

soned

soned for religion & escaped away by a miraculous meanes:
not withstanding in the very first triumph ouer the Lutherans, they burned his picture . When he was sette and
brought afore them, being taken for a good honest man, they
asked him what the woman ment by talking of such a number of Lutherans &c. but he forthwith forcing a laughter,
fained himselfe to meruaile much at thē, in ẏ they perceaued
her not to be besides her selfe, declaring vnto them that she
had bene in that plight by ẏ space of 2. or 3. monthes, in so
much that he was constrayned to beat her and binde her, as
was to sée by her shoulders that were both blacke and blew,
and by the print of the Irons on her legges: adding moreouer, that he for Gods sake and in the way of charity kept
her at his house : from whence she brake loose causing
him and his whole household to séeke her ouer all the citie:
howbeit he was now right glad that he had once met wyth
her agayne and found her safe. As for the Lutherans whom
she prated of so much, he told them, that during the time of
her fits, she had none other song, as most commonly madde
folke wilbe alwayes talking of some one speciall matter
or other . And for the fetters wherein she was chayned at
his house, if it were theyr pleasure either to send any to sée
them, or to make enquiry of the neighbours about him, they
should find all thinges so as he had reported, and therefore
besought them, that some of theyr seruauntes might take
and bynde the woman and bring her home agayne to hys
house . Whereat the woman fell into a great rage and exclamation, that all the castle range withall, saying she was
not madde, but he was the greatest and starkest Lutheran
in all the Citie, that laded her with Irons and scourged her
dayly most pitifully . At which wordes they all fell in a
great laughter, and thereupon commaunded theyr seruauntes to take and bind her, and to cary her to her olde
home agayne, and to her colde Irons, commending hym
greatly for hys good worke in taking vppon hym so great a

F.ij.   charge

charge as to deale with a madde woman, & to seeke meanes
to amend her, aduising hym henceforth to make her surer,
leaft she should chaunce to breake loose hereafter, and make
as much bussines at some other tyme. Thus the Inquisitours forgetting them selues and theyr owne practises, loft
at this time as great a pray, as all that amounteth vnto
which they had bene scraping and gathering together in the
haruest time & increase of the church for 2. or 3. yeres before.
But to returne to our matter. It is furthermore to be cõsi-
dered & obserued in this holy Court, that ý Promoter neuer
speaketh in open Court agaynst any person, but onely the
Fiscal, who is, as it were, an Atturney generall to moue the
Court in all the matters that are brought vnto hym, and to
take all the informations, and pursue them accordingly, so
that the Promoter serueth him for a witnes. Wherof, like
(as of other thinges) I nede not to bring any other proofe or
testimony then their owne. Let euery man therefore iudge
by what right or reason they do it.

The confutation of the witnesses.

Then after 3. or 4. dayes, the party is commaunded to
come before them, and to put in his aunswere to the depositions. And wyth hym commeth also his Aduocate. But
here I should not forget to tell you by the way, that whereas it is the part of euery Aduocate in all iust causes, diligently to conferre with his Client about his depositions, and to
aduertise him, which be the chiefe and principall poyntes
that require aunswere, and not onely this to do, but also to
drawe the aunswere himselfe, and set it in such order as
most may further his Clientes cause (els whereto doth an
Aduocate serue but for such purposes) they leaue the simple
man to hymselfe, to deuise and dispose it so well as he can,
hauing none in the world to help him, saue God alone. And
if you aske this holy Court the question why they do in this
behalfe

behalfe breake and contemne thys custome, which doubtles proceeded of the very lawe of nature, they can yeld you no reason for it, nor make you any other aunswere, but onely this: Forsooth there is a great difference betwixt thys holy Court and other common Courtes. In very deede they say truth, and so it is: for al their nice quiddities were not worth a strawe, if the parties might there franckly and freely defend themselues by such meanes as are to them by all lawes allowable. But when the party hath alredy framed hys answere so well as he can, then in good time hys Aduocate commeth in, to play his part at the length. Who very warely (I warrant you) & circumspectly (as he knoweth full well it standeth hym vpon, dealing in so daungerous a case) least he likewise, ere he be aware, fal into the Inquisitous hands by some litle ouersight, declareth vnto his Client oprly before the Inquisitours, which depositions they be that touch him nighest, and what be the great matters that are proued agaynst him, who be witnesses with the witnesses, and who not, and that there is no good to be done any way but one, to gesse if it be possible who is his accuser, and to deuise exceptions agayst hym. And yet it is not best for the Aduocate here to be ouer busy in prating to the party, or to put hym in minde of any further matter that myght do him good, more then he by aduisement and leasure can picke out of himselfe. Onely this counsell he geueth hym, to remember himselfe and call his wittes together when he is most at leysure, with whom he hath fallen out at any tyme, because it may be that some of his enemies hath accused him for some old grudge. For if there be any apparant matter of some special quarel that hath bene betwixt the party and his accuser, this is all and the onely cause of challenge that this Court will admitte agaynst any witnes, whatsoeuer. Furthermore, he declareth vnto him that he may refuse peremptorily such witnesses as haue varied in theyr tales, or be his enemies, as is aboue sayd: or if he can bring mo wit-

nesses

nelles, to proue that he hath alwayes bene an aduersary to that whereof he is accused, and one that hath rather frequented and dayly bene conuersant in the contrary. And here is al the helpe ÿ the poore Client hath at his Aduocates hands. Wherupon he is remaunded to prison agayne, with this Item alwayes, that he vtter the truth, wyth a fewe menacing wordes now and than enterlaced, more then wel do befeeme them, that if he will not be ordered in time, they will extorte it out of him by extremity of lawe: whereby it is geuen the party to vnderstand, that he shalbe henceforth more straitely examined, and more hardly dealt withall: in fo much that after 3. or 4 dayes respite geuen hym to call his wittes together and to remember himselfe, they send for him againe, & aske him whether he hath yet bethought himselfe, and haue ought to say. But whether he hath, yea or no, his Aduocates questiõ is: if he haue hit on the names of any of his witnesses or accusers. Wherein if the party can call any thing certainly to minde, he declareth it vnto the Inquifitours, praying them to consider, whether such and such men be not his accusers, betwixt whome and hym there hath bene an old grudge, which as yet refteth betwixt thẽ vncompounded. Howbeit if he gesse not aright, besides this, that his answere is not worth a buttõ, both hys whole three or foure dayes labour spente in gessing, is quite loft and his accusation abideth ftil vntouched. But if he chaunce to gesse right, his aduocate asketh him what exceptions he can take againft such as he hath named, but dares not for his lyfe directly tell him that he hath gessed aright, for it is not good for him iwisse to talke so playnly. Yet when the Aduocate hath heard his Clientes exceptions, & taken ÿ names of such witnesses as he nameth vnto him for profe thereof, being now at more liberty then before, he taketh vpon him the charge to examine those matters by interrogatories, & further demaundeth of his Client, if he be able to bring in proofe for his better purgatiõ, that he hath bene a frend to ÿ Fryers and Monkes and familiarly acquainted with them,

and

and diligently obserued and kept all and singular the cu-
ſtomes, rites, and ceremonies of the church of Rome , and
vſed to come often to ſhꝛift, and to receaue his maker, & in
paſſing by any image oꝛ croſſe, if he haue done to them their
due reuerence, ꝥ it may appeare that he is none of Luthers
ſeꝏ. Finally if he cã be able to pꝛoue generally, that he hath
bene quite contrary to that whereof he is nowe accuſed.
Which if he pꝛofer to do particularly, the Inquiſitours by
ſolemne acte in law do opély declare in Court, that they are
cõtét that he make his purgatiõ accoꝛdingly within 9. dayes
next after. The whole charge whereof, after that the party
hath geuē in ꝥ names of thoſe witneſſes that depoſed againſt
him, reſteth wholy on ꝥ Aduocate, as I haue ſaid a litle befoꝛe. Howbeit euery mã hath not thus much fauour ſhewed
him to make his purgatiõ on this ſoꝛt, but only in ſuch caſes
where the witneſſes in their depoſitions agræd not wᵗ their
fellowes, noꝛ greatly with themſelues in their owne tales.
Foꝛ otherwiſe they haue but ſmall ſuccour oꝛ none at all
to auoyde them by making their owne purgation, but only
are admitted to take exception agaynſt the witneſſes (as I
ſayd befoꝛe) if they can deuiſe who they be.

And when the party is pꝛocæded thus farre, let him per-
ſwade himſelfe that God hath bꝛought him thether foꝛ triall of his faith, whether it be pure and perfeꝏ, yea oꝛ no. Foꝛ
if he vppon hope to auoyde the pꝛeſent perill of the body, determine to vſe ſuch ſhifts foꝛ hys ſuccour in pꝛocuring hys
purgatiõ by meanes afoꝛeſayd, albeit he be thoꝛoughly quit
in this Courte concerning his duty and obedience to the
church of Rome and her Idolatries: yet be he wel aſſured, in
that generall day of doome which wilbe ſo terrible to all
creatures, and in the iudgement of gods true church , it will
fall out againſt him farre otherwiſe. It ſhall therefoꝛe ſtãd
a man vppon in this caſe to looke well about him, and to enter into his owne conſcience, and ſecretly debate wyth himſelfe the cauſes of his impꝛiſonment diligently . Foꝛ if it be
foꝛ the gloꝛy of God, and the frée pꝛofeſſing of the truth, and

he forſweare Chriſt treading the bloud of his teſtamēt vn¬
der his féete, and denying the truth whereunto God hath
called & raiſed him, out of that déepe dūgeon of darckenes,
ignozance, and ſinne, hoping by theſe curſed and damnable
meanes to eſcape the tyranny of men, perhaps he may do ſo
foz a ſeaſon, and purchaſe the fauour of men agayne: but let
him be moſt aſſured that he ſhall neuer eſcape the ſharpe
and moſt iuſt iudgement of God, from whoſe truth he is
reuolted: whoſe power is not alonly ouer the carcaſſe to kill
the body, but afterwardes to throw ẏ ſoule into vtter darke¬
nes. Therefoze if he haue any ſparcle of grace left aliue
within him, oz any zeale either of Gods glozy, oz loue of his
owne ſaluation, oz that the authozity of our Redemer may
waigh with him any thing at all, ſaying: *who ſo denieth me*
before men, him will I deny before my heauenly Father: and he
Math. 10 *that acknowledgeth me before men, him wyll I alſo acknowledge*
before my Father and his Aungels in heauen &c. he wil who¬
ly reſt vppon that authozity, and ſticke to his tackling in
that pinch, and vtterly reuouncing with hart and mouth all
theſe meanes to ſaue this tempozall lyfe, offered vnto him
by his Aduocate and the Iudge (whereunto he cannot geue
his conſent without great diſhonour to hys creatour, and
daunger of hys owne ſoule) will yeld a plaine and open con¬
feſſion of his fayth, thinking him ſelfe a thouſand tymes in
better caſe, that God hath pzeſerued him to that inſtant,
to ſuffer ſome affliction foz Chriſts ſake, battering in péeces
this earthly tabernacle (that is to ſay, a full weake & wea¬
riſh body) foz ſo noble a quarell, as is the honour of God and
the building vp of his churche. Foz theſe curſed meanes to
ſaue a mãs life (which that holy houſe the very ſack of ſinne
and iniquitie vſe of like curteſie and compaſſion as is in the
Crocodile to graunt to theſe pooze ſoules) are not here repoz¬
ted to the end, that the godly ſhould learne hereby the ſhiftes
to ſaue themſelues, but rather, that by knowing them they
ſhould vtterly auoyde and abhozre them, and that the wozld

may

may sée that all the deuises and policies of this holy Inquisition tende to no other ende, but after they haue layd theyr
cruell hands continually stained with ẙ bloud of some of the
Saints, vpõ any person, if he relent & recant gods glorious
truth, so to destroy him both body and soule: if otherwise,
yet at ẙ least to kill his body, ouer which alone theyr power
is able to extend it selfe in such as liue in the feare and seruice of God only and truly.

Thus, after that the party hath endured 2. or 3. moneths
in prison at the discretion of these good Fathers, they send for
him foorth once againe to the place of this christian combat:
where the Inquisitour beginneth to declare vnto hym, how
that the witnesses which he brought for his purgatiõ, haue
bene heard what they can say, and therefore he desireth
to sée what he can say for himselfe or els to draw to an end.
And after their accustomed maner falleth to exhortation
that he tell the truth, which is alwayes one péece of theyr
talke: so that I beleue a man should tell them a good longe
tale, ere they would be satisfied. Wherunto the party maketh them such reasonable aunswere as he thinketh best for
his owne case. Howbeit vnto diuers they vse to put sundry
questions, and oppose them in their owne aunswere exhibited vp by thẽ in writing, quarreling at euery letter & silla-
ble, like subtil Sophisters. When the party hath spoken all
that he hath to say, the Fiscall concludeth vpõ his sayings, &
lastly, the Inquisitours with the assent of their Counsell &
Assistances geue sentence when and what they list or like
themselues, the Diuines and Monkes & other of the Clergy first weying and considering such thinges as the party
hath vttered touching doctrine and fayth, and so valuinge
it after their owne rate and measure, and trying it by their
owne touch, which they call the Qualification of doctrine.
At what time if the party be able to proue substancially,
that he neuer dealt in Christs Gospel, which they by a new

name

name of their owne coyning commonly call Luthers hereseyes, either they absolue him and geue him his Quietus est, oz els most commonly, vse to ozder the matter & geue iudgement accozdingly as they haue him in a certayne ielousie and suspition still either moze oz lesse : Pzouiding alwayes that none passe their handes without such markes and badges as he shall cary with him to his graue, in token that he hath ben within the Inquisitours pawes. The markes are commonly these: Confiscation of their goods: Impzisonment during life oz foz a great part of it: A white linen garment with a red crosse called a Sambenit, and last of all a perpetuall sclaunder and ignominy to all his stocke and posterity, such as neuer wilbe wozne out, as shalbe hereafter declared. But if the party shzinke not foz the matter, but constātly continue so cōfessing ÿ truth, oz disaffirme the depositions that be against him, hauing not excepted against the witnesses, he is sure to try the tozmentes : wherof I haue now to say somwhat.

The Inquisitours cognisance. *(marginal note)*

¶ *The condemnation to the racke and the maner of the execution therof.*

THe state and condition of the godly (gentle reader) hath bene euermoze from the beginning hard and very miserable, in comparison of the pzosperitie which the wicked and vngodly enioy in this wozld. Foz accozding to Chzistes owne saying in his gospell after Iohn, they thinke they doe God great good seruice, which slay them vpon euery light occasion, and study daily by new deuises and pzactises to circumuent them: wherof you haue heard some sufficiēt pzoofe befoze. And albeit the iniurious dealings and subtile pzactises which I haue declared already, be such, as any good natured people, oz that can be content to be ozdered by lawe, reason, oz equitie, would wozthely thinke intolerable : yet in respect of these that shall ensue hereafter, which I haue now to shew, they will seeme not onely sufferable, but very

reaso

reasonable and full of equitie & good conscience. For they do farre excæde all barbarousnes, yea I may well say all brutish & beastly madnes, that a man can not more aptly liken thē to any thing in the world, thē to that which they do most liuely resemble, and from whence they procæde : that is to say, Sathan their Syre: so that the deuill though he should force himselfe thereto, is not hable in matters touching mē, no nor in any thing els in ye whole world, to go beyond them in these their most monstrous and deuilish examples of tiranny : Neither hath he any mans harte in hys belly, that can without teares reade or heare these thinges that hereafter ensue, which in rifling this butchery wherin many a good soule vpon trifling occasions, yea diuers of thē giltles (God knoweth) are made away, we will lay open before the face of the whole word, and plucke of theyr hoode of holines, wherwith they haue bleared all mens eye, and abused the whole world hetherto.

After the sentence be once geuen (except it be to the racke) the party is not sent for agayne, till the great day of theyr glorious shew, at what time he commeth out into open audience with the other prisoners that come to heare theyr iudgementes pronounced vpon them, and euery man forth with to receaue his punishment accordingly, vnlesse he be found not gilty, and so quite by proclamation . For then is he kept in prison still by the space of ij. or iij. dayes after the Triumph, that the world may thinke that he also departed out with the rest. And this forsooth is one of theyr holy deuises, because they would not be thought to lay theyr handes vpon any person rashly or without good cause why : as they are wont oftentimes to tell the parties by the way, in such exhortations as they make vnto them to vtter the truth. The holy House is so persuaded of theyr owne doings, that what extremitie so euer they shewe vnto the prisoners, yet they thinke they do vnto thē none iniurie . Howbeit diuers of them vnto whome they shew speciall fauour for certayne causes to them known, are set at libertie and sent away to

theyr owne houses two oz thze dayes befoze the great day of
their solemnities, causing it to be noysed abzoade that they
were accused by false witnesses . Pet is this their slye dealyng open inough to any man that list to marke it, euen by
this one thing, that a man shall neuer sée any such false witnesses openly punished therefoze , which in all other causes
are accustomably most sharply séene vnto. But if they be determined to put any man to the racke at suche time as he
least loketh foz it, thé shall he be sure to be bzought into the
Audience where all the Inquisitours oz the greater part of
them, sitte in their seates of maiestie, and besides them the
Prouisor, as they terme him, oz deputie Ozdinary of the dioces, like a shepheard redie to slea one of his owne flocke, who
of duetie ought to be pzesent , aswell to heare the sentences
geuen , as to sée execution ministred . At thys Courte
day they declare vnto the pzisoner howe the Inquisitours
with all their learned counsell haue depely considered hys
whole case, bearing him in hand, that they haue found it out
foz a suretie that he will not wholy declare the truth , and
therefoze are resolued, that he shall ride the racke, and there
be spurred certayne questions , and so by hoke oz by croke
will wzing it out of him, will he, nill he : therefoze they aduise him to do it voluntarily, as he will auoyde the payne
and perill of the racke . Whereunto they ioyne a certayne
exhoztatió, which they intermedle with some sowze speach
of high and thzeatning wozds, and set it out with greate seueritie of countenaunce, rehearsing vnto thé all the seuerall
tozments of ý racke, as terribly as they can describe thé, to
make thé quake in euery ioynte of thé. Pet whether he confesse, oz not confesse, all is one, foz to the racke he must goe.
Whereuppon they send foz the Officer, and commaund him

The place
where the
pzisoners
are tozmen
ted.

to haue the partie into that place where the Racke standeth,
which commonly is a dépe and a darke dungeon vnder the
ground , with many a doze to passe thozowe ere a man can
come vnto it, because such as are put therto , should not be

heard

heart to ſhrike or cry. In the which place there is a ſcaffold reared, where the Inquiſitour, the Prouiſor, and the Clearke do ſit, to ſée the Anatomie made of him that is brought thether. Then the linckes being lighted, and al the players entred that haue partes in this tragedie, ẏ Executioner, who taried laſt to make all faſt (as they ſay) and to ſée euery mã in befoze him, commeth alſo at the length, and of him ſelfe alone maketh a ſhew worthy the ſight, moze thẽ all the reſt of that route, being wholy ꝑraped all ouer from ẏ toppe of hys head, to the ſole of his foote in a ſute of blacke canuas, ſuch as the ſuperſticious Spaynardes weare one Maundie thurſday when they ſcourge and whip thẽſelues, as the cuſtome is in moſt places vnder popery, if not in all (much like that apparell that the deuils in ſtage plaies vſe here with vs in Englãd) Mozeouer his head is couered w̃ a long black hoode, ẏ recheth ouer al his face, hauing two litle péepe holes to ſée thozough, ꝗ all to this end, to make the poze ſoule the moze afrayd both in body and mynde, to ſée one tozment him in the likenes of a deuill. O Lozd, ſuch are their holy guiles.

The diſcription of the Tozmenter.

After the Lozdes be ſette downe ech in theyz places, they beginne with him agayne, and erhozte him a freſh to ſpeake the truth fréely and voluntarily: otherwiſe at hys owne perill be it. Foz if either his arme, oz his legge, oz any other ioynt be brokẽ in the Racke, as it happeneth to diuers, ſo that he chaunce to dye thereof (foz moze gently then ſo they meane not to deale with him) let him blame no mã but him ſelfe. Foz they thinke that after they haue geuẽ him this faire warning, they are now diſcharged in conſcience both befoze God and man, and therefoze are giltles, what harme ſoeuer come vnto him by meanes of the Racke, yea though he dye thereon as innocent as is the childe newly bozne. After this, with ſharpe rebukes ꝗ menacing wozdes, they commaund that the party be ſtriped ſtarke naked, be it he oz ſhée, yea though it were one well knowen to be the moſt honeſt and chaſt maiden oz matrone in all the citie (as

G.iii.   they

they be neuer lightly without ſundꝛy ſuch in this their (ſtá‑
bles) whoſe griefe I dare well ſay is not halfe ſo great in
reſpect of any toꝛmentes that pꝛeſently they endure, as it is
to be ſéene naked in ſuch a pꝛeſence, and of ſuch maner of
perſons. Foꝛ theſe wicked villaines without any regard of
humanity oꝛ honeſty, (which me thinketh they ſhould ſom‑
what reſpect, if it were but only foꝛ their long beardes and
ſide gownes, with the name and countenaunce of grauitie
and holynes which they pꝛeté᷉d, ſeing that neither foꝛ Gods
ſake, noꝛ foꝛ the honeſty of the good and Godly matrones ⁊
ſober maidens they wil not foꝛbeare one iote of that barba‑
rous impudéry) cauſe thé first to be ſtriped into their ſhirts
and ſmockes, and then out of them alſo welnigh (ſauing
your reuerence) vp to theyꝛ pꝛiuityes, dꝛawinge on a
cloſſe linnen bꝛeech, and after that make bare theyꝛ armes
alſo to theyꝛ ſhoulders, as though the wꝛench and racke,
wherewithall they are about to toꝛment them, were not
able to perce theyꝛ linnen, oꝛ as though theyꝛ linnen bꝛéé‑
ches would moꝛe manerly couer thoſe partes, which they
may be aſhamed to diſcouer, then could theyꝛ ſide ſhirtes oꝛ
ſmockes. And here thoſe ranke Rammes declare how they
will not loſe that deuiliſh pleaſure, which they take in that
ſhamefull and vnſéemly ſight, though the pooꝛe wꝛetches
that ſuffer this, buy it both with payne ⁊ ſhame enough full
dearely. The which thing ſurely is a good occaſion, why that
after this ſhameful ⁊ impudent dealing of the Fathers of
ẏ faith be once noyſed ⁊ bꝛuted abꝛoad, they whoſe wiues oꝛ
doughters either haue alredy, oꝛ may heareafter fall, oꝛ pꝛe‑
ſently are in this ẏ holy fathers foule há᷉dling, ſuffering this
ſhameful villany, ſhould be vtterly abhoꝛred and ſhunned of
al the people whereſoeuer they go, aſwell of Papiſtes as of
other, becauſe they ought to eſteme the honeſty ⁊ chaſtity of
theyꝛ doughters and wiues aboue all other treaſures. But
to returne to our purpoſe.

    When the partyes are thus ſtripped out of all theyꝛ
clothes,

clothes, be it he or she, into their linnen breeches, they
signifie vnto the Tormenter by some token, in what sort
they would haue the partie ordered. For thys is one o∫
ther péece of their arte, to talke by signes and watch-
wordes like to pedlers french, wherein from the highest to
the lowest all the packe of them in that cursed Court, as
well Jacke Jayler, as my Lord Judge can vnderstand one
an other very redely As for the torments by the which these
holy Fathers vse to bring mē to their beliefe, as they be ma∫
ny in number, so in sortes they are sundry, yea moe by a
great many thē any one pore soule is hable to enduro or can
come to the knowledge of.

But the most vsuall be the Icobit and Pullie with wa∫
ter, cordes, and fyre: whereof I meane to speake seue∫
rally. And yet haue they one other cast at him first or he go
to his punishment, perswading him a fresh to vtter what∫
soeuer he knoweth either by himselfe or by others of his ac∫
quaintaunce: In the meane space while they are thus com∫
moning with hym, one commeth behinde hym and bin∫
deth his handes with a corde, 8. or 10. tymes about: and be∫
cause nothing should be thought to be done without autho∫
rity and order of lawe, the Inquisitour calleth vpon him to
straine ech harder thē other. Being thus bound to the rack,
they begin yet once againe to perswade wt him & besides the
bynding together of his hands, they also cause his thombes
to be bound with some smaller line drawen very straite, &
so fasten both the lynes that tye both his hands & thumbes,
to a certain Pullie which hāgeth on the Icobit. Thē knocke
they great and heauy bolts vpon his héeles, if the party haue
none already, or els hang betwixt both his féete vpon those
boltes which he hath, certaine waightes of Iron, at the first
tyme but of 5. pound, and so hoyse him vp from the ground.
Whiles ý pore wretch hangeth in this plight, they fall to
their perswasions once againe, cōmaunding ý hangman to
hoyse him vp on high to the very beame, till his heade touch
the Pullie. Then cryeth the Inquisitor & the Clerke vpon

The Ico-
bit or Pul-
lie.

G.iiii. hym

him to confesse somewhat, promising to let him downe out of hand, if so be that he wilbe ruled : otherwise, they tell him that he is like to tary there till he would be glad to declare whatsoeuer they would haue him. After he hath hong thus a good space, and will graunt nothing, they commaund him to be let downe, and twise so much Iron more to be layd on hys héeles, and so hoysed vp agayne one inch higher if it may be, threatning hym that he shall dye none other death, except he declare vnto them the truth in such matters as they demaund of him, and therefore charge the hangman to let him vp and downe, that the waight of the Iron hanging at his héeles, may rente euery ioynte in his body from other. At which intollerable paynes percing all the partes of his body, if the party shryke or cry out (as he hath good cause to do) they are as loude on the other side, roaring and yelling vpon him, to declare the truth then, or els they tell him he shall come downe with a vengeaunce. Neyther will they only say so, but the party shall finde it so. For if he continue in the same minde, they go on forward as fast in their madde moodes, & bid the hangman to slip the ropes suddenly, that he may fall downe with a sway, and in the halfe

The Strip pado. way to stop and geue him the Strippado: which being done in a trice, al his whole body is out of his frame, both armes, shoulders, backe, legges, and all the rest of his ioyntes by reason of the exceding great waight hanging at his héeles, and the suddayne sway tearing ech part from other. And yet here is no ho with them neither . For renuing theyr exhortations and threates, if he will not yeld vnto them, they cause more Iron to be added the third time: so that the poore wretch being in that pitifull plight, halfe deade and more, is by theyr commaundement heaued vp once againe, and to mend the matter withal, besides ý extremities of his griefes, they beginne to raile vppon him, calling him dogge and heretike that will stand so obstinately in concealing the truth and at the length tell him that he is very like there to make

his

his end. Now if the pitifull creature in the middest of hys panges call vpon Chrift (as for the moft part, all that are thus perfecuted for his truths fake doo) that he would vouch-fafe to ayde & affift him, thus miferably tormented & almoft flayne for his fake, then fall they to mocking & deriding hym, faying, Iefu Chrift, Iefu Chrift. Let Iefu Chrift alone and tell vs the truth. What a crying out vpon Chrift makeft thou? confeffe what we afke thee & make vs no more a doe. In much like forte (as a man may eafely iudge) were the blafphemous fpeaches of the Iefves agaynft our Sauiour himfelfe faying : Behold he calleth for Elias . He trufteth in *Math. 27* God, let him deliuer him novv if he vvill : for he calleth *Pfal.22.* himfelfe the fonne of God. Whiche is a true token and moft euident argument, that it is Chrift agaynft whome they kicke and make all this broyle , whofe name when it is called vpon by fuch as fuffer for his fake, their eares do fo ill digeft that they can hardly abide to heare him named or once fpoken of. But if the party at any time defire to be let downe, promifing to tell them fomewhat , and performe it in deede , that is the very redie way to make him be worfe handled then before , becaufe they thinke that now he be-ginneth onely to broch his matters. For as foone as thys tale is at an end, they begin a frefh to exhorte, to threate , to racke him, geuing charge to hale him vp, & to let him down agayne in fuch forte as is before declared. This execution for the mofte parte continueth from nine of the clocke in the morning till high noone, or an houre after , and when they are difpofed to leaue him and let him downe for that time , the Inquifitours for a pollicie afke the Iayler if hys other inftruments be in a redines, to put the partie in feare of further torments being almoft dead with thefe alreadie, the Iayler anfwereth that they are readie, but that he hath not brought them with him. Then fee (fay they) that they be made readie agaynft to morrow and looke that nothing be wanting . For we will try one way or an other , whether

we

we can get the truth out of this fellow, yea or no: and so departe, geuing these and such like wordes of comforte to the poore wretch ý lieth distracted in euery limme: Hovv novv Sirrha? hovv like ye this geare? haue ye enough of it, or no? Well, see yet betwixte this and to morrow, that ye call your wittes to you, and bethinke your selfe what to say, or ells looke to dye none other death but this; and yet we promise thee that al this is but a fleabiting in comparison of that which thou arte like to feele, and so departe. Then beginneth the Iayler to play the bonesetter so well as he can, & to put his armes and legges in their right ioynts agayne: and putting on his clothes, bringeth him backe to hys prison, or carieth him rather hauing neuer a legge to stand vppon, yea somtime draggeth him by the armes or legges two two pitifully: and then forsooth for fashion sake and to seeme somewhat mercifull (minding in deede no such matter) telleth him that a Surgeon shalbe sent for if neede be.

¶ But if they be determined to put the partie no more to the racke, then within two or three dayes, they send for him forth againe into the Audience, and prouide so, that in the way from the prison, as he passeth by the place where the racke stocke standeth and is commonly occupied, the hangman shall stand for the nonce, to shew him selfe in the selfe same likenes of a Deuil, the which I haue before described, that the partie in passing by, may haue a sight of him, and thereby be occasioned the more to remember his former torments. Who comming into the Courte, findeth the Inquisitour, the Ordinarie and the Clerke redie set ech man in his place, which after their maner fall in hand with him, sometime by persuasions, and sometime by earnest intreatie, mouing him to vtter somewhat. At which time if they preuayle not, ne can get any thing out of him, they cause him to be caried to prison agayne. But if he declare any thing, they presse him the more, & such matter it may be his happe to disclose, that it may chaunce to purchase him the racke once more, vppon hope of getting some greater matters at

his

his hands. Marie if they were resolued before to put the party
to the racke once agayn, then about .3. dayes after his last be
ing there, when the ache in his ioyntes is most greuous
and painefull vnto him, they send for hym agayne to come
before them, and what with earnest entreatie and with terrible threates, they labour to haue him shriue him selfe of al
his opinions and hereties, and to appeach as well such persons with whome he hath had conference in such matters,
as also all other whom he knoweth to be of the same minde
and opinion. Otherwise, they will him to make him selfe
readie for the racke, wherein, if it be his chaunce eyther to be
maihemed in any part of his body, or to receaue his deaths
wounde, let him blame no man but him selfe. And if he
continue still the same man that first he was, the keper is
commaunded that once agayne he prouide the racke, all the
aforesayd parties taking their places, as before to see hym
stripped out of his clothes and put to it once agayne in such
sorte as is before declared, or somewhat woorse, after thys
manner.

The partie hauing his handes bound behinde hym, and
hanging at the Pullie, they bind both his thighes together
with small but very strong cord, and so in like manner, hys
legges aboute the calfe or midlegge. Then put they betwixt
the cordes and his legges a short pece of woode, wherewith
they wrest the stringes so stiffe till they be so deepe suncke
into his flesh that they are past sight: a very extreme and a
terrible torment and much woorse then any that as yet he
hath endured. In this plight the poore soule lieth by the space
of two or three howers, abiding the Inquisitours good will
and pleasure: who neuerthelesse cease not to mislesse and
trouble him all this while, either by questioning, or entreating, or persuading, or flouting and mocking hym, or disquie
ting him one way or another. Or in stead heereof, they practise as they thinke best, any other kind of torture, which, albeit it be vsed vppon offenders in other places aswell as in

D.ij.   this

this, yet for one especiall poynte of crueltie added by them, we may iustly ascribe it to their holy Courte as a deuise of theyr owne. The name of it as it is comonly called, is Burrio or Aselli, and the manner of it is this. There is a benche made of masse timber, wrought somewhat hollow on the vpper parte lyke a trough, so large that a man may lye open in it on his backe, and therabouts as his midriffe lieth, there is a sharpe barre going crosse ouerthwart, wheron a mans backe resteth that it cannot settle to the bottome, because ȳ partie should find the lesse ease, where otherwise he might stay & rest his backe against the bottome of ȳ trough: beyng also placed in suche sorte that hys heeles shall lye higher then his head. When the partie is layd hereon, hys armes, thighes, and legs are bound with very stiffe & small cordes about the middest of the maynebone, which afterwards they straine with certaine stiffe wresting stickes or troncheons put vnderneath ȳ cordes til the cordes be setled downe within the flesh and pearce almost to the very bone, in so much that they be cleane out of sight, and then commeth in this deuise of their own addition: First they take a very fine and a close laund or linnen cloth, and ouerspread ȳ parties mouth therwith as he lyeth vpright, so as it may stoppe his nostrels also, that when the water is poured into hys mouth, he should take in no ayre at hys nose. Then take they a certaine quantity of water, so much as it pleaseth the Inquisitours to appoint, which they poure vpō the cloth not by droppes, but in the manner of a long streame lyke a threede, which hauyng somwhat a high fall, beareth doune with it the fine linen cloth into ȳ furthest part of his throte. And here, who so should behold the poore wretch in this pitifull case, would thynke hym (I dare say) to be in as great an agony as any man is at the geuing vp of the ghost. For in all other torments a man may haue liberty to draw his breath: onely here he cannot, by reason that the water

stop-

Burrior Aselli.

The Torment by water and the land.

ftoppeth his mouth and the cloth his noftrels, fo that when they plucke it out of the bottome of hys throate (as many tymes they do, to fee whether he will aunfwer to their de-maundes, yea or no,) the cloth is fo wet with water & bloud together, that a man would thinke the very intrals would come out of his body. And thus the party continueth in thefe panges fo long as pleafeth them, with promifes of fharper fauces, then any that he hath tafted as yet, and fo they fend him to prifon agayne.

But if thefe good fathers be difpofed to deale with him fur-ther, and proceede to other greater tortures (for their luft is law in this lawles Court, where right nor reafon can take no place) then within a moneth or two, or thereaboutes, as they thinke beft, the party is once agayne brought to the racke, and fome twife, thrife, foure, fiue, or fixe tymes, and therin entreated eafily or roughly as it pleafeth the Inqui-fitours to appoint. And fome are tormented in an other forte that is no where els vfed but in this Holy houfe, the which is termed by fire, the defcription whereof is fhorter to fhew then the reft, but the paynes and cruelty as great al-together. They take a charcole panne of Iron full of whote coles which they fet hard ouer againft the foles of a mans feete, before he go to the forefayd racke, and to the ende that the fire might haue the more force to bruffe them, they bafte them with larde or bacon.

The Tor-ment by fire.

Thus after they haue occupied and vnedged all theyr tooles one after an other, and are paft hope of hauing any thing at the parties handes, they refpite him for a feafon to take hys reft, and after a while call him before them agayn and fall to queftioning with him, inquiring and requiring many thinges in a farre other order then they vfed before, in fuch termes as euery word may minifter matter enough to quarell at. The queftions alfo are framed fo cunningly and fo fubtilly (for this is their onely fhift that neuer fay-

leth

leth them (that by graunting one thyng, they muſt nedes graunt another, and deny the contrary to that. Foz theſe Fathers are paſſing good Logicians, and meruailous ſubtill Sophiſters, their craftes maſters I warraunt them, which notwithſtanding that they are daily in vre with ſuch matters, will not ſticke to take a little paynes, and vpon ſtudy to coyne caſes and queſtions foz the nonce, which to helpe their memozy withall, leſt when the time cōmeth that they ſhould haue vſe thereof they might fozget them, are witten and layd open befoze them: ſo that if the party when any thing is demaunded of him, be neuer ſo litle recheleſſe, it is not poſſible foz him to auoyd them but that one waye oz other they will ouertake hym. The onely helpe foz a man therfoze in this caſe is to haue a perfect remembzance of all ſuch things as he hath deliuered vp into their handes: foz it is but in vaine foz him to craue, to haue thē read vnto him, becauſe, either they will not graunt him that, oz if they do, yet will they read vengeably amiſſe. Wherfoze if he do miſtruſt his owne memozy, let hys aunſwere be this, that he wholy referreth them to his fozmer doings and ſayings and in any caſe auoyd reaſoning with them. Oz if by their ſubtilties of Loogicke, they inferre any thing therupppon, which either he knew not of, oz els neuer affirmed, let hym take héede in any caſe how he aunſwereth it, leaſt eyther they entrappe him in ſome new matter, oz els dziue hym to the denying of Gods truth moſt wickedly. And the readieſt way will be, to cut of all their queſtions with a quicke and a round aunſwer, and to tell them plainly that he was neuer ſet to ſchole in all his life to learne theſe quiddities in argument, ne exerciſed in any manner of diſputation. Foz theſe fellowes are ſo cunning herein, and ſo full of interrogations and ſtrange deuiſes, beſides, ſo troubleſome therwithall and ſo impoztunate, that many times they will get that out of a man by theſe meanes, when all the racking in the wozld will do no good.

As

As at Siuil not long agone they apprehended a certain ogoly Matrone, whose husband they haue burned a litle before, & so made her widow. But because her confessiō while she was on the racke and there tormēted most cruelly, was by their owne decrees insufficient either to condemne her to the stake or to confiscate her goods such as they were, and yet, if they could but get only thus much out of her, that she knew full well that the churche of Rome had determined cleane contrary to that which she affirmed, this shoulde bee sufficient cause to make her to forfaite that poore remnaunt of her riches that she had to kepe her selfe withall in her widowhode, though poorely (God wots) they did rather compel her by their importunity, then compasse it by their Sophistry, that she was content to say so much. For perceiuyng that els they would neuer make an end thus to molest and trouble her, in deede (saith she) I confesse that the church of Rome hath so determined, and therfore I pray you enter in myne aunswer to be so, and let me depart quietly, and afterward as you shall see cause determine what shall become of me or mine at your pleasure. Wherunto they gaue her neuer a worde, but onely wrote as she had said and sought no further. For whether it were so yea or no, what care they, so the party say so much, that they may haue the spoyles whatsoeuer, either by hooke or by crooke.

¶ Certayne other deuises to driue the prisoners to confesse such matters as the Inquisitours are desirous to vnderstand of.

Wen the extremity of tormēts with the subtil practises before expressed will do no good, but that the party constantly endureth the one, and auoideth the other very cunningly, then fall these good fathers to other farre better setches to their thinking, wherin who so is able in deuise to go beyond the rest, is counted a chiefe champion, and therfore hath yelded vnto him the preheminence of place aboue

other

other in this holy House being therefore past all hope of hauing any thing at the parties hands by foule meanes, they deuise to compasse him by faire, shewing themselues very mild and mercifull and so affectioned, as though the misery and affliction which they sée the other in, went to their own hartes. They wéepe with him, they entreat him, they comfort him, they geue him their aduise, & deuise for him some secrete meanes to ridde himselfe out of his misery, making him beleue that they tell him that in secrete, which they would scarce tell to theyr owne fathers, or brethern, or dearest frend that they haue aliue, with many other like wordes. And this they vse commonly to do to such as be the simpler sort of people, but specially to women, which for the most part are not so cunning to discerne forced and fayned teares. Therefore when the Inquisitours beginne to vse them so gently, and to profer them such kindnes, then let the party sée to himselfe warely and learne betymes to discerne whereaboutes they go in vsing such flattering speches, assuring him selfe, that they are but faire baites put vpon sharpe hookes: whereof I will of a number report vnto you one example.

The very first time that they beganne to burne for religion at Siuill, which was about 8. or 9. yeares agoe, among certain other that were for ẙ same cause apprehended, there was a very Godly Matrone with two of her owne Daughters and one of her sisters children, who hauing passed all these aforesayd pikes with manlike constácie, were pressed very sore to betray some of their brethern, but especially one to appeach an other. One of the Inquisitours counterfaiting a meruealous kinde of compassion towardes these séelie women, sent for one of the daughters to come vnto him. And when she was come, they two being alone together, he began to make a long preachment vnto her in way of consolation, and afterwardes sent her to prison againe. This he vsed to do diuers times and vppon seuerall dayes,

always

alwayes towardes the euening and there helde her a great
while, declaring vnto her, how great a griefe it was to him
to sée her in these troubles: and therwithall would interlace
some other pleasant communication, moze familiarly many times, then did wel become him. Which tended to none
other end (as it fel out in pzoofe) but to perswade the maiden
that he of very good affection sozrowed to sée her in such distresse, that in seing him so fatherly aduise her what the best
were both foz her selfe and her mother and sister to doo in
this case, should wholy committe her selfe and her cause to
his ozdering. After that two oz thzée dayes had bene thus
spent in such like conference and familiar communication,
weping (as it were) ouer her, foz ŷ miserie which she was
in, with other many moe argumentes and tokens of compassion, wherein he vttered the affections and sozrowes of
his hart foz her pitifull estate, with often pzotestation of
his good will and best furtheraunce to his power: after all
these pollicies (I say) when the wilie Wolfe was sure that
the simple shéepe was within his reach, he beginneth to per
suade with her to disclose vnto him the truth of the matter,
as well in such thinges as touched her mother, sister and
aunte, as any other that were not yet appzehended, binding
himselfe by an othe, that if she woulde so do and disclose to
him whatsoeuer she kneswe concernyng those matters, he
himselfe would stop all these gappes well enough, and find
a meanes that they should all depart home agayne quietly
to their own houses. The maydé being but simply witted,
was soone induced to credite the fayze pzomises and allure-
mentes of this flattering Father, and therupon beginneth
to open vnto him certayne pointes of religion wherof they
were wonte to conferre among themselues, in manner almost, as if one shoulde geue holy thinges to a dogge oz caste
pearles befoze a swine. The Inquisitour hauyng gotten
this thzede by the end, laboured to vnwind the whole clew,
and therfoze calling in the mayden many times befoze him

I.i. to

to the end that her depositions might be entred by order of law, made her beleue that he would take it vp and end it so reasonably, that she should receiue no maner of harme ther-by, & in the last day of hearing made a repetition vnto her of all his former promises as to sette her at liberty againe, and such like . But when the time came that she loked verely for the performaunce thereof, there was no such matter, but contrariwise my Lord the Inquisitour and his adherents perceauing how this deuise had brought som-what to light, which al their extremities otherwise could in no case do, to the end to make her confesse the residue, deter-mined once againe to haue her vpon the racke, wherein she indured most intollerable paines, both vpon the Pullie and the trough, vntill they had, as it were, in a presse wrong out of her aswel her belief, as also forced her to accuse those per-sons whom they had hunted after so long. For the damosell through very extremity of panges and tormentes, was dri-uen to betray her owne natural mother, and sisters, and di-uers other, that were thereupon immediately apprehen-ded and afterward put to the tormentes, and at the length sent to the fire.

Moreouer, the selfe same mayden within a while after played a notable parte in testimony of her belief. For when she was brought vp into the solemne scaffold with other of her companions there to be séene of all the people, and euery one to heare sentence of death pronounced vppon them, as she returned thence to her place agayne, hauing heard her iudgement, which was to be burned, she came to her Aunt who had bene her Schoolemaistres, and taught her her cate-chisme & belief (for the professiõ wherof she should presently be executed) & with a bold courage without chaunge of coũ-tenaunce, bending her head downward maidenly, gaue her most harty thankes for that exceding great benefite, in ta-king the paynes to instructe her , and prayed pardon at her handes if at any time she had offended her, for that she was

now

now at the poynt of taking her death, and departing thys
life. Whome her Aunt on the other side comforted as stoutly, willing her to be of good cheere, & to let nothing disquiet
her, for she hoped in God that she should be with Christ ere
it were long. And this did she in the presence and hearing
of all the people, but specially of all those of the holy House
and their adherents. This Aunt of hers was the selfe same
woman, which a yeare or two before being mad had detected the whole congregation to the Inquisitours, whereof I
made mention before: who being restored to her former
wittes againe by the goodnes of God, so wel as the reliques
of her disease would let her, did now both confesse his truth
and for the same endured most horible and lothsome imprisonment and tormentes: moreouer, was openly whipped,
and so remayned in prison during the rest of her life. But
to returne to their practises.

Certaine other more secrete practises.

The passing excellency of these practises which presently
I ented to discouer, is such, y they rather deserue to haue
some speciall place by them selues, then to be thrust in here
confusedly among these other grosse and common deuises.
For they do as farre passe all the other that haue bene spoken of heretofore, as there is difference in dignitie betwixt
a Court of Pipowders & the high Courte of Parliament.
The first wherof in order as it falleth out, and the most mi-
sticall (& I beleue as beneficiall to their bore as all the rest)
is y abuse of their sacramēt (as they terme it) of Confession,
which by their owne decretals is no smal offence. But al is
law in this holy House (as I said before) whatsoeuer they
list. Theyr deuise is this: Whensoeuer any of the prisoners
beginneth to be but a litle crased, they aske him whether he
be disposed to go to holy shrifte. The which is done for two
especiall cōsideratiōs. The one is, to proue whether he like

well

well of theyr holy confeſſion, yea oꝛ no. The other to ſee it
perchaunce he wil be perſuaded to ſay ſomwhat vnder Benedicite, either touching himſelfe oꝛ any other, that this holy houſe may be ſette on woꝛke. If the party be willing, at
hãd is Sir Ihon and a clearke behind him with penne and
inke left behind the pꝛiſõ doꝛe, and ſo the ghoſtly father falleth to his Confiteor: in pꝛoceſſe whereof he examineth the
ſicke man fir̄ſt generally, and thẽ ſpecially, whether he hold
any of Luthers articles, chiefely in this oꝛ that article, oꝛ
haue at any time conferred with any other concerning the
like cauſes : finally of whom and by what occaſion he hearᵭ
them.&c. Willing him boldely to confeſſe it and to feare nothing, neither to thinke any ſuch villany to be in him as
to reucale it, ſaying that he hath authoꝛity immediatly frõ
the high Commiſſioners to abſolue him of al, ſo that he diſcharge his conſcience: with other ſuch like talke to the ſame
effect. Now if the party follow him ſo farre that he beginne
to confeſſe ought, then is he ſurely caught. Foꝛ whẽ he hath
poured out all & ſayd what he can ſay in theſe caſes (though
he doe it thꝛough the earneſt and wicked perſuaſions of the
pꝛieſt) then doth he charge him further to confeſſe the ſame
befoꝛe a Notary, otherwiſe he telleth him that his abſoluti-
on is nothing auailable vnto him. And if the party yeld vnto him ſo much & be content ſo to dꝺ, then the Clerke, who
lieth lurking not farre of, is ſtreight way ſent foꝛ, and ſo is
this matter diſpatched. But if he refuſe, either miſtruſting
him altogether, oꝛ ells halfe in doubt to credite hym, yet is
he no leſſe indangered by diſcloſing it to the pꝛieſt, then if
he had confeſſed it befoꝛe a Notary. Foꝛ this kind of confeſ-
ſiõ is not right Auricular, but all is done aloud, by meanes
that ẙ crafty Cõfeſſoꝛ repeateth ẙ woꝛds after him & ſo dꝛi-
ucth the party to anſwer him almoſt in the ſelf ſame note:
who knoweth not noꝛ feareth any ſuch matter that there
lurketh any body ſo cloſly behind the doꝛe to harkẽ oꝛ wꝛite
what he ſpeaketh. Then after they haue gotten thus much,
either

either they charge the party therewithall, oz ells by occasi
on hereof examine him further vpon greater matters, and
therupon pike a further quarell vnto him to the intent to
vse moze extreme kind of toztures. Neither doth thys good
ghostly father eyther feare excommunication, oz feele any
trouble in his conscience, foz reuealing his ghostly sonnes
confessiõ, both because he is persuaded, that a litle loud spe
king and in somewhat a higher note then the secretes of cõ
fession would wel allow, is not to be accompted any disclo
sing at all, and foz that, whatsoeuer he did, was done in the
seruice and behalfe of the holy House.

Iulian Apostata (as histozies of very good credite do re
pozte) spoyled the Chzistians of all that they had, and colou
red hys theste wyth a false glose vpon the Gospell, where
as Chziste commaunded all hys disciples to loue pouerty,
and to be careles foz thinges of this wozld. At an other
time he persecuted them most cruelly, and exhozted them to
patience, saying that Chzist had geuẽ thẽ an example. And,
no doubt, these holy Fathers haue bozrowed one of theyz
deuises of him. Foz when they sẽ any constantly, and like a
good Chzistian mã to continue as wel in his faith towards
God, as charity towardes his bzethzen, they hedge hym in
wyth this argument: Now surely Sir, ye are but a faynte
Chzistian by lyke. Foz you pzetende the doctrine of the A
postles and Pzimatiue Church: and the Apostles and Mar
tyzs in those dayes being bzought befoze the Ethnike Ma
gistrates, and examined whether they confessed Chzist oz
no, aunswered playnely that they did: and being further
demaũded, what fellowes and companions they had, would
tell the truth at the first. Therefoze syth you pzofesse your
selues to be followers of them and theyz examples, in lyke
sozt should you confesse of your selues and of your fellowes.
And this is theyz godly reason ÿ they make. In very deede,
Iulianus Apostata spake truth, that Chzistians in the time
of affliction should not be wauering noz geuen to the gathe
ring of these earthly treasures. Euen so say (the Inquisi-

tonrs) fhould a chziftian man comming befoze a tempozall iudge, and there eramined of his beliefe, yelde a playne and euident declaration of the fame. But they lye both of them (by their leaue) when they fay that the Chziftians in thofe dayes did of like zeale betray their bzethern bnto the Eth= nike iudges, as they did make open confeffion of their faith: foz that were flatte agaynft the rule of charity, And therfoze it is a playne matter that in al other things the Inquifitozs are altogether as bad as euer Iulianus was, becaufe they bfe the felfe fame reafons that he did, and all to one effecte : that is to fay, to make wafte in the Church of Chzift, by cutting down the bzaunches therof, making but a ieft of the lawes of true religion.

As there was once an Inquifitour, and one of the chiefeft of them, whome it fhall not be greately amiffe to touche by by name, becaufe if it be his chaunce to reade this, he may acknowledge it to be true that I will repozte of hym. His name was Iuan Gonçales, bozne at Siuill, and Bifhop of

Tarracon. It was his common faying (which I beleue o= ther of his fellowes lerned of him) fpeaking of fuch as were bzought befoze him foz the pzofeffion of Chzift, that it was a wonderfull thing to cōfider, how firmely thefe heretickes haue ingrauen in the tables of theyz hartes this commaun= dement : Thou shalt loue thy neighbour as thy felfe, which will neuer be bzought to confeffe of their fellowes, till they be almoft tozne in pæces with tozments, and yet cā ye not get it out of fome of them by thefe meanes neyther ; Such notable teftimonies hath true religion oftentymes, euen of thofe that are her deadly enemyes. Foz the law of God concerning bothe the Tables, is perfectlye wzitten and fealed in the hartes of true Chziftians, and the pzynte of this feale of Gods lawe is not elfwhere to be founde but in thefe onelye. But all the Lawes of the flefhe are fig= ned with this marke: To day mine ovvne man, and youres

to

to morovve. And surely me thinketh a chzistian Byshop ought to haue bene very much ashamed to be so blind & ignozaunt therein, and not alonely so to be, but thereunto to adde such blasphemie besides.

The selfe same bishop (seeing we haue begunne to talke of him) was sent from the kinges Courte to Siuil to be one of the Commissioners in the Inquisition there, about two oz thzee yeares befoze, at what time so greate a multitude of the faythfull were firste espyed, of the which euen till thys day, at certayne tymes appoynted there be diuers sente to the fire. Foz all hys Predecessours were not wozth a strawe in comparison of hym, neyther halfe so stout as he, noz so cunning in bzinging their matters about as was this one man, and specially such as concerned the holy Inquisition. Foz vntill his tyme there was neuer an hable man, that was thought so pzouident as to pzeuent so great a mischiefe befoze it happened, oz otherwise hable to vpholde the church of Rome dzouping, as it were, by meanes thereof and in daunger of ruine. But foz any other good qualities that were in him to cõmend him to this Office, oz sufficiency to discharge it, I repozt me to himselfe, I repozt me to them that chose him to this office, yea I repozt me to al that euer knew him, if there wer any thing in him at all that might pzeferre him specially and aboue his fellowes, either apparance of learning, oz skill in Diuinity, oz knowledge in the ecclesiasticall Histories, oz any great reading of the auncient fathers oz the late wzyters, (whose autozity the church hath wozthely in great estimation) oz if he were greatly seene in matters of faith, wherof they terme them selues the Inquisitours and iudges, as it were, both of oyer and terminer, in these cases: to be shozt, if there were anye knowne and appzoued godlines of life and conuersation in this man: wherein the whole packe of them flatter themselues so much, that they arrogate vnto themselues a very gaye and glozious title thereby : but

rather becaufe he was moze cruel and vnnaturall, & fome
what moze flie in the deuifes and pzactifes of the inquifitiõ
then the reft were. In refpect wherof he obtained both a
difcharge from his feruice, and a fat bifhopzike befides in
recompence of his trauayles, and partly in confideration
that he was an olde fozwozne fouldiour, and hauyng nowe
good leyfure like a wicked impe of Rome returned to hys
old occupation agayn. At the felfe fame time whiles he remayned in commiffion at Siuil, fo many were appzehended
foz pzofeffing his Gofpell, that he was dziuen to beftowe
fome of them in his owne lodging becaufe all the pzifons
in the towne were not able to receaue them, the nũber was
fo great. Yet his reuerend Lozdefhip wanted neither tyme
noz leafure to take his pleafure abzoad and row vppon the
riuer in Barges tilted with purple and filke, with fuch pzeparation as had better befemed one of Sardanapalus fchollers, then any fober man oz Chziftian bifhop: accompanied
with Mufitians, but not with the Mufes, hauing a verye
great trayne after hym befides, and fo paffyng to his gar-
dayne adioyning therunto, all the whole people gazyng vppon him & runnyng in heapes and thzonges to fee his fight.
In very dede thefe triumphes and Jolities were not greatly out of the way foz him and his mates to delight in, theyz
matters beyng in fuch ftate as they were, and the churche
of God wherunto he was pzofeffed an enemy, fo ful of troubles, vexations, and afflictiõs. But to returne to their pzactifes agayne.

　　Whenfoeuer thefe good gentlemen are defirous to
learne out a certaintie of fuche as liue together all in one
pzifon, (whome they fufpecte to haue fonne conference in
matters touching faluation, either by way of exhoztatiõ oz
by comfozting and confirming one an other in the faith, being in fo great mifery as they are)they fend a flee amonge
them (as the pzifoners vfe to terme him) whom the Inquifitours caft in pzifon craftely & foz a colour to marke euerye
mans talke, who after two oz thze dayes that he hath once
　　　　　　　　　　　　　　　　　　　　crept

The In-
quifitours
flees.

crept into their acquaintaunce, wil begin a farre of to offer
some talke in matters of religion, makyng as thoughe he
would be glad ether to teach other oz to learne himself, & by
these subtil deuises many of ȳ simple sozt are soone beguiled.
Wherefoze let euery man take heede after this faire warning, that he be not ouer light of credite in trusting straungers to far (I meane such as are put in pzison with them)
hauing no maner of acquaintaunce with thē befoze. And to
the intent that they may know such a slee the better, I will
geue them one sure token: to wit, he will commonly be the
first that will offer talke and pzetend a zeale towards true
religion, both beside tyme and without occasion, and then
shall they do well to let him pzeach alone till his chaps ake,
geuing him neuer a wozd. Foz if he chance to get any thing
out of any of his fellowes, that he longed foz, so soone as the
Jayler cōmeth to visite his pzisoners at his accustomable
houres, he is straight way in hand with him to pzay a day
of hearing foz him, as the maner is that sometimes the pzisoners wil sue foz. But so soone as he is out, I warrant thē,
the rest that tary behind shal shoztly after feele the fruites of
his fellowship, little to their likyng. A meruailous matter,
doubtles, that men should be so diuelishly bent, to be content foz a small gayne of a little money, to serue in such offices, so much to their owne hinderaunce, that to obtayne
their purpose they sticke not to lye in pzison with others
bounde and chayned as they bee, by the space of two oz
thzee monethes, and there to endure all the other miseries
incident thereunto, as hunger, filthe, stenche, whiche
the other pzisoners can in no case away withall by theyz
willes, and yet can these men with all their hartes. Besides
this (a moze wonderfull thing to consider) they wil so passe
from one pzison to an other, that they are no sooner out of
one, but by and by they will be in an other, and so in the second, and third &c. and be content to endure the same extremities twise, thzice, oz foure sundzy and seueral tymes, yea

R.i.   all

all their lyfe long to féede vppon these dishes of daynties. And when this good fellow is out of prison and come before them to yeld accompt of his office, he doth not onely declare what he hath heard the prisoners say, but also what counte∣naunce they made him, when he called these matters of re∣ligion into question, and how they tooke it, whether as li∣king or misliking therwithall, or what opinion he hath of thē, though they neuer aunswered him one worde. And this mans accusation is of as great force as the strongest & most allowable witnes that is or can be, and is without all excep∣tion, be he neuer so meane a mā either in calling, or credit, or common reputation of men: yea though he be but a gōg∣farmer and serue in thys rowme for a small reward, yet is he reputed a worthy member for that purpose, well beseé∣ming such a head as is that holy House of theirs. It happe∣neth also many tymes that some suche as are apprehended for religion, fall into the company of some other that are layd in for speciall matters, who to curry fauour with the Inquisitours will villanously accuse their fellowes whom they haue heard conferre together in pure & sound doctrine: and the testimony of such persons is of the greatest credite that can be, & most highly estemed in their holy House. For to the state of the matter or Qualification as they terme it, a great respect is to be had of the circumstances, as the pri∣son, the person of the accuser, and the party accused.

Other Flees there be also which serue the holy House to do the like feate abroade out of prisons, secretly and slily go∣ing about to compasse in by like wyles suche as are among the common people suspected to be Lutherans, whereof some do make so good wing, that they will flye quite ouer the sea into very farre countreis to take such as are content to leaue Spayne and banish themselues thence, to the ende that they may liue ẙ more safely in other places elsewhere: such is the ernest zeale which these good fathers haue both to the glory of God and the health of mēs soules. But to kéepe

within

within the bounds of Spaine, and to speake onely of those that flye about the Cities there where this holy Court is kept, there are a great sort of ghostly fathers, both Priestes & Monkes, which are not behind with their partes in playing the Flees. To whome if a simple man and one whome God hath sent some light of his worde vnto, do chaunce to resort, and in processe of his confession open his conscience vnto hym, either doubtingly, or els as one already perswaded, praying to be further instructed and confirmed, they labour not onely to quenche that lighte which beganne to shyne in his harte, but some of them are in hand with hym either by gentle entreaty, or sometyme by threatning hym terribly to the end to get him to go to the holy House there to accuse himself, promising him in the behalf of the Lordes the Inquisitours, that he shall haue all fauour shewed him that may be, so that it commeth to passe many tymes that the poore soules lyke sely Sheepe will runne of their owne accord into the Wolues mouth to be torne in pieces and deuoured euery morsell.

Another pollicy they haue which they put in practise likewise, more vnhonest by a great deale then this, whiche is also borowed out of y Inquisitours bowdgets. After they haue groped a mans conscience that suspecteth no such trecherye at a holy mans hand, specially vnder their blessed Benedicite, they dissible the matter for that tyme without contrarying him, willing him to resort vnto them the next day whē they shall haue better leysure, to heare him thoroughly, & to talke with him more frely in those matters, & so send hym away halfe shriuen, with halfe a confession ilfauouredly cut of. His meaning is this, that when the party commeth the next morrowe, and communeth with hym of the selfe same matters out of shrift, he may frely and without daunger of reueling his confession, complaine of hym to the Inquisitours: neither doth this their purpose want his performaunce. This religious route (forsooth) can choke wyth a

gnat & swallow downe a camell. And of such craftie dissem=
blers, diuers haue gotten this good by their trauaile at the
Inquisitours hands, that if any thing escape them ignorat=
ly or for want of hede taking (as it happeneth many times)
which had bene inough to haue heaped coales enow vpon
an other mans heade, though the same things were proued
against them so manifestly, that they could not be denied,
yet can the Inquisitours be content to wind vp such mat=
ters, and winke at thē wisely, accompting it a greater losse
to forgoe the gaines that commeth trolling in by such fel=
lowes, then the spoile were worth that might be gotten by
taking aduantage of them. Of the which sort I could, if I
were disposed, recken vp a great number by name, and sure
they well deserue it for their wicked dealings in this kind
of seruice, to be so serued. But I meane to suppresse their
names in consideration of Gods great might and mercy,
who may hereafter shew his fauourable countenaunce vn=
to them, and graunt them grace to repent (as I know he
hath done vnto diuers) and then should I repent me to late
that their names were made so infamous and execrable to
the Congregation by my meanes, though for their own de=
merits. For truly a great number of these at the first knew
the truth, yea some of thē preached and taught it to others.
But so sone as the storme beganne to arise, and to trie ech
mans building vpon what foundation it stode, on the rocke
or on the sands, they thought it wisedome for them to goe
backe with that legge betimes. And being moreouer assu=
red that diuers had thē in a great ielousie for so doing, they
imagined that they could not spunge out that staine by any
other meanes, then if they should become promoters of such
as had bene their fellowes and companions tofore, and so to
become daily Ghestes and stoute Seruitours to this Holy
House : and thus were persuaded that they had taken a
ready way to saue them selues from the Inquisitours. But
what consciences they cary about within them, and what

testi=

testimonies of the terrible iudgement of God prouided for them, they know best them selues. It shalbe sufficient that I geue this Item by the waye, to consider that it is not any zeale in the Inquisitours of the truth or cutting down here sies, that moueth thē to such butcherlike slaughters as these (ỹ which things both they pretend to do, & the cōmon people are likewise persuaded of them) though we should yeld vnto thē so farre that they be erronious opinions which they correct so seuerely. For if it were so, then should they not haue fauoured them that haue done them so profitable seruice, & procured them so great gaines as is said before. Nay all the zeale which they haue is, rather to fil the kings Treasory & their owne purses. Yet if we respect ỹ chiefe cause that moueth thē to make so many poore innocēts to be so miserably punished and tormented & afterwards put to death, besides their wiles, their guiles, their villanous breach of fayth and the deuillsh deuises, by the whiche they do procure their matters, it is a sting of *Sathan* him selfe who hath bene a murderer of the childzen of God, the Father of lyes, and Patrone of such practises from the very beginning. For who is so blind but he may easely espy, that this kind of dealing can procede of none other spirit? or who wilbe so blasphemous to referre it to ỹ spirit of God as author thereof? Moreouer, one other good lessō to the godly may be this, that they take diligent hæde, whome they deale withal or admit into theyr company and familiar acquaintaunce, and not to trust euery man. For truly the saying of *Ieremy* *Ieremy.* that, euey brother vvill supplāt an other, and euery neighbour vvill beguile an other, may as well be verefied at this time, and in these matters, as euer it might in any other age or case heretofore.

Yet haue ỹ Inquisitours one other net more, which albe it they cast not but at aduēture, yet commonly they draw a great draught whensoeuer they vse it. If they chaunce at

any tyme to apprehende any notable and famous fellowe
whome they knowe, eyther to be a greate teacher or preacher to others or els to haue great resort made vnto him for
learninges sake and for their better instructions, as some
Doctor or Preacher of some name and fame, then their maner is to cause it to be bruted abroade by theyr Familiars,
that the same person beyng on the racke, hath detected diuers of hys Auditours, and for the further confirmation
thereof, they suborne some of the next neighboures in the
prison adioyning to sooth it, and to affirme that they heard
the greate shrikes whiche he made beyng vppon the racke.
The which rumours are coyned out of this their holy Mint
to this ende, that such as haue bene his scholers should come
to the holy House and there make open confession of theyr
faultes, and pray pardon betymes before they be sente for,
or the Sergeaunt attache them. For they persuade the common people that who so will come vncalled and vnsent for,
and confesse their owne offences, shall either escape scotte
free, or els very easely: and their punishment at the vttermost shall be onely the doing (as they call it) of a little penaunce. Thus by this meanes they deceaue a great number
which if they had taried til they had bene called, might haue
taried stil til this time vncalled, or if it had so happened that
they had bene sent for, they should haue bene no worse entreated then they were, being so doltish as to credite the inquisitours so farre vpon their faire and flattering promises,
and to follow their folish aduise.

How the prisoners are delt withall
concerning their diet.

THe prisoners within the Inquisition concerning theyr
meate and drinke and other necessaries, are vsed in all
respects accordingly, as they are in credit with the Inquisitoures and the residue of the officers of the holy house. For
the common estimation of them is no better then as they
terme

terme them, dogges, heretickes. &c. And yet they deale not
with them altogether so well, as most men will doe with
their dogges, that doe them eyther seruice or pleasure: but
as men commonly vse to intreate those men, whome in derision of all humanity they terme dogges, and so esteeme of
them. The discourse whereof shall neyther be altogether
nedeles, nor impertinent in this place, because it may doe
much good to the Godly in many respects. First to doe them
to vnderstand the miseries of their poore afflicted brethren,
that they may departe with some thinges for their reliefe,
euery inā acording to his hability: Secondly, to put them in
mind that the staffe stādeth at their dores, and theyr turne
therfore to be the next, and that God hath reserued them for
a time that they may follow the other in this fight, & serue
him in this most glorious kinde of seruice by confessing hys
holy name before the world. Thirdly and lastly, that thrs
horrible & most barbarous tyranny of these holy Fathers
may appeare to all the world, among other of their cruell
pranks, which we are to report of them, and of their bloudy
butchery. Happy therfore, & thrise happy was that preacher
of Siuil, Constantino (for so Solon accōpted him happy that
had liued in honoure and estimation, and dyed accordingly) who being imprisoned (as I will declare hereafter), for
the testimony of Christes gospel, tasting theyr tyranny and
lifting vp his voyce to God many times with these wordes:
O my Lord God, was there in all the wide world no Scy-
thyans, nor cruell Cannibals into whose handes I mightest
haue deliuered me, and let me escape these men? An other
named Olmedo a man singular both for vertue and learning, falling likewise into the Inquisitoures handes for the
self same cause that purchased vnto Constantino his death,
first vppon his imprisonment fell sicke, and afterward dyed
amiddes the filth and stenche of the prison, and was wonte
to say in like sort: O Lord God, do with me what thou wilt,

B.iiii.   Throw

Throw me headlong whether thou wilte, so thou geue me not ouer to these men, whose entertaynmente is suche as may more rightly be termed a perpetuall Torture, then a place of imprisonment. For first & formost, the place wher=

The descrip= tion of the prisons.

in ech of them is shut vp seuerally, what with the straight= nes therof, and the euil ayre, and dampe of the earth, if it be below, may more properly be likened to a graue the called a prison: but if it be aloft, at the time of the yeare by means of the extreme heate, more lyke a frying fornace. And in e= uery of these holes, for the most part (specially if theyr pri= ses be so many that there be moe seuerall persons then seue rall roumes) two or three of them are thronged together, so that they haue no larger scope, then to lay them downe and rest them in, saue onely a foote in compasse perhaps, which serueth for theyr stoole of easement to stande in, and by it a pitcher of cold water to quench their thrust. Neither in the day time is their light any more then may come in at a key hole or at a litle long rift no greater the a mãs finger. How= beit there be certayne prisons that be somewhat larger, but they are also more then somewhat costly, and do serue for such as are not greatly suspected for religion. Againe, other there be, lesse in compasse the the former, and worse a great deale to lie in, for that they are not a mans legth: in so much that they which enter into one of the, lightly neuer goe out till they be halfe rotten or dye of a consumption. All which places and prisons are bestowed according to the qualitie of the person, and of his or theyr deserts, and many times as it pleaseth my Lordes the Inquisitour and maister Jayler to bestow them in, according as they beare affection to the par ty either good or bad. And thus much concerning the place of theyr imprisonment.

The maner of their diet and their allowaūce.

The order of their diet is answearable to their lodging. The rich pay very large fees to the holy House, & euery pri= soner is rated at the discretion of the Inquisitour. Out of the which there is deducted an allowance for his dayly char=

ges

ges.30.dipondia commōly called Maruedis, wherof.17.make
a dutch batte.8.and a half, a french souse.10.a flemish stiuer,
which amounteth in our reckning after ŷ English rate, to
vi.pence well nygh. Howbeit if any of them be disposed to ex
cæde & haue any other dainties, he may at his pleasure, so ŷ
he pay for it on his own purse. And yet they deale not so fauourably with euery sort of prisoners, but onely with such
by whome they loke not for any bootie, being layde in
but for trifling maters. For if they be such prisoners, as they
know by ŷ informatiō geuen in agaynst thē, lykely to lese
all that euer they haue, they will not suffer thē to excede in
such sort, but let thē fæde onely vppon a little browne bread
& a curtsy of colde water, not sufferyng them in any case to
haue any special cates besides their ordinary, be they neuer
so rych, because they make this accompte that the more
is spent in that sort, the lesse shalbe theyr parts whē it commeth to reckening and rifeling. Notwithstanding, if any be
so poore that they are not able to liue of their owne in pryson, the king alloweth them a certayne for theyr dayly diet,
ŷ is to say, halfe a riall of plate, which is as much as a dutch
batte, & is worth two souse french, that is thræ pence ster-
ling. Out of the which pore pittance is to be defrayed theyr
Stevvards and Launders wages, and what soeuer other necessary charges grow besides, must be thence also deducted
Moreouer, of this allowaunce geue them by the king, there
commeth not the one halfe to theyr vse, for whom it was
specially limited and appoynted: for it passeth through two
or thræ mens handes that wilbe ready to finger some of it.
First thorow ŷ office of Receipt (for so I thinke they term
the treasorie) who is accomptant for al the reuenewes that
come into the Escheequer & disbourseth for suche and other
like vses. And this is the swetest office in all ŷ holy House,
and therefore not graunted but to special men, especially fauoured. Next to him the Stevvard or cater wyll haue an o-
ther pece, who will commonly for one penny bestowed, de

(margin note:) Fees deduc
ted out of
the priso-
ners allow
aunce.

maunde two to be allowed: then the Cooke that dzesseth their meate, and last of all the tythe whiche is the Iaylers fées, whiche many time alloweth the same vnto the poze pzisoners of his owne beneuolence. This I haue described the moze largely, because all these Officers haue theyz certaine fées out of this small allowance of the kyng, whiche passyng thozow such limed fingers is so fléced, that it commeth not to the pzisoners but euery of these Officers will take not only Tole, but Tithe ere it passe his handes. For in this house both maister and man from head to fote, are all couetous & geuen to the spoyle. Now if it happen at any tyme by a special grace of God, that any of these are touched with compassion to pity the poze pzisoners, & of very almes do relieue them by any meanes, that is counted such a heynous offence in this their holy House, that it will go neare to cost him a scourging till the bloud follow, that doth any way relieue them.

As it chaunced within these few yeares, a certayne man to be appointed keper of the Inquisitours pzison in the Castle Triana at Siuil, that was not very euill disposed, for as yet he had not learned ẙ trickes of that holy House, noz wel digested their couetous and cruell lawes; beyng otherwise very curteous, and a man not farre striken in yeares; hys name was Petro a Herrera. Who entreated the pzisoners very well, and shewed them such gentlenes and fauour as he could, but closely and couertly, because he knew the Inquisitours in that poynt well enough, how much they were enclined to tyzanny. It happened in his time (as oftétimes it doth when a number are appzehédeð at once) that among other pzisoners a certaine honest Matrone was committto to his warde, with two of her own daughters, which being put into seueral pzisons, had a great longing to sée one another, and ech to cófozt the other in their distresses. Whereupon they besought theyz keper to suffer them to come toge ther, if it were but only foz a quarter of an hower, oz ẙ space

that

that ech might but embrace other. The keper being of a good
nature was cõtent they should so do, and suffered them to be
together by the space of halfe an houre, and after they had a
litle shewed their affections, and done their ducty ech to o-
ther, the daughters to theyr mother, and she to them again,
he brought euery one to her owne prison where she was befoze. Within a few dayes after, ŷ keper seing the same persons in most terrible tozments, and fearing lest the very extremity therof would driue them to confesse that litle curtesy and fauour which he shewed them, in suffering them to
méete & talke together but onely foz halfe an houres space,
went to ŷ holy House, cõfessed his fact, & prayed pardõ therfoze, supposing like a fœle, by his owne confessiõ to haue escaped the penaltie therof. But the Inquisitous (to whome
it is incident to abhozre all kinde of humanitie) déemed it so
haynous an offence, that they commaunded him fozthwith
to be hayled into prison: wherin, partely by meanes of the
greate extremitie that was shewed vnto him, and partly of
very thought and a certayne conceite that he tœke therupõ,
(being therwithall somewhat melancholike) fel beside him
selfe: and yet his infirmity & madnes notwithstãding, they
released him no iote of his punishement. After he had bene
... a whole yeare in a vile prison, they brought hym vpon
theyr triumphing stage, hauing a Sambenit on hys backe
and a rope about his necke like a fellon, and there gaue sentence vppon him: first to be whipped about the citie in the
high strœtes, and to haue two hundzeth stripes bestowed on
him, and afterwardes to serue in a Gallie as a slaue, foz sixe
yeres. The next day following, as he was bzought from the
Castle Triana with theyr accustomed solemnity, to be scourged, one of his madde fittes that was wõt to take him ech o-
ther hower, came at the same time vpõ him very pitifully,
so that in casting himselfe of from the Asses backe wheron
he was sette in despight, he fell vppon the Alguazil, & doubtles had slayne him with a swozde which he snached out of

his hand,if the people that gathered about him had not so
denly layde handes on hym, and set him vppon the Asse a
gayne,binding him somewhat surer, to the intent that he
might receaue the rest of his payment. And after he had re
ceaued his two hundred stripes,the Inquisitours commaun
ded,that for his misdemeanour shewed towards the Algua
zir,he should continue in the Gally foure yeares moe,ouer
and aboue the other sixe,to make vp a iust halfescore . So
well do these good and godly fathers, reward charity & good
deedes,and curtesy,with cruelty and extremity, so that a
mad man with them,may not play a mad touche.

   Howbeit there was one that was this mans predeces
sour called Gasper de Benauides,for couetousnes & cruel dea
linga monster rather then a man,in so much that he was
grown to such a gredines,that he would defraud the poore
prisoners of part of their small pittance & allowance,beyng
both euill of it selfe for want of good cookery,& woorse a great
deale by meane of his filching: of which victuals so lurched
and purloyned from thẽ,he would make good Marchandise
& sel thẽ in Triana. Moreouer, such allowance of money as
should haue bene payd to a Laundres for washyng the priso
ners clothes,he conuerted wholy into his owne purse, no
thing regarding how sluttishly y prisoners wẽt for a great
space together,without any shifte, and thus deceaued both
the Inquisitours & the Treasourer,who allowed the keper
in his accompts for such and such money payd and receiued
to y prisoners behoofe,for whose weekely expences,it was a
poynted.And herein marke I besech you thẽ notable negli
gence & slipper dealyng of both parties:First y wincking of
y Inquisitour at the kepers behauior : & secondly the kepers
vniust oppression of the poore prisoners. But to say truth,it
is no very hard matter to deceaue thẽ that wyll neuer take
paynes to boulte out a truth.   For if any of the prisoners
receauing neuer so much iniury at the kepers hand, had cõ
playned at any time or grudged any thing at all,the cruell

tyrant

tyzant would find the meanes to be with euen them: foz he would take and remoue him from the place that hee was in befoze, and thzufte hym into some déepe Dungeons, whiche they call Mazmorra, and there woulde keepe hym alone foz two oz thzee dayes, geuyng him not so muche as a little ftrawe to lie vpon: and as foz his diet, neyther should it be wholesome noz yet sufficient to hold life and soul together, but like to kil him oz at ý left to bzede some extreme sicknes, al the which should be done without commission oz warrant frõ the Inquisitours, & yet would he very craftely and maliciously bear the pzisoner in hãd that he did it wholly by the Inquisitours speciall commaundement. Now if any that had bene so iuiuriously dealt withall, meanyng to make complaint therof to the Inquisitours, shoulde desyze hym to pzaye a day of hearyng (as none maye sollicit that matter saue onely the Keper) the crafty knaue suspectyng that hereby he should make a rod foz his owne tayle, would beare the pzisoner in hand that he had so done, and therwithall tell him that it would not be graunted at that tyme, and thus with such fozged answeres would kepe ý pooze pzisoner in that déepe dungeon twelue oz fiftene dayes, till he thoght his anger were somewhat afwaged and hys courage thorowly cooled: and then at the lengthe woulde remoue hym thence to his olde pzison agayne, makyng the pooze man beleue, that he had cause to thanke hym foz it, which of mere compassion and pitie that he tooke vppon hym, trauayled to the Inquisitours, and became an earneft suter to them to get hym released. In summe, suche filtchyng he vfed, and such extremitie he shewed towardes the pzisoners, that diuers men of very good credite and eftimation with the Inquisitours, did make complaintes thereof. Wherupon he was committed to pzison, and being found guilty of diuers kindes of trecheries, yet notwithftandyng in geuyng sentence vppon him, he founde the Inquisitours his very good Lozdes and maifters, who knewe full well that he had

bene

bene a full sure stake to their holy House, and a trusty serui-
tour: so that his iudgement was easy enough, nothing like
as was geuen vpon the other his successour, that onely suffered the mother & her daughters to méete and talke together for the space but of one halfe hower: albeit for his mis-
déedes well known & proued by him, he deserued to be dealt
withall in as euill sorte altogether, as the other was for his
pitie and mercifulnes. But to procéede. His iudgement in
the end was this: to stand vpon the scaffold holding a waxe
taper in his hand, and afterwards to be banished the citye
for.v.yeres. And wheras they vse wholy to confiscate other
mens goods, they did onely put this man to his fine of forfai-
ting the fée due to him by reason of his office, that shuld haue
bene paid vnto him by the holy House: and this was done
rather to satisfy his accusers, then for any great zeale of punishing such offences done by their holy Officers.

The very same man had a maideseruant in his house
while he was in office there, who pitying the miserable e-
state that the poore prisoners were in, pyned and hunger-
sterued by meanes of that wicked Iew her Maister (for she
her selfe fauored the Gospell) did diuers times speake vnto them at the grate, comforting and exhorting them so wel
as she could, to arme them selues with patiéce, and did sundry times put vnder the dore, some good & wholsom meates
for their weake and féeble bodies, declaring no lesse charitie
in déedes, then she had before vttered in wordes. Whose
zeale (no doubt) was so much p̄ more meruailous, that wanting of her owne to depart withall to Christes afflicted mé-
bers, she would priuily conuey from her Maister some of the
meate which he had lurched from the prisoners of their due
allowaunce, and so restore vnto them their owne. And to
geue vs the more cause to wonder at the miraculous prouidence of God, which of euill séede sendeth not alwayes the
worst corne, but somtimes the best, this maiden had a little
damosell her maisters owne doughter to helpe her in these

her

her conueyaunces. Moreouer by this maydens meanes the prisoners came to vnderstãd one of an others estate, and to know in what case euery of their afflicted brethern was: the which thing was both a singular comfort to themselues, & a speciall furtheraunce to their affaires. At the length, this also came to the Inquisitours eares: who, after that they had kept her in prison a whole yeare, and there made her pertaker of the like hardnes that the other prisoners were in, caused her to be brought out vpon the day of their trïuph and set vpon the scaffolde where they gaue sentence vppon her, to weare the Sambenite and to be whipped about the towne with like infamy and extremity as had bene vsed to other before, with two hundreth stripes : the whiche was wholye performed the nexte day following. Besides this, they did also banishe her the City and the suburbes for ten yeares, with this writyng on her heade . A fauourer and ayder of heretikes. An other thing also that so sore incensed the Inquisitour against her, was this : for that it was cõfessed vnto them vpon examination of others, that she had disclosed vnto diuers citizens, after what sort the prisoners were entreated at the Inquisitours handes, as well in their diet as otherwise. The which example being cõpared with the former concerning the fact of her maister, and the punishments that eche of them had therfore, is euidence enough to shew what indifferency they vse in punishing malefactors. But to my matter.

It is a thing that hath neuer bene séene nor heard of before their tyme, that either the most gally slaue, or he that endured the worst kinde of bondage that euer was deuised by man, should bée restrayned and forbidden the solace of song, to recreate himselfe withall in the middest of his sorowful dumpes, to driue away fantasies, and to relieue his pensiue and heauy harte with some kind of lightning. But this holy House passing and exceding all the tyrannies that euer haue bene practised by or vppon any, depriueth ỹ poore

The prisoners restrayned the libertie of for--.

wretches

wretches of this small solace in their greatest miseryes and extremities. For if any of the prisoners beginne to sing any Psalme to the intent to ease hys present griefe somewhat, or do recite any text of scripture, the more that the saying or singing thereof doth ease the sæly soule, the greater matter do ỹ Inquisitours & theyr offycers make of it, taking it to be a great hinderance to their affaires, if the prisoners be at any time light harted, because theyr purpose is to keepe them in perpetuall slauery & thraldome, wythout hauynge any one good day in al their liues. Therfore, so sone as they heare any of the prisoners to sing or say ought aloud, by and by is there a limme or two of the Deuill, that is to say, one Notary or other, wyth the kæper of the prison to commaūd them silence, and to charge them in ỹ Inquisitoures name to make no countenaunce of mirth vpon payne of Excommunication. Whych if he seeme to contemne and make light of, or els to laugh at (as in dede it is no better worthy) he shall haue a bit on his tong, and be taught his obedience, will he nil he, & thenceforth be taken for a rebell and a contemner of the Inquisiours authority, and shall not be suffered to speake but in a very low note, whereof they themselues will apoint him the tune, and Sol fa it before hym. This is done for two speciall consideracions. The one to bereue the pore soules of al kind of solace (as I sayd before): the other, for that the crafty old Syers learne by dayly experience, that such singing of Psalmes or other songes made out of the scripture, is a meruailous comfort vnto them, and a great incouraging and hartening to others theyr weake brethren, that lye a great distaunce from them in other prisons. There is also a third cause why they enioyne them silence, for that by song or loud speaking they might one know of an other. Therefore it happeneth many times that a man and his frend, the father and the sonne, the husband & the wife, shall be all within one prison house, by the space of two or thrée yeares together, and neither of them

know

know of the others being there, till the time come that they ſée one and ther at the great Doome day vpon the ſcaffolde. And vpon this conſideration eſpecially, thys is wont to be one of their common queſtions in euery day of hearing: Whether the priſoners of ſeuerall priſons haue conferred or communed together, or the one to know of the others being there: & if they find it to be ſo, ſtraight vpon it, they ſhift priſons & examine thē vpon an other interrogatorye to beat one thing out of an other: if they haue had any maner of conference, or what counſell ech of them gaue to the other.

And this is the whole order of the priſoners diet: ſo that ſuch as goe not to the ſtake, for the moſt part peariſh there, either of the greate filth and ſtench of the priſon, or if they be deliuered thence, die ſhortly after of the Frenche diſeaſe, growing vpon them by reaſon of their corrupt and noughty diet: either els of aboundaunce of Melancholy become altered in their wits, or at the leaſt haue ſuch quaſie bodyes diſpoſed to theſe or to ſome other greater maladyes that they conſume away by litle and litle, leading a farre more miſerable life, then were any death that they could die. For proofe whereof, out of a number of examples, that might be brought only out of the Inquiſition at Siuil. I wil chuſe one worthy to be reported in all Chronicles, for a ſpeciall example of their barbarous dealings

Not many yeares agoe, there arriued a certaine Engliſhe ſhippe in the porte S. Lucars, which the Familiares going a bord vpon, to make ſearch for religion (as their maner is to do before any man of them may be ſuffred to come on land) they tooke and caried with them to priſon dyuers Engliſhmen that were in her, vpon ſuſpition which they had on them to be profeſſours of the Goſpell, by certaine tokens and likelihoods which they eſpied in them, and knew them by. In the ſame ſhip there was alſo a little boye not paſſing 10, or 12, yeares of age, ſonne to a very rich marchaunt of England, that was owner (as they ſayd both of

M.j.   the

the shippe, and the most part of her lading. Amonge other they toke also thys yong childe (as they pretended) for hauing in his hands Dauids Psalmes in Englishe. But who so doth indifferently vnderstand of theyr couetousnes and naughty practises, may well thinke without any offence to the holy Inquisition, that the fathers wealth was the occasion, both of the childes imprisonmēt, and of the other misery that did befal him afterward. Wherupō, they made Sequestration of the ship and goods, and caried the childe to prison with the rest of his company, where he aboade by the space of. 6. or. 8. monthes. This child was so well broughte vp by his parēts in vertue and good discipline, and the same toke so deepe roote in him, being dewed with ye grace of God, that notwithstanding his tender age and hard imprisonment, he ceased not still to geue most euident tokens of the same: hys good and godly education: in so much, that many and sundry times, but specially euery morning and euening, he did accustomably vse to lift vp his eyes to heauen, and to call vpon God, from whence he was taught to loke and hope for a helpe and succour. And as his keeper espied him now and then making his prayers in that sort, whereas he ought to haue ben ashamed of himselfe and of his paganisme, to see in so tender age, such a paterne of piety and godlynes before his face, in steade thereof, so sone as he behelo him lyfting vp his eyes to heaue, saying some Psalme or other prayers in Englishe, now surely (sayth he) this boy is become a pretty heretike alreavy. After the childe had continued the foresayd space in that darke dungeon (being tenderly broughte vp tofore in his fathers house) by reason of the moisture and dampe of the prison, and of his corrupt diet, hee fell into an extreme sicknes. Whereof as sone as the Inquisitours had intelligence, they gaue commaundement to remoue hym thence, and to cary him to the Cardinals hospital til he were recouered. The hospitall is a house that serueth for suche as fal extremely sicke within any of the prisons belonginge to

the

the Inquisition. Howbeit they are not delt withall there in any thing more gently then they were before in their persons, sauing only that they haue phisicke, which is allowed them very liberally by the Hospitall, and may tender their bodyes somwhat more charely for their helthes sake. Neither may any man be suffred to resort to the pacitt, but his phisitian and the seruaunts of the hospitall. But so soone as the pacient beginneth to be on the mending hand, thoughe he be not altogether sound, and perfectly whole, he is caryed thether from whence he came. Mary this child being by reason of a great sicknes which he caught in hys long and paynefull imprisonment, remoued into this Hospitall, became benummed in his legs, neither can any man tell any certainty what became of him afterward. Let euery man weigh now with himselfe and consider, whether it beseme these good Fathers so rudely to deale with a child & a stranger, or if there be found any such vnreasonable kind of dealing among ye wild Scythians, to ouerpasse the great spoyle of the shippe and her Marchaundise with silence.

At the same very time wel nigh there was a certayne Turke taken and caried to the same prison, who had voluntarily forsaken and abiured the Mahometicall impiety, and was newly come from Marrocke, the chiefe Citie and head of the realme of Mauritania, into that part of Spayne ylyeth directly ouer against it, deuided by Midland sea. But sauouring as yet of that venemous licour, wherewyth he was poysened in his cradle, and fed withall from his infancy (for as yet he had not taken out any one lesson of Christianity for want of a teacher) and finding moe faultes and worse enormities among the Christians, then he had left behind hym among his countreimen the Mores, supposing himselfe to be in good safety there, and therefore more carelesse, happened to say on a time, that the Morish law (mea- *The Hospitall for*ning their religion) was farre better then the Christians, *th Par*for the which saying he fell into the Inquisitours hands, *ners in the Inquisition*

M.y. who

who to the ende that they might bring him into a better mynde, schooled and cathechised hym in such sort, that he confessed in prison playnly, that from the first day of his Christendome, it neuer repented hym that he was become a Christian, till he came within the Inquisitours iurisdictiō, where it greued him to see, force and violence, wrongs, iniuries, and tyranny of all sortes executed with extremitye.

The prisoners visitation.

IT hath bene a custome generally receaued in all places which haue sought to be renowmed by sitting in y seat of Iustice and equity vprightly & indifferently, that certayne tymes should specially be appointed for the visitatiō of prysons, to the intent that the kepers should not oppresse theyr prisoners, but that such iniuries as ether they had alredy or thereafter might receiue should be redressed, and preuented, by the ouersight of the chiefe rulers and iudges, so oft as nede were. A thing which both conscience craueth, and the law of nature, and all policy and good gouernement, last of all God by his word commaundeth, wherin the case and poore estate of such as lie in bonds, is recommended vnto vs, & geuen vs specially in charge to be cōsidered. Wherfore, to resist a number of wrongs (besides other that come not to our eares) which the report was that the holy House had done to their prisoners, where there was no good to be done any way but one (I meane by the visitation of prison houses) marke I beseech you the Inquisitours, & consider ye what hipocrits they ar: which in respect of their holy House & Consistory, with their glorious titles, and the very name of Sanctitie, wherin they seeme to excel al other prophane & tēporall Courts, should haue bene by all reason more bountifull and gentle, more full of comfort and charity, and in withstanding iniuries, moste iust and vprighte, carefully prouiding for the necessities of the poore afflicted and duely punishing such as had wronged them any wise, ether by couetous or cruell dealing: yet were they so farre

from

from doyng their duties herein, that it semeth rather their visitation was deuised of purpose to a cleane contrary end: in so much that the dayes when they kepe their visitations may be more worthely termed dayes of Doole to the poore prisoners, then be thought meanes of ease or reliefe of their miseries: as it appeareth most euidently by their common maner of dealing, on such dayes, apointed for the visitation. Wherof we purpose here to make rehersall.

The visitation of prisons is commonly once or twise euery moneth kept by the Inquisitours, a Notary, and the Keeper, and for the most part vpon the Sonday or some other festiuall day. The manner of it is in this wise. At the very firste entraunce into the prison, the Inquisitour demaundeth of the prisoners these questions : How it is with The maner of their visitations. them, what they wante, whether their keeper geue them any euill language, or threaten them, or vse any woordes of despight or reproch towards them : if he geue them their full allowance in their diet duly and truly, or prouide them shifte of shirtes with such woordes. For in very deede there is no hope of one droppe of comforte at their handes for all this busines: but are onely woordes and questions of commō course, and speciall articles prescribed vnto them to inquire vppon, wherunto they neither adde any more in woordes, nor performe so much in deedes. As if the prisoner be halfe naked, or want a couch to rest him on, and should pray that his necessitie may be considered and prouided for, they shape him such an aunswer as serueth them both for winter and sommer. And their aunswer in sommer is thus, in very milde & fatherly termes: wel (say they) now the weather is warm you may liue full well without either clothes or couch. And for winter in this sort: True it is, it hath bene a great frost of late, but nowe that it thaweth and the colde is come downs & resolued into snow and rayne so that the ayre is open & cleared, you shall haue a more seasonable time. Care you for the garmentes: wherwithall you should clothe your

M.iii. soule

soule, which standeth in vttering the truth and discharging
your conscience before this holy Youte: for this shold be your
speciall care. And here is all the promisso which they make
for them, for all the questioning at the first, & so departyng
as they came, their visitatio in the end turneth but to a iest:
so that, if their visitations were daily, ye see all the comfort
that the prisoners should haue at these holy Fathers hands.
Yet notwithstanding true it is that some such whom they
owe special fauour vnto, receaue some curtesy at their handes, and easy it is to iudge who they be that finde it, where
couetousnes and cruelty kepe their Court.

Likewise if any of the prisoners either learned or vnler-
ned, desire to haue some good boke, or the holy bible permitted them to reade, to the intent to passe that troublesome &
carefull tyme away to some profite, they shift him of wyth
the like aunswer for a boke, as they vse before to him that
was naked and without garmentes. For the Inquisitour
wil aunswer him like a graue counseller, that y true boke,
is to speake the truth, and to discharge his conscience in that
holy Courte, and that he ought to be occupied in that boke,
that by recounting and recording therof, he might lay open
his woundes and sores to theyr Lordships, that were most
ready to geue him a plaister: & this (say they) is y true boke
&c. But if the prisoner be earnest and importunate in cra-
uing the same, eyther at that or the next visitation: he shalbe taught to hold his peace and to be answered with reaso.
For if he be so bolde to aske what liketh him, they will be so
good as to deny that liketh not the. To be shorte, they seeme
to be wholy bent vpon this thing of purpose, diligently to
see vnto it, that the prisoner haue nothing to loke or thinke
vppon, but onely his present estate in misery, that the grief
therof grating vppon hym, may force him the rather to sa-
tisfie their requestes in as much as may be. Howbeit, if the
prisoner haue any frendes or kinsfolke, that are able to relieue his misery by any meanes, perhaps they will send the

Inqui-

Inquisitour some pretie present or other, to obteyne hys
fauour and good wil, that theyr kinseman may be somwhat
more fauourably entreated. Now, all the hardnes of thys
matter resteth on thys poynte to gette the Inquisitour to
take it. But for any other vnder officers, it is an easy mat
ter to brybe them, so it be done priuilie or by night: for suche
fellowes will sone be corrupted. Mary their masters make
it somwhat more deintie and strange: yea it were a thynge
impossible if a man woulde take their first naye. Whiche
commonlye is after this sorte: that this holye Courte is a
Court incorrupte that can away with brybes in no case &c.
For sith their answeres are from the teethe outwarde, all
this a doo in excusyng themselues and refusyng the profer
is a plaine token that they would be content to haueit with
all their hartes. Therfore is the Inquisitour for the moste
part neuer without some of his brethren or sisters childrē
about him, or some one seruaunt to whom he sheweth speciall fauour and good will: the which seruaunt must be ten-
dered and regarded as much as himselfe. Then is there also
an other wayter that standing by, and seyng this great ado
betwixt the Inquisitour and the other party, the one profe-
ring and the other refusing as fast, when the party beginneth to relent, shall come vnto hym immediatly, and teach
him a trick how to obteine hys purpose, and entryng talke
with hym without any manner of occasion, will poynte
him to one with his finger and saye. Sir, see ye yonder the
young gentleman that standeth at my Lordes elbowe? He
is my Lordes Nephew. Nowe is there none so verye an
Asse that hauing made so much a do in temptyng the Inquisitour, bnt he maye easely perceaue that there is one
ready to hold the poke & to receiue his profer, though the o-
ther refused it. And so by this meanes at the length the pore
prisoners get somwhat released. Wherby it is apparaunte
what spirite this holy house is gouerned by, whē couetousnes is able more to preuayle with thē to further a deede of

charity

charity, then charity far her own ſake could euer haue gotten or obteyned at their handes.

The acte conteyning the publication of the Sentences.

Here remaineth now ŷ laſt Acte of the Tragedy, which
is the very winding vp of al that is to be done in this ho
ly Court Wherin both parties are pleaſed & haue their deſire. The Inquiſitours, in obteyning their pray: the priſoners, ſeing the terrible and continuall torments, the ſubtill
ſlights and practiſes of the Inquiſitors with their extreme
and cruell dealinges grow to an end. For thē do they heare
their finall iudgemēts, after their matters haue bene toſſed
to and fro many yeares in open Courte, and in ſo greate an
audience and aſſemblie, as there hath not bene ſene a greater, no not in Olympus it ſelf. This Act of Faith they commonly call El Auto. And ſurely good cauſe why. For then is
the priſoners fayth tried to the vttermoſt, & ſheweth it ſelſe
what it is, eyther by denying and abiuring Gods truth in
open and ſolemne audience, or els by ſtanding ſtoutely and
manfully therein, in like ſolemnitie of ſhew and view of all
the people, thronging together purpoſely. Let the Inquiſitours therefore deriue the worde and deſcant of it as they
pleaſe: we do conſtrue it thus, as in a ſence moſt agreable to
Gods iudgement.

This acte hath many Iole deuiſes, or to ſpeake more
aptly, this Paſchall of Gods people Peſah: that is to ſay.
this paſſage out of Egipt to the lande of promiſe, I meane
from the world to God, hath his Euen, his preparation. Ioa.
13. For a few dayes before this feaſt, the Inquiſitours vſe to
call into the Courte ſeuerally one after other, all ſuch perſons whoſe goodes are confiſcate examining thē what lands
or goodes they haue, and where they lie, charging them earneſtly that they conceale not one iote, declaryng vnto them
further, that if afterward it can be proued that they haue
kepte any thing backe, both fellonie ſhall be layd to theyr
charge

charge, and they also in whofe handes it is found fhall pay
foz it moft affuredly. After they haue côfeffed y whole truth
of all their other gœds & fubftance, befides fuch as were taken & found in their own houfe at the firft time of their ap-
pzehenfion, and fo fequeftred, and that all be eftreited into
the accomptes of the Efcheequer, they returne euery one to
his owne pzifon againe, being affured to lofe all their gœds
howfoeuer they efcape with their liues.

  But the right Euen is the daye nexte and immediately going befoze the Feftiual day. Foz the towards night
they caufe all the men to be bzought together into a
large pzifon houfe, fuche as are appoynted to be bzought
fozth the next mozow to doe diuers kindes of penaunce befoze all the people accozding as it is enioyned vnto them
in their feuerall fentences. This wozd penaunce, is a wozd
bozowed and vfurped by them, vpon the vfe of the olde pzi-
mitiue church, foz certaine penalties and punifhmentes v-
fed towards offenders. Into an other like pzifon they bzing
all the women together likewife. But fuch as are iudged to
death are put ech in their feueral pzifons againe, and about
9. oz. 10. of the clocke at night , there is fent to eche of them
fome pelting Pzieft to cary them this heauy tidings, and to
be their ghoftly father. And now at this laft inftant , the
man to whom God hath geuen the fpirite of conftancy and
boldnes, maketh his laft pzoteftatiô of his faith, to y fhame
of his Confeffour, & confufion of all that hellifh army. But
on the other part, he that hath not bene conftant tofoze, noz
is at this pzefent, hath now a time to cal foz grace at Gods
hands (the only geuer of all gifts and graces) thofe efpecial
gifts of conftancy and patience. Yowbeit both foztes haue
much to do with their ghoftly fathers : the one in maynte-
nance of theyz faith now in their laft hower and moft dangerous time of all : the other in hopeles entreating and
pzaying their pardon of lyfe . Yet is there neyther of them
bothe but in that night they are occupied on euery fide, fu-
ftaining (no doubt) a greater temptation, both in that their

flesfe is frayle,and the deuil sturring,and yet sure it is that
the heauenlye Father fozgetteth not hys childzen in that
hower.Yea thys night wherein his members suffer suche
agony,may be well resembled vnto that, which God hymselfe the heade of all,suffred,both foz the anguish of the paci-
ents,and the comfozt that came from heauen.

The next mozow by ŷ breake of day,the familiars & all
the rest of the officers pertaining to the Inquisition,assem-
ble together euery man to do his office about this holye Sa-
crifice, and do attire such pzisoners as are to be bzought out
befoze the people euery one in his aray verye curyously, in
such sozt as was by the sentence pzonoūced and pzescribed.
Wherof,such as stode stoutly to their tackling & defended
their pzofessiō against their detestable falsehodes,weare the
Sambenit vnto the very stake,whiche is a linnen garment
of the coulour of earth,made lyke to a coate armonr and
all to be painted with black deuils,ouer whom the manful
souldiour of Chzist triumpheth in token of victozy.On his
head he hath a hat,long lyke a turret,whereon is pictured
the image of a man burning in the fire,wyth many deuels
about hym,plying him with fire and fagots. It is muche
after the maner of a fough ten field, as I may liken it. Foz
there is the whole skirmish,with the ouerthzow of his enemyes set foz a greater glozy and shew of conquest and victory. Mozeouer their tongs are nipped and pinched wyth a
cleft pæce of wod which they call Mordaza, of the Latine
wozde Mordeo to bite, because the pzisoners should not
make any pzotestation befoze the people either of theyz innocency,oz of their beliefe, hauing besides this about their
necks new cozds made of bentes, and their hands fast boūd
behind them. Whereby he declareth(in myne opinion)like
a god champion (though hys desertes in other respectes be
somwhat)yet that he reposeth no trust oz confidence in thē,
but in the only and vnspeakeable mercyes of God, foz the
confessing of whose holy name he is ready to die ŷ most ter-
ribls

The dis-
cription of
the Sam-
benit.

rible death, and so wil appeare before the iudgemente seate
of God: wheras if God should deale wyth him craftlye ac=
cording to the letter and the law, notwithstanding al those
glorious workes that make him so famous amonge men,
he should well find there were nothing remayning for him
in the end, but the destiny and reward of a villanous thiefe.
And on this sort come these constant martirs disguised, and
bearing these badges: first vpon the stage, and so consequent=
ly to the stake. Likewise, they that by reuolting and deny=
ing the truth haue brought ỹ Fathers in some hope of their
saluation, haue iudgement of deathe neuertheles, and are
arayed in like sorte, saue onely that in stæde of the Deuils
pictures, there is the image of the crosse, hauing their hands
bound in like sort: that as the other haue born the ensignes
& cognisance of true fayth and manly courage so these may
also cary the badges of dastardy and false faith. And in lyke
sort do all the rest come forth, arayed as the other, and be set
with like badges, more or lesse, as it pleaseth the Inquisi=
tours to disgrace them in the sight of the people.

But at what time ỹ prisoners are ready to passe out of
the Castell Triana where they were imprisoned, then the
holy house affecteth of purpose to sæme ful of pitye and cha=
rity towardes them, in the sight of the commõ people. For
after that they be disguised on this sorte, and euery man set
in his order as he shall issue forth, they are commaunded to
pause a while, and forthwith are certayne tables spread for
them as they stand, and a very plentifull breakfast in shew
of rosted hennes, kidde, and such like prepared, wherewyth
they woulde blind the common sorte and persuade them,
that they had ben none otherwise vsed in prison beginning
now at the last to make them amendes for the euill inter=
taynment which they had before. Howbeit the poore soules
are in that taking at that tyme, that they will do the meate
no great harme, and therefore those cutthrotes the Famili=
ars which vse to gard the prisoner on ech side, do common=

ly snatch the meate from befoze them and deuoure it without either checke oz controlement. As foz the pzeparation,
such is their ruffe in that triumph, as neuer was the like
pompe in Perſia, noz triumph in Rome comparable thereunto. Firſt ¢ fozmoſt go the Childzen of y̅ Hoſpitall where
the youth is bzought vp at learning, who both with their
apparell, and ſong, and array which they are kept in by certayne Clerkes that walke vp and downe by thē in ſurpluſ-
ſes, moue a pzety deuotion. Their ditty is the letaines : the
one part of y̅ Quier anſwering an other, and y̅ foote of theyz
ſong is, Ora pro illis. After them go ſuch as do penaunce,
placed as it were in certain degrees, ſo that ſuch as haue the.
eaſieſt puniſhments go next in ozder vnto the Childzen, and
are to be diſcerned from other by theſe tokens : tapers in
their hands vnlighted, ropes about their neckes, and Barnacles vpō their tongus, with hats of paper, bareheaded, except they put on thoſe hats, but without clokes like ſlaues:
and the better oz richer man commeth alwayes hindmoſt.
Nexte vnto theſe go they that are diſguiſed in Sambenites,
that is to ſay, a linen garment ſhaped like a coate armour
with a red croſſe ouerthwart, obſeruing the ſtate ¢ condition of euery perſon as is ſayd befoze. But ſuch as haue ben
beraied with their Ozders are pzeferred befoze others both
foz eſtimation ¢ place. Laſtly commeth in the third ranke,
thoſe that are condemned to the fire : of the which ſort, ſo
many as haue refuſed Gods truth and betaken them ſelues
in ſtead thereof to lyes, in hope of mercy at mans hand, do
well deſerue to go befoze the reſt that remayned conſtant
to the end, whom the Inquiſitours place in the rereward as
the fitteſt place foz them euen in their owne iudgementes,
in reſpect of their vertue ¢ fayth. Alſo, on ech hand of euery pzifoner, there goeth a Familiar all armed to gard him,
and beſides them two Monkes oz Theatini (as they terme
them) attēding on euery one that is ready to ſuffer, to per-
ſwade them tooth and naile, not to cleaue vnto that doctrine

now

The ozder
of the Jn-
quiſitours
triumphe.

Theſe be
the Jeſu-
ites.

now at their departure out of this world, wherin they haue bene trained and taught hetherto. Which wicked importunity, is as great a grief in my fanſie to him that conſtantly hath perſeuered hetherto, as any torment that he hath endured. Immediatly after the priſoners, do follow in order, as the maner is in all ſolemnities, firſt the whole ſtate of of the city which conſiſteth vppon Alguaziles, Conſtables, Gouernours of the 24. Wardes, the Shirifes, the Regent or the Viceroy and Aſſiſtent, and after them a great troupe of noble gentlemen on horſeback: next vnto them the ſtate eccleſiaſtical. In the firſt ranke the Clarkes, Vicars and Curates: in the ſecond, the whole Chapter of the Cathedrall church, commonly called Cabildum eccleſiæ maioris: in the third place the Abbots and Priors with their couentes: and laſt of all, after all theſe followeth the holy Houſe, whiche triumpheth in dœde, and is in a ioly ruffe that day. Before whom as they paſſe, there is a way made in reſpect of their honours and a compaſſe kept, wherin the Fiſcal, one that taketh no ſmall paynes in the holy Houſes behalf towards the obtayning of this victory, hauing a flagge of red damaſk diſplaied in warlike faſhion (for all the world) occupieth the place of the Standardbearer.

The flagge is of turkie worke, ful of much good workemanſhip, and hath on the one ſide the Popes armes that firſt graunted the Charter of the Inquiſition, and on the other the armes of king Ferdinando ý firſt gaue it the countenance all very ſumpteouſly embrodered with ſilke & purple & in the toppe of the ſtanderd is fixed a rich croſſe of ſiluer & gilt with the crucifixe, which the people make after, more ſuperſticiouſly a great deale, then they do after any other croſſe, onely becauſe it is the croſſe pertaynyng to the holy Inquiſition. Laſt of all come the Fathers themſelues a very ſofte ſet pace for grauity ſake, triumphauntly as chiefe Emperours of that côqueſt. Hard at their heeles follow the Familiars and promooters belanging to the holy Houſe, all

on horfeback,as the maner was in the triumphes at Rome
foz euery Captaine conquerour to haue his fouldiours hard
at his elbowe. After the which,come the common people
hand ouer head wyth a wonderful preffe. With this pompe
they paffe from Triana where the Inquifitours prifon is,to
a certayne fcaffold made of wood and reared bp a good height
in the middeft of the high ftræte and chiefe of all the Citye,
foz the Penitentiaries to ftand bpon in biew of all the peo
ple,there to heare fentence pronounced bpon them. Beynge
come bpon the fcaffold,they caufe them to fit downe,euery
man and woman in the fame ozder that he oz fhe came in.
Right ouer againft ý which there is alfo an other ftage fet
bp of like quantitie,wherin is erected a ftately kind of Cō
fiftozie foz the Inquifitours where they fit in their maiefty
like Gods,with all their trayne about them that followed
them thether.

The maner
of the pe-
naunce vfed
int he Pri-
mitiue
church.

Here it would not be impertinent(as I iudge)to difcourfe
a litle in comparing the Triumph of our aduerfaries with
the publike penaunce vfed in the Primitiue Churche,and
fet out by the godly bifhops and Paftoures in thofe dayes,
wherein was nothing but meare godlines fought, wyth a
feruent and bnfained zeale of the amendment and faluation of the repentantes:into the which neuer any entred but
he departed thence to his great comfozt, though with fome
fhame. And his fhame was foz his offence,but the eafe of his
grief and the plaifter which the paftours and preachers applied to his ruptures,was the perfect plaifter & true Sana-
tiue,that healed his wounded and cozrupt confcience. Neyther was it theyr manner that prefcribed the penaunce to
triumphe on that day,oz to fend foz their braueft futes out
of their wardzobes,to go and fhew themfelues abzoade in,
in token of ioy and bictozy:but came themfelues in mour-
ning wæde,and fo likewife did the whole congregation,de-
claring by that outward fhewe of fozrow,that their hartes
wer touched inwardly with the fal and infirmities of their
bzethzen

bꝛethꝛen. In fo much that many times the Cenfors themfelues haue bene fene to fhæd mo teares then haue ẙ Penitentiaries, vnfainedly foꝛowing the fhame which the other
fufteyned (as right ⁊ reafon was) foꝛ theyꝛ mifdeedꝛs. Neyther was any of them put to any kind of death one oꝛ other
oꝛ fo fmartly fcourged that by means of the ftripes percing
fo dæpe, a mã might haue fæne the bare bone, noꝛ the vtter
fhame and difcredite both of them felues and their whole
pofteritie fought hereby: but whatfoeuer was done, it was
referred to this end, that they might recouer the good name
againe among the congregation, which they had loft befoꝛe
by theyꝛ mifdemeanour. As foꝛ any of the pꝛeachers oꝛ Mi-
nifters, none of them had any allowaunce oꝛ fæs from the
Efcherquer oꝛ any one flæce oꝛ locke of wool frõ the backes
of any of his flocke, neyther was any thing founde in their
houfes that came by fpoyle of the pooꝛe. Ezechiel, 34. Efay 3.
V Vo be to you fhepherds &c. Againft ẙ which albeit there
be good caufe to complaine and cry out pꝛefently, yet may
there perhaps be fome other opoꝛtunitie elswhere to doe it.
My meaning in this place is, onely to make a platte without any oꝛder oꝛ fafhiõ, that fuch as haue any fenfe at al left
within them in this vniuerfall time of ignoꝛaunce and do-
tage, may beginne to weigh and confider what difference
there is betwixt thefe triumphes fet out with fuch pꝛepara-
tion and iolitie, and the publicke penaunce vfed in the pꝛi-
mitiue church which the holy houfe bꝛaggeth fo muche that
they retaine till this day.

Thus, when euery mã hath takê his place in oꝛder, one
beginneth a Sermon which is purpofely deuifed muche in
commendatiõ of the holy Houfe, and the cõfutation of fuche
herefies as they are pꝛefently about to perfecute. But the
greateft parte of it is fpent in fhamefull and fclaunderous
repꝛochẽ, wherwith they charge the good chꝛiftiãs, addyng
one trouble and griefe in the necke of an other. Which if
they fæme to take in good parte, fæing them felues fet there

as wondering stockes to all the worlo and marks for them
to shoote all theyr diuelish dartes of shameful and reprochful
sclaunders at, either it is because they beare them of with
the sure buckler of faith: or els by reason that they haue ben
acquainted therewith, and their hartes hardened with such
continuall exercise, like senceles men they feele nowe
no touch of them. When the sermon is finished, they beginne to read the sentences geuen vpon the Penitentiaries in order as euery man came, or in place as they
sit, beginning with such as are to haue the easiest iudgements and punishments first. This part of the Acte is somwhat long, & because it is the chiefest part, therfore it requireth some speciall treatise, but hereafter in more conuenient place. The Sentences being thus orderly all pronounced, the chiefe Commissioner for the Inquisition singeth certayne shorte prayers for the Conuerts (as they call
them) whych neuertheles must dye also: the effecte whereof
is, that God would vouchsafe to extend his mercy and fauour towardes them, that they may perseuer in confessyng
the doctrine of the Church of Rome, and die therin. Which
done they beginne to sing Miserere the 51. Psalme for the obteyning of Gods fauoure & mercy towardes the Penitentiaries, and that the discipline and absolutions done and executed vppon them by the Fathers, may be effectuall and a-
uailable vnto them to true repentaunce. The sentences
are most commonly these. Death without mercy: VVhipping
with extremitie, that the parties eyther not at all, or els very hardly escape with theyr liues: Condemnatio to the gallie
and Forfaiture of all theyr goodes, with such like penaltyes,
wherein the good mother church of Rome extendeth her pity and compassion towards her children, by ÿ Inquisitours
as by her meanes, thinking the profe and the effect of true
repentaunce necessarily to consist therein. Now surely the
whole world may see & perceiue (not alonely such as haue
dronke of her cuppe) ÿ outragious tyranny of such Terma-
gaunts

gaunts as haue bragged and boasted of théselues, that they are the true church of Christ, and be occasioned therby to remember themselues and to esteeme of them as they are.

The Psalme being ended which they abuse to theyr purpose most impudétly and abbominably, in a plain mockery (as they do commonly all other places of scripture) the chief Inquisitour singeth a sort of Uersicles, and the whole Quire aunswereth them with their Responces, in a high & a loud note, strayning their cunning and pipes to the vttermost. Which done, the Inquisitour of his absolute authority pronounceth absolution in a kind of note, wherein he absolueth all such as are come home to the church of Rome (but forsaken Christ) from all theyr errours wherof they shewe themselues penitét, forasmuch as they haue swerued from the Romish church. Howbeit this absolutió must haue none other constrution, then hath the Romish absolution a *culpa tantum*, but not a *pœna*. That is to say from the fault onely not fró the penalty: For they must forthwith (notwithstáding this their recantation) abide the penalties without either mercy, iustice, or conscience.

After the absolution, the Inquisitours haue yet one other notable deuise to vphold theyr kingdome withall as it were with anker & cheine cable, which is a manifest prœfe that they are halfe in doubte, least they nor their kingdome should not lóg cótinue. And the deuise is this: That all the people gathered together at ý tyme, whereof some come to sée ý solemnity aboue 20. leagues of, take a solemne othe before them and bind themselues therby, vowing the perfor-mance therof, that they will liue and dye in the seruice and obedience of the church of Rome, and by all meanes possible, to their power defend and maintain it, hazarding both life lands & gœds against any whosoeuer shal go about to ouerthrow it. Moreouer, they make thé to forswere & curse, whatsoeuer is contrary to that which the churche of Rome holdeth & affirmeth for true. Also that to their power they

Conspiracy to vpholde the Inquisition.

D.i. shall

shall mayntaine and vphold the holy House, and defende al
the officers therof, &c. In witnes wherof and for a further
surety of the matter, they take record one of an other. And
thē may a man see the sæly commō people, & those of higher
estate and degræ crouche to the earth with great deuotion,
and through ignoraunce take their othes against God and
his anointed, rashly & wickedly conspiring together euery
man to his power to be a promooter and setter forward of
the Inquisition. Now if you talke with any man about the
abolishing of this monster of all wickednes and iniquitye
out of the world, though he confesse of himselfe, and graunt
in dæde, that there is much cruelty & tyranny vsed therein:
he will tell you a tale agayne, of his solemne oth taken and
vow vowed, in open and solemne audience, and what can
ye reply to him then . Mary (sir) thus. How that certayne
of the Iewes of very blind ignoraunce and superstition did
bynd thēselues with an oth, and made a solemne vow, that
they would neither eate nor drinke til they had slaine Paul
Act. 23. And these men (say we) sinne thrice so dæply as they,
and therefore are lesse bounde to sæke to saue their othe; so
wickedly takē and so vngodly. First, for that they of a blind
and therfore a wicked zeale, in defence of their law, do fight
against the Gospell of Christ. Secondly, in abusing and ab-
hominably prophaning the name of God, swearyng by hys
holy name, with all their might and mayne, to maintayne
an euill quarel and oppresse a better which lyeth not in thē
to do. Thirdly, wheras they should in tyme reuoke and re-
tract all thinges begonne against God and his holy worde,
they do still procede & go forward in their purpose lyke the
stubburn and stifnecked Iewes. Can any mā come in now
& auerre y contrary? But when it shall be most manifestly
proued, that the Inquisitours haue gone about busilye and
of purpose to destroy of kingdome of Christ, as did the wicked Iewes, then shall it also bee euident and apparaunte,
that such as haue vowed this solemne oth, though it wer of

ignorance

ignozaunce haue incurred all thofe thzée feuerall offences.
Wherefoze, if they will take vp them felues, and learne to
be wife in time, this wilbe one way and meanes foz them
to recouer their faluation. Firft, to côfider diligently what
kind of quarell the Inquifitours do take in hand to mayn-
tayne. Secondarily, to weigh with them felues, whether
they fight vnder the Inquifitours banner foz Chzift, oz a-
gainft Chzift, and fo let them kéepe oz bzeake their othe, as
they fhall thinke good, after they haue debated ý matter thorowly. Now to our purpofe agayne.

After all thefe things thus done and finifhed, if any there
be among the Penitentiaries that deferue to be fo ferued,
they are ftraight way difgraded: and the Bifhop that mini-
ftred the ozders to the party playeth that part, arayed all in
his Pontificalibus. The ceremonies vfed about the actuall
degradation (as they terme it) of him that is to be executed
that day, are both ftraunge and tragicall. Firft they apparel him in his maffing robes, as though he wer ready to doo
maffe, and afterwardes difpoyle hym agayne of euery trin-
ket one after an other, vfing both dogtrickes, and termes
of côiuratiô about euery of ý oznaments, in côtrariwife to ý
that they did befoze at ý firft putting on thereof, whê he entred into ozders. Thê ar his hands, lips, & crown, fcraped wt
a bzóken glaffe oz fome fharp knif, in tokê ý they fcrape of ý
oyle that he was greafed withall at his firft initiation. All ý
which is done in the full view and wonder of all the people,
fome pitying the poze man and fome curfing him woze
then Iew oz Pagane, being in déede moft happy if it be but
foz this one thing, that in the latter end of this life he cryeth
abrenuntio to that greafie & ftinking oyle, fcraping away
that Baals marke and that Apifh patch fo well as it wilbe,
and fo departing. But fuch as haue not iudgement of death
are difgraded onely verbiliter (as they terme it) that is
to fay, by wozd. Which is in effect a fufpending from all
function and pzeferment during the Popes pleafure.

An other ceremonie they haue that in no cafe is to be o-

The maner of Degrada-tion.

mitted wherin the holy House most shamefully and wythout any kind of colour in the world, mocketh both God and
man, and all the whole company present, geuing all men
good cause iustly to laugh at their folly, and that is this. In
the ende of their sentence pronounced vppon suche as haue
iudgement to be burned (their conuersion to the church of
Rome notwithstanding) they adde moreouer & cause there
openly to be proclaymed, that forasmuch as the holy House
mistrusteth that the party is not truly conuerted nor from
his hart, but counterfayteth: and do feare therefore, least a
wolfe lurke still vnder a sheepes clothing, for all hys semblaunce of conuersion, they do geue and bequeth him to the
seculer power, wyth thys humble request vnto them, to
shew the party so much fauoure as may be, and to breake
neither boone, nor perce any skinne of his body. But such as
nothing was able to remoue from their godly profession
(whom they terme V Vilful and Obstinate persones, they
commend to the same power, with these words. Forasmuch
as we haue laboured ernestly and taken great paines with
this man, to bring him home to our mother church of Rome
and can doe no good on hym, but that still he continueth ob-
stinatly in his opinions &c. We therefore deliuer this fellow to the seculer power, to do execution on him according
to order of lawe: yet praying them by the way that if he
shew any tokens of true repentaunce, to deale as fauourably with hym as they may, with other such like speach. And
what impudency (I pray you) is this? They haue already
geuen sentence vppon hym that he must dye, and thereupon deliuer him to the seculer power to be brent, in so much,
that if they that should see execution done, should either suffer the party to make an eschape, or els keepe him and not
burne him, they themselues should be assigned to supply his
place: and yet they require thus much at their hands, to vse
as much mercy towards him as they may. But what kind
of pitie or mercy is it I pray you, that they shew vnto them

them-

théſelues, which bring the poore ſoules forth into that place
diſmembzed & ſhaken al into péeces in euery limme & iopnt
of theyz bodyes, with neuer a whole bone in their ſkin,
yea the very ſinewes, bayues, and guts within the bzoken
with their moſt cruell tortures, wherewith diuers haue pe-
riſhed pzeſently, euen betwirt their hands: and yet wil they
ſue to the ſeculer power, to bzeake neither arme noz legge,
noz any other member, noz to dzaw one dzop of bloud on
them. Forſooth it is becauſe the harme that they haue done
to the poore wzetches already, is wholy within the fleſh, and
becauſe they haue dzawen no bloud of them, eyther with
knife oz launce, but onely at his mouth with a fine Lawne
let downe his thzote, they forſooth are frée from bloudſhed
and bzeaking of bones. They themſelues haue entreated
hym tootoo pitifully, and without all mercy oz good humanity, with exquiſite deuiſes, & ſuch kind of crueltye as was a-
boue meaſure and moze then barbarous, and fall they now
to entreat the tempozall iudges to ſhew him as much mercy as may be? Perhaps theſe flouting marchauntes ſuppoſe
that by this only ſhift of deſcãt, in pzaying mercy foz them,
they haue cleanely auoided their Canon, which holdeth the
accurſed and excommunicate, whoſoeuer being of the clergy ſhall ſhéd any bloud, oz geue any mayheme: foz they can
wype away ſuche a foolíſhe penaltye, in compariſon of ſo
great an offence, with as foolíſhe and ridiculous a ſhifte.
And theſe moſt impudent toyes of mockery, both the Pzin-
ces and the whole people, but chieſly the tempozall magiſtrate heareth & ſuffreth, without ſaying any thing thereto:
otherwiſe there is no man ſo boid of all vnderſtanding, but
he may eaſily perceiue, that their pzaying of mercy and cra-
uing of fauour foz them, is but a very ieſt, imagined, to ſlout
all the whole company withall, and ſpoken the, when they
meane it leaſt. Loe here is the pitie and tender compaſſion,
and motherlike mercy of their holy mother Church, which
this holy houſe ſheweth. This alſo may the reader ſée and

marke by the way, were he neuer ſo blind, that this chiſte of
theirs to ſend ſuch to the fire of whoſe conuerſion they ſtand
halfe in doubt, ẏ is to ſay, leſt they leaue a wolfe in a lambes
ſkinne, is yet one of the cunningeſt trickes, that the holy
houſe hath in all her bouget.

I tould you before, that the chifeſt part of the Acte conſi-
ſted in the reading and pronouncing of the ſentences, and
therfore moſt worthy the marking: foraſmuch, as they do
not onely by ſingular falſehood miſereporte ſuch thinges as
the party vppon examination hath confeſſed, but alſo father
theſe thinges vppon hym moſte deueliſhly, which he neither ſpake, nor thought in all hys life time. And theſe hath
the holy houſe deuiſed againſt the party, whereof part is
moſt filthy, part ſhamefull and abominable, and part blaſ-
phemous, to the intent to diſgrace his perſon, and to make
both him and his doctrine the more abhorred of men, and encreaſe theyr own eſtimation and credit, as moſt neceſſary
mẽbers, to ſcoure and ridd the world of ſuch peſtiferous perſons. Whiles all this geare is in rcherſing to the people,
they clappe vpon the parties toug a clefte peece of wood in
maner as it were a barnacle, to his great and intollerable
payne, ſo that he can anſwere no gaynoſay nothing in defence of him ſelfe and his owne innocency. For if he might
be ſuffered and let alone, he would openly geue them the
lye to theyr faces: as it hath hapened diuers times. Howbeit ẏ controuerſy wer not like long to continue. For ſtreight
way the felow ſhould be ſure to haue his mouth gagged, or
his toung ſtocked, to teach him to be quiet, ẽ to ſay nothing
openly. Moreouer, that which is the parties cõfeſſion in very dæde, is ſo peruerted and corrupted, with the wordes ſo
changed, and rechanged in reading, that in a maner it may
be very well ſaid of him, that he neuer ſpake nor thought
any ſuch thing. Wherof I will here ſhew ſome ſpeciall examples, becauſe they be matters of weight, and ſuch as can
not eaſely be contraried, foraſmuch as the whole world ſæth

and

and knoweth them well enough.

After that all this sentences be red, and the actuall degradation wholye finished, the Temporall magistrate taketh them into his handes very solemnly, accoording as it is enioyned him by the holy house, and so conueyeth them to the place of execution, with a sorte of the deuils own Proctours about them, calling and cryeng vpon them with great importunity to forsake the truth which they haue receaued and professed. And many tymes it chaunceth that suche as constantly perseuer in confessing the truth to the ende, doo breake their neckes against the stake with a trice, and then they noyse abroad among the commõ people, that such, and such repentantly recanted their heresies at theyr very last hower, and came home agayne to the church of Rome, and therfore felt no force of fire at all, by reason of the Inquisitours mercy and pity extended vppon such as became conuerted. By these, & such like subtil practises, they goe about to bury the truth, as though God the auenger therof were not able to raise it vp againe out of darkenes and dungeõs. The residue, which be not condemned to dye, are caried backe to prison agayne: and the next day after, are brought out & whipped, such as had like sentence pronounsed vppon thẽ: wherof diuers are afterward sent to the gally: other remaunded to perpetuall prison, eyther to Triana the speciall prison for the Inquisition, or to some other place els where altogether as euill as a prison. wyth thys Item vnto them ere they go : that if they happen hereafter to call any thing to minde, that erst they haue not disclosed, they immediately resorte to the holy Houle and declare it whatsoeuer it be: for if it be founde otherwise , that they haue craftely and closely conceyled any thing, they shall be reputed (say they) as persons wythout remorse of conscience, and lyke to bee sharply and seuerely punished therfore. But the chiefest mater that they geue them in charge is, in no case to reueale any thyng that they haue eyther heard or sæne duryng the

D.iij. time

time of theyr impzisonment, concerning the maner of their
entreating in any respect, either of punishment, oz impzisonment, oz otherwise, how and after what sozte they haue
generally pzoceded in Court agaynst them, and theyr other
fellow pzisoners, but foz ye time of their being there, should
take and repute themselues altogether as dead persōs. Foz
if the contrary can be pzoued by them, oz that it come to the
Inquisitours eares, that they haue vttered any of their secrets, they shalbe taken foz persons relapsed (as they terme
them) and be punished with most seuerity. And the iudgement appoynted foz suche, is death wythoute redemption,
which surely is a deuise aboue all the rest and might worst
be spared. Foz by this theyr so strayt enioyning them silēce
vppon payne of their liues, they cope them (as it were)
with nedle and thzede, and so kepe in al theyr knauery and
tyzanny as sure as vnder locke & key, both close and secrets
to themselues, They know full well Iwis, that if the kyng
who authozised them, should by any meanes vnderstande
their false play whiche they vse, the violence and iniurye
that they offer, the slaunderous repoztes which they make,
the wonderfull fetches, and deuilishe deuises whiche they
pzactise to entrappe diuers and sundzy poze innocentes,
chargynge them with many matters, whiche neyther
they sayde, noz sawe, noz hearde at any tyme, but speciallye
if he vnderstwde of their couetous and cruell dealinges and
(as I may say) moze thē barbarous, growing of that gredy
desire of theyzs: he would (no doubt of it) turne the Inquisition on theyr owne neckes, and fozesee the safetye as well
of his own subiects, as the common weale of the countrey,
and pzouide foz it accozdingly: but chiefely he would se to
the execution of Justice, whereof he is appoynted by God
a lawfull Pzotectour, rather, then the enrichyng of hys
bagges & cofers wonne by such vnlawfull meanes. Oz els,
if the king slacked herein to do that apperteineth vnto him,
the common people would be ready to fire them, that haue
bene

bene so fierce with fire to others.

Furthermore, they labour so earnestly to bury the truth, & are so carefull lest their cruelty should come to light, that among other great penalties which they enioyne to diuers men of worship & good reputation, and some of honor and in authority, after they haue kept them in prison a season, and caused them to suffaine open infamy they inhibite them the company and conference of any other, then such as they shall appoynt and allow them : neither will suffer them to write to any frend of theirs without making them priuy vnto it, that they might haue the perusing therof . Their colour for this matter (forsoth) is very prety, lest that by conference or writing of letters, they should publish their heretical opinions. But in very déede their very drift is, lest such men as haue good frends & be wel alied, should complaine the selues & make their mone to their frends & alies, of the iniuries y haue bene done vnto them, & they make means to the kyng to enquire further of their doings, & so bring the practises of the holy House to light. Wherof this is proofe sufficiét, that they vse not this kind of punishmét to any of y meaner sort, but only to them that be of good bloud and parentage.

For at the very first beginning, whé the maner of theyr Triumph first came vp and was executed vpon the Lutheranes (as they cal them) they that were present at the sight and beheld the order and fashion well, were wont to write vnto theyr frendes both within the Realme and abroade, of all such things as there were done and séene, especially of such as did penaunce : also what sentences were pronounced vppon them, with the causes and circumstaunces of all their other punishments and penalties. But the holy house (as dayly practise maketh euery one hys craftes maister) grew so cunning in their affaires, & straight way they beganne to smell out the matter, that it might in tyme turne them to some displeasure, & therewithall that the doctryne which they so greatly detest and abhorre , myght be publyshed

P.i.

thed and spread further then they woulde wysshe it, so that many, which otherwise would haue cōtinued in their blindnes still, if they had neuer heard nor seene any such reports, should be occasioned thereby, to open their eyes and vnderstandings, and to confesse as wel the doctrine it self, and receaue it, as also espy the wickednes of thē that persecute it. Therfore, for remedy of this mischiefe and inconuenience, the holy house prouided, by making & publisshyng certayne presidentes of such like reports, briefe, and in such wyse as were not likely to do any great harme: that who so were disposed to certifie their frendes of such matters, should follow those presidentes in any case: and therfore appointed certain great penalties for the transgressours hereof, ȳ should make their reportes in any other more large or ample manner, then was by their order prescribed. The manner whereof

The Presidentes for letters appoynted by the holy House.

was this; that after they had told who & what maner of mā he was ȳ was punished or executed, they should adde moreouer: because he held with Luther, without naming any of his opinions (which notwithstādig were specially recited before) was burned, or thus, or thus punished or executed, according to the truth of the matter.

Moreouer, as the holy house wel may erre (albeit men now adayes are so bewitched with superstition and flattery, that they dare affirme the contrary, beyng ordered and guided (say they) by ȳ holy ghost) so it cōmeth diuers tymes to passe, that some be causeles apprehended, some vppon very smal and light complaints, very few vppon any lawfull and sufficient information. And the greatest part after they haue bene imprisoned in such miserable sort as I haue before declared, for a yeare, or two, or more, til their causes were thorowly examined, at the last beyng tried and found guiltles, so that necessarily they are to be discharged, within a day or two after their great day of Triumph, they bryng them into the Courte, and there beginne to set on them againe as freshly as euer they did, willing them to vtter the

truth

truth, as they will auoide theyr displeasures and the extremitye of law, threatning them the racke, and saying, that
there is now come in sufficient matter by information a-
gainst them. Thē if any wil be feared with this facing, and
be brought but to vtter one worde of any suche matters as
they are desirous to heare of, they send him straight to ward
agayne, and renue theyr sute against him from the beginning. But if nothing can be got out of him by this meanes,
nor that they haue any thing els to charge him withal, they
leaue of threatning, and fall to flattering : saying, that they
haue better opinion of him then so, and therefore are resolued to send him home againe to his owne house : for the
which fatherly fauour extēded towards him in sauing both
his life and his goods, he is to accompt him selfe much beholding and bound to theyr Lordships, willing hym to persuade himselfe, that what fauour they haue shewed him already, they meane to continue towardes him, for the good
liking that they had of him at the very first biew, but specially for the good example of pacience which he shewed during the whole time of his imprisonment. With these and
suche like Lenitiues the good and vpright iudges, thinke
to supple the rest of his sores that were of theyr owne making, and so send him home to his house at the last, with speciall charge ý he be silent . Yet sometime they detaine him
in prison a good while after, notwithstanding ý he be found
not guiltye, nothing regarding what any, be he neuer so
giltlesse, suffer at their hands, and there do kepe him closely
& craftely til a day or two after their great ruffe and iolitie,
that being dismissed nere about the time that the other are,
the common people may thinke he receiued his punishment
amongst the rest, though in some lesser degrée, and thereby
be persuaded that the holy House neuer vexeth any man
without sufficient information. And marke I pray you one
other new foūd guise that these rauening wolues haue got
to obtaine their pray and spoyle withall : that such persons

as among other parcels of their punißments are condem=
ned either to perpetuall imprisonment, eyther during the
Inquisitours pleasure, oz foz a certayne seaſon, albeit they
remaine no longer in Triana, that is the Inquisitours pzo=
per and peculier pzison, becauſe they ßall thinke them=
ſelues quite and clere diſpatched, & to haue no moze to doe
with ŷ holy Houſe: yet wherſoeuer they be appoynted their
place of aboade as an impzisonment, there be ſpies alſo to
marke diligentlye how they take the matter, and whether
they put it vp quietly, yea,oz no, oz what they ſay vnto it.
Foz if they be cherefull,oz do any wayes make but a coun=
tenaunce of mirth in this time of their trouble, they ßal
both incurre the Inquisitours diſpleaſure therfoze,and fele
a greater ſmart beſides. They alſo that do remaine in ſuch
apoynted places,are likewiſe biſited ſometimes by the In=
quisitours,but in ſuch ſozt as hath bene deſcribed of ŷ other
and to the very ſame end and purpose, that is to ſay, that ŷ
common people might ſée how full of mercy and pitye they
are:howbeit it is to this ende,to bzing them moze in feare
and awe of them,and of theyz diſpleaſure. Foz then begyn
they(as it were)to kéepe Court & to make inquiry,both of
the pzisoners themſelues and of the kéepers, whether ſynce
their departure out of Triana, they haue heard any of theyz
fellowes ſay any thing touching matters of religyon, who
it was that did ſo,and what countenaunce other that heard
it made thereunto. Also,whether any manne do grudge oz
finde himſelfe greued foz any puniſhement that he hath en=
dured,but eſpecially, whether they haue diſcloſed any mi=
ſtery oz ſecret of theirs,oz whether anye man haue compaſ=
ſed oz imagined to make an eſcape,wyth many other ſuch
like queſtiõs. And if they find no ſuch matters,they return
as wiſe as they came. If otherwyſe there appeare any euy=
dent matter againſt them, thé commence they their ſute a
new againſt him oz thé.   Not many yeares a go,it chaũ=
ſed in Siuil in ſuch a like biſitation,that a certayne pzyſon=
                                                    ner

ner,after he had remained in prison for certayne yeares at
ÿ chiefe Inquisitours pleasure, whose name was El Licentiado Gasco, made very earnest sute vnto him for his discharge and deliueraunce thence. This Gasco was a man
wel learned in both the lawes,as it seemed, who straining
him selfe to speake somewhat wisely, made this graue and
godly answere vnto him, passing all wisdome or good reli-
gion.Now Sirs(saith he)you must take your affliction paciently,for here you suffer for the sinnes of the people, & for
ours as well as for your own.Howbeit I wil moue the rest
of my Lords in ÿ matter,& what may be done,shal be done.
But vppon these and such like foolish and blasphemous speches,neuer any Comissioner made inquirye:& thus departed he out of the Parler wherin he had made such a clerke-
like pece of worke to the poore prisoners in way of consolation,and so like a gay diuine, casting a word out to the keeper very solemnly,and charging him by vertue of their Office to looke to the narowly,that none escaped. For if there
did, he should both seeke the at his own charge, & be punished
besides for his negligence,in loking so slenderly to his duty.

My Lord
the chiefe
Inquisi
tours occa
sion to the
prisoners.

The interpretation of the sentences.

THere be also certayne speciall termes which the Holy
house vseth for euery kind of penaūce seuerally.Wher-
in,seeing there lieth also some secret mystery,it shall not be
greatly impertinent to declare them in this place, expoun-
ding them after the Inquisitours owne sense and vnderstanding. First,concerning the iudgments, some are to be
burned quicke, and that is for such as haue constantly perseuered vnto the ende, in the confession of a pure and perfect
faith : and these men they call obstinate. Other are to be
burned also, but after they be dead,being first strangled at
the stake. Such are they that being once wonne by their
owne frailty and weaknes, haue bene content to submit
them selues vnto the Inquisitours, and to doth whatsoeuer

the other will say, and yet haue by certaine euident and sufficient tokens, geuen the Inquisitours good cause of suspicion, to thinke that they remaine the same in heart still, notwithstanding their mouth hath confessed the cótrary. After
the same maner are diuers also of the former sorte, whom
they terme obstinate, strangled ere the fire be kindled, to
make the people beleue, that so soone as they were set to the
stake, they abiured & renoûced all their heresies, and returned to the holy mother church of Rome. But of these I haue
made mention before. An other sort of sentences there are
that haue a shew of more mercy, which they call reconcilia-
tions, because such as haue renounced the truth, are as it
were purged and clensed by doing that peanaunce in way
of satisfaction, and therby receaued againe into the very bosome of the Romish church. Such for the most part, cary in
theyr handes tapers vnlighted on the greate day of theyr
Triumph, with ropes about theyr neckes, and Sambenites
vppon theyr backs aboue theyr other garments, as badges
and tokens of guilt: and these they weare either during life,
or for some certaine number of yeares, or ells are close
kepte and shut vp in some monastery, or some other priuate places, whereof as there be sundry sortes, so are there
likewise seuerall names. Some are Perpetuall wythout
redemption. Some only perpetuall. Some for a certayne
season: the which being expired, they must notwithstanding remaine there still, during the Inquisitours pleasures:
and some be no longer limited at the first, then duryng the
pleasures of the chiefe Inquisitour, the Generall they call
him, because he is chiefe iudge aboue all other Courtes of
the holy Inquisition throughout ȳ whole realme of Spaine:
there be also some at the pleasure of the inferiour iudges,
that gaue the sentence, in theyr owne Courtes and priuate
iurisdictions. These diuersities of prisons are lyke the
properties of purgatory for all the worlð, for excepting as
well certaine cases in matters of penaunce, as also degrées
of

of affinitie and bloud in cases of mariage. For they are deuised to gleine all the money out of the poore Penitentiaries purses, more or lesse, accoording to the quality of the offence, and after the rate and proportion of the penalty asseassed on ech of them therfore. And al this (forsoth) must be vnderstand to procede from the Inquisitours clemency & mercy of theyr owne mere good wil, by the only meanes wherof, the party that otherwise must necessarily perish for abiuring the truth, may stand in state of grace againe, and be in possibility to recouer his owne saluation.

When iudgement is geuen to weare the Habite, (for so they cal the Sambenite by a more clenly terme) and to perpetuall prison without bayle or maynprise, it is to be vnderstoode, that there is no talke to be had of any remission therof, til the party haue woorne that garment and suffred imprisonment, the space of whole nine or ten yeres except the party haue so good happe, as by meanes of his frendes to obteyne his pardon at the kings hand, who only may by hys prerogatiue pardon it at his pleasure. But after those yeres be expyred, vnles the party haue geuen some cause of suspicion againe, the chiefe Inquisitour is commonly wonte to remitte the residue, howbeit with great crouching first, and with much entreatie.

When they adiudge a man to weare the Sambenite and to suffer perpetuall imprisonmente, without addyng any more, it is commonly taken for 3. yeares if the chiefe Inquisitour do so thinke good: vppon whose pleasure it resteth eyther to geue the prisoner his discharge after those thre yeres or els to his perpetuall ignominie, there to deteyne him all his life long. But when they say, that a man shal weare the Habite and suffer imprisonment so many yeares or moneths, so soone as that certaine time is expired the party is set at liberty, except it be added moreouer besides the limitation of time certayn, that it shalbe further referred to the discretion & appoyntment of the Inquisitours. The which

clause

clause, they commonly vse to put in the latter end, in the win ding vp of al, to choke men therwith, to make them thynke themselues much bound to them while they liue, for relea- sing the same: But if the sentence be, to weare the Sambe- nite with imprisonment during the chiefe Inquisitours plea sure, it is left to their discretions to pardon, or punish accor- dingly, as they shall thinke good. In summe, how or after what sort soeuer their sentence be, the matter is wholy re- ferred to them and to their ordering.

Now the meanes to redeme this imprisonment, and to dispense with the wearing of these robes, is the more common and ordinary, by reason that the kyng hath in hys Courte dyuers younge gentlemen, to whome in respecte of their seruice he vseth to graunt pardons for those matters. Then, such as get the graunt hereof, do commonly make in- quiry for such persons as are therunto adiudged, who they be, and where they remayne, to the intent to make theyr market of those pardons to their most aduauntage, as they can agree of price either more or lesse, respectyng alwayes, both the ability of the person, and the quality of the sentêce. For such as had iudgement without redemption pay more other for release of perpetuall imprisonmente, lesse; other for certaine time and during the Inquisitoures pleasure, lesse agayne: and least of all, that which onely resteth vpon the discretion and will of the Iudge. Likewise, at somtimes the kyng of his like liberality and gracious goodnes vseth to graunt vnto diuers, such money as should be leuied for par- don of the Sambenite and other punishment towardes the redeming of their brethern and alies being taken prisoners by the Turks or Mores. And yet whosoeuer sueth vnto the king for any such pardon must first in any case make ÿ In- quisitours and the Clarkes or other officers of that Court his frends otherwise both the kings own charter, and the payment made by the party besides notwithstanding they will auoyd him by hooke or by croke, and tell him plainly

be

be it the king o2 the Pope him selfe that graunted the pardon, he must be better enfo2med how the case standeth ere
he may departe so lightly. Then, if the matter be b2ought
to that passe, it is an easy thing fo2 them to imagine, that
the party is not so cleared, but that there was good cause a
while to make a stay.

But when any hath iudgemēt of Imprisonment during
the chiefe Inquisitours pleasure, who fo2 certaine secrete
occasions to him knowne will not be entreated, and yet
can not well with honesty reiecte the suters (albeit he doe
them manifest iniury to detaine thē so long) he wil conuey
the matter full cunningly, saying that he is content to referre it to the Inquisitours by whom the iudgement was
geuen. And when the party reso2teth to thē, then straight-
way is he possed ouer from them backe againe to the high
Inquisitour, alledging that the determinatiō hereof belongeth vnto him, & so by meanes that one of thē vnderstādeth
the others meaning, they dally and p2olong the po2e mans
imp2isonment, d2iuing him of from day to day, so long as
it pleaseth them. In like maner, when the punyshment is
limited by the inferiour Inquisitours. Fo2 when they are
loth to be entreated, they passe it to the high Inquisitour &
so one of them serueth an other: and therefo2e except the
party go conningly to wo2ke & b2ibe either the Clerke o2
some other Officer of the holy house, & that with no small
gubbe, and there beginne the ground of his sute, all his labour and cost bestowed vpon the redeming of his imp2i-
sonment is quite lost. But if any of the Inquisitours o2 any
chief Officer of the Court do make intercession fo2 the party, then straight way the other vnderstand, that it is done
vpon some such speciall occasions as they know, whereupon the suter is moued to pitie the state of the po2e p2isoner,
specially if he vse the o2dinary wo2des knowne and vsed a-
mong themselues in cases of petition. Which is on thys
so2t. My very good Lo2des, my humble sute to your good

Lordships is, that such a prisoners cause may be fauourably considered, of whose good life and conuersation, but spe-
cialty of his pacience in the tyme of his imprisonment I
haue bene sufficiently and substancially enforced. Here are
intermedled two or three words in his commendation, but
moderately, lest it should be thought that he were to carefull ouer him: The conclusion then is, that it would please
their Lordships to determine, whether the party shalbe re-
leased.yea or no. And of such as escape thus hardly through
the breares, it costeth some the one halfe of their goods:some
all, and some a piece, as it pleaseth the Inquisitours to deale
with them. For they are persuaded this to be the nyghest
way to bring them home againe, that are any thyng gone
astray or become aliens from the fayth. Or perhaps the
holy house thinketh it to be against Gods forbod, that an
heretike should haue wherupon to liue. Or els belike, they
haue a found out an Aphorisme for their purpose: that as a
surfeter must vse a temperate and a thinne diet: so must an
heretike also be kept low, lest he swell and grow vp therin,
and therfore take it for a soueraigne medicine to kepe hym
so hungry that he must be fayne to begge his bread.

Moreouer, of these (as is abouesayd) some haue iudgement, besides the wearing of the Habite and suffering imprisonment, to be also whipped. Some both to be whipped
and afterward set to the gally. But these sharper kindes of
punishments, they comonly vse to strangers, be they neuer
so small offenders, to be euen with them this way, because
they make so light of wearing the Sambenite, for most of
them make but a iest of it. And all these proceede from the
Inquisitours owne mercy.

The last & least penalty is appointed for such as in theyr
iudgements haue committed but a light offence: that is, to
be brought vppon the scaffold barcheaded and wythout any
cloke, hauing in his hand a waxe taper: wherof some are
com-

commaunded to make Abiuration ex vehementi: some
ex leui. Abiuration de vehementi they call, when it appeared not in the hearing and debating of any mans cause,
what is certainly to be determined, for wont of sufficient
proofe, and because ẙ party him selfe confessed nothing that
deserued any maner of punishment. Therefore, vppon such
a fellow, whom they may neither by iustice condemne for
an heretike, nor of their consciences can absolue and set at
liberty for a good catholike, specially hauing some apparaut
tokens of scarce good belief, they geue sentence vpon him as
as vpon one vehemently suspected: and so accoding to their
suspition, they cause him to abiure. And such a mã being afterward found guilty, be it in the least title of papistry, they
take for a relaps and condemne to ẙ fire. Abiuration de leui,
is much after the same maner, but that it is enioyned vpon
smaller offences in their iudgements, whether the matter
hath bene apparaunt or no. Howbeit, no such person though
he be taken with the same maner agayne, shall be reputed
for a relaps or haue iudgement of death therefore: albeit the
qualifying of the second offence, that is to say, the iudgement
and estimation thereof, be referred to the Inquisitours. And
this kind of abiuratiõ is for the most part vsed in other matters, then concerning Luthers doctrine, as for example, for-
nicatiõ (forsooth) betwixt single persõs, as though it were no
sinne: therefore, it is accustomably punished but as a trifling
toy, by carying of a waxe candle, and by abiuration de leui.
Yet at some times they punish this sinne with the whippe,
and that very extremely, but if the party offend a thousand
times after, so that he put himselfe vpon the Inquisitours
mercy, he is sure neuer to die therefore.

Loe, these be the godly meanes wherby these good fathers
bring into the right way the weaklings in faith, as Paul ter-
meth them. And thus much concerning their deuises practised in the Inquisition, till the time come that we may
see the fall of that arke of Iniquity with the hidden secretes

D.ii.   and

and misteries therof further disclosed, and all those thinges fulfilled and accomplished which in tyme (no doubt) must be reuealed and come to passe vpon this Holy Inquisition, these good Fathers, and their holy House, finally vppon the whole man of sinne, which God threatneth by his prophete shall fall vpon al such wicked hipocrites, which to the ouer-throwing of Christes kingdome, and the vtter defacyng of his glory, lyke shameles men, most wickedly doo pretende the defence, and zeale, and the earnest aduauncement of the same. *Malach. 2. And now to you this precept (sayth he) O ye Priests. If you will not geue eare, nor purpose in your harte to geue all glory to my name (sayth the Lord of hostes) I wil curse you, yea I wyll curse your blessinges, nay I haue cursed them already, because ye do not consider it in your hart Behold I wyll destroy your siede, and wyll ouerspread your owne faces wyth the filth of your solemnities, and it shall cleaue fast vppon you, and you shall knowe that this commaundement touchbeth you onely.* Repent ye.

¶ *Certayne speciall examples wherein a man may more playnely see the trecheries &* legier de maynes *of the holy Inquisition in very practise and exercise.*

HEre haue I thought good to annexe certain special examples of their practises: wherin a man may euidently see a great sort of their trecheries heaped and shuffled together ouer and aboue suche, as I haue heretofore made relation of in their special places, to the end that their cruelty in the execution hereof, with their vnsatiable couetousnes, and all other abhominable iniquity in the peruertyng of all good lawes, may be liuely described and (as it were) painted in tables, and set forth to the shew, that such as do behold thē, may take the full view therof. And partly I do it for theyr sakes, who for the professing of the gospel, and the abiuring of an abominable religion, haue bene ouertakē by the same

meanes

meanes seruing these holy Fathers in steede of a bouty to
pray and rauine vpon, because I thinke it expedient for the
church to continue some memory therof. Now therfore, let
all Christendome open their eies, that they may know and
discerne these rauenous wolues, Lions, & Dragons, the very
generation of Vipers whome (notwithstanding theyr tyranny) they haue till this day had in great reputation and
honoured as Gods, to the greate decay and vndoing of all
Christian common weales: that learning to knowe them,
and stripping them out of their clokes of piety and godlynes, wherof they haue gotten speciall commendation, they
may banish them al Christendome ouer. But as for any examples wherof I meane presently to make rehersall, they
are taken out of one onely Court of the Inquisition holden
at Siuil, whose secrets alone the reporters hereof were able
to disclose, hauing had the most part of them practised vpon
themselues. By relation wherof, a man may haue a prety
gesse, what a number there would be if a man should likewise course ouer all ŷ other Courts of Inquisition throughout the whole realme of Spayne. Neither are these ŷ hereafter ensue, or the other reported before in my whole treatise of any long collection: but al within the compasse of 6.
or 7. yeres next after they began to persecute the Lutherãs
that grew vp in Spaine in great multitudes vpon a sodain
specially in Siuil and valladolit, which was from the yere of
our Lord God 1557 or 58. til an. 1564.

About the which time there was apprehended for religion and brought before the Inquisitours of Siuil, a certain
Englishmã whose name was Nicholas Burton, a very godly man, whom afterward they burned for that he cõtinued
constant in his profession and beliefe, detesting vtterly all
their wicked and abominable religion vntil his liues ende,
Immediatly after his arrest, all the goodes and merchaun-
dise which he brought with him into Spaine by way of tra-
ficque, were according to their common vsage seised and ta-

ken

ken into the sequester: among the which they also rolled vp
much, that appertayned to an other English marchant,
wherwith he was credited as Factour. Whereof so sone as
newes was brought to London, aswel of the impꝛisonment
of his Factour, as of the Arest made vpon his goodes, he sent
his Atturney into Spaine with authoꝛity frō him to make
claime to his goodes, and to demaund them. When his Atturney was landed at Siuil, and had shewed all his letters
and wꝛitings to the holy House, requiring them that such
goodes might be redeliuered into his possession, answere
was made him that he must sue by bill, and retaine an Aduocate (but al was doubtles to delay him) and they, foꝛsoth,
of curtesie assigned him one to frame his supplication foꝛ
him, and other such billes of petition, as he had to exhibite
into theyꝛ holy Court, demaunding foꝛ ech bil. 8. rials, albeit they stode him in no moꝛe stead thē if he had put vp none
at all. And foꝛ the space of thꝛee oꝛ four moneths this fellow
missed not twice a day, attending euery moꝛning ⁊ after-
none at the Inquisitours Palace suing vnto them vpō his
knees foꝛ his dispatch, but specially to ẙ bishop of Tarracon,
of whom I made mencion befoꝛe, who was at ẙ very time
chiefe in the Inquisition at Suil, that he of his absolute authoꝛity would commaund restitutiō to be made thereof: but
the botie was so god and so great, that it was the harder to
come by it agayne. At the length, after he had spent whole
foure moneths in sutes and requests, ⁊ all to no purpose, he
receaued this answere from them, that he must shew better euidence and bꝛing moꝛe sufficient certificates out of
England foꝛ pꝛofe of his matter, thē those which he hath alredy pꝛesented to ẙ Court. Wherupon the party foꝛthwith
posted to London, and withal spede returned to Siul again
with moꝛe ample and large letters testimonialls and certificates, accoꝛding to their request, and exhibited them to the
Court. Notwithstanding, the Inquisitours still shifted him
of, excusing them selues by lacke of leisure, and by occupation in greater and moꝛe weighty affaires, and with such an-

ſwers

swers delayed him whole other. 4. monthes after. At the
last, when the party had well nigh spent all his money, and
therfore sued the more earnestly for his dispatch, they referred the matter wholy to the Bishop. Of whom, when he re-
payred vnto him, he had this answer : that for hym selfe he
knew what he had to do: howbeit he was but one man, and
the determination of the mater appertained vnto the other
commissioners as well as vnto him : and by thus posting
and passing it from one to an other, the party could obtaine
no end of his sute . Yet for his importunitie sake, they were
resolued to dispatch him, but it was on this sorte : One of
the Inquisitours called El Licentiado Gasco a mā very wel
experiēced in these practises, willed the party to resort vnto
him after diner. The fellow being glad to hear these news,
and supposing that his goodes should be restored vnto him, ⁊
that he was called in for that purpose to talke with thother
that was in prison, to confer with him about their accōpts,
the rather through a little misvnderstanding ; hearing the
Inquisitour cast out a word, that it should be nedeful for
him to talke with the prisoner, and being thereupon more
then halfe persuaded, that at the length they mēt good faith,
did so, and repaired thether about the euening. Immediatly vppon his comming, the Jayler was forthwith charged
with him, to shut him vp close in such a certayne prison,
where they appoynted him . The party hoping at the first
that he had bene called for about some other matter, and seing him selfe contrary to his expectation, cast into a darke
dungeon, perceaued at the length that the world went with
him farre otherwise then he supposed it would haue done.
But within two or three dayes after, he was brought forth
into the Court, where he began to demaunde his goodes:
and because it was a deuise that well serued theyr turne,
without any more circumstance they bid him say his Aue
Maria The party began and said it simply and plainely on
this sorte, after the English fashion: Aue maria gratia plena

D.iiij. dominus

dominus tecum, benedicta tu in mulieribus , & benedictus fructus ventris tui Iesus. Amen. The same was written word by word as he spake it: and without any moze talke of claiming his goodes, because it was booteles, they commaund him to prison againe, and enter an action against him as an heretike, foralmuch as he did not say his Aue maria after the Romish fashion, but ended it very suspiciously, for he should haue added moreouer: Sancta Maria mater dei ora pro nobis peccatoribus by curtalling whereof, it was euident enough (say they) that he did not allow the mediation of Saints. Thus they picked a quarel to detaine him in prison a longer season, and afterwards brought him foorth into their Stage disguised after their maner : where sentence was geuen that he should lose all the goods which he sued for, though they were not his owne, & besides this suffer a yeares imprisonment. His name was Iohn Framton a citizen of Bristovv.

In the confiscation of goods, it is neither any great noueltie, noz a thing so rarely seene in this holy house that straungers goods should be also seised among other mens. Otherwise (say they) it might easely be wrought, if they should geue eare or credit to such allegations, that many by meanes therof might coulour their goods vnder an other mans name, and by some false & forged Certificates proue the to appertaine to other men, & so defraude the kings Escheequer. For remedy whereof, and for the better auoyding of al couins and collusiōs, the holy Youse thinketh it the safer way to offer wrong then to suffer any. As within these fewe yeres there arriued at Siuil a certaine rich Marchant straunger, whose goods were afterward confiscate for religion. Among the which they seised a very faire and a goodly ship, such one as by all mens iudgements, there neuer road a better noz a fairer vpon Guadal queuir. The party brought sufficient proofe that the ship was none of his own, & yet not withstanding the Inquisitours found a meanes that the

law

law went on their sides, so that the ship fell out in triall to be theirs. And this marchaunts name was Reuchino.

Moreouer in the same Court of Inquisition at Siuil, there was one of the citizens, a very goodly and a vertuous man, seuerely persecuted by the Inquisitours for religion, howbeit not executed therefore. And among other of his punishments, this was one péece : that all his goods whereon he liued and maintained himselfe, reasonably well and honestly among his neighboures, should be wholy confiscate, and he committed to close prison for ten yeares. Wherein, after he had remained by the space of two or thrée dayes, liuing there full barely (God wots) of a poore stocke, that diuers wel disposed persons had gathered for him of their deuotiõ, hauing somtime liued in reasonable good estate, one of the Notaries of the Inquisition, came vnto him with a bill signed and subscribed by the Inquisitours, charging him to pay to the Notaries handes. 130. ducates for his commons and other expenses, during the time of his aboad in Triana their prison for the Inquisition. The party made aunswere (as the truth was) that those good Fathers had taken from him all that euer he had, so that nothing was left him, and wher nothing was, they could nothing haue. Howbeit this answere contented not the Inquisitours, but they sent the Notarie vnto him once agayne, straitly charging hym either to pay the money out of hand, or els to be remoued from that priuate place, & cariéd to the common iayle, and there to remaine till he had discharged it. What mad fooles were these, to confiscate all his goodes, and charge théselues by attompt for them into the Eschequer, not foreseyng to demaund allowance for his charges?

About the same time welnere, the House of ÿ Inquisition at Siuil apprehended a certain noble womã whose name was Dõna Iuana de Bohorgues, ÿ lady & wife of one dõ Frácisco de vargas, a noble gentleman, & baron of Higuera, daughter to one Pedro Garsia xerelio a very rich citizen of Siuil.

R.i. The

The caufe of her trouble was, for that a fifter of hers called Maria de Bohorques a very vertuous Virgine, & one that afterwardes was burned for her profeffion and fayth, had confeffed in the extremity of her torments, that fhe had cóference with her fifter in thefe matters of religion diuers times. This Lady, when fhe was firft committed to prifon, was gone with childe well nigh halfe a yeare: in refpecte wherof, neither did they fhut her vp fo clofe, nor dealt wyth her otherwife fo hardly, as they vfed to deale with others, for the regard of that which was within her. Notwithftanding within foure dayes after her deliueraunce, they tooke the child away from her, and the vii. day nexte after, they fhutte her vp in clofe prifon agayne, entreating her in all thinges as they did the other prifoners, and with as much cruelty as they vfed to any: in fo much that in all her miferies the only comfort that fhe had, was, of the good company of a certayne vertuous mayden that was her fellow prifoner for a tyme, but afterwardes fent to the ftake. Unto whome fhée bare fuche good wyll, that being on a tyme caried foorth to the racke and recaried to pryfon, fore ftrayned there on and fo fhaken in péeces, that hauynge a bedde of flagges whiche ferued them bothe to couche on, more paynefull a greate deale then eafefull, whereon fhe tumbled her felfe, fo well as fhe could (though hardly God wots and to her great payne and griefe) the good Lady beyng not in cafe able to doo her any other good, yet dyd fhe inwardly fhewe fingular tokens of loue and compaffion towards her. The fame mayde was fcarce recouered, or her ioyntes well knit agayne, but the fayd Lady was likewife caried out to be ferued in the fame fort, and was fo terribly tormented in the Burrie and Trough that by reafon of the exceding ftrayt ftrayning of the ftringes, percing to the very bones of her armes, her thighes, and fhinnes, fhe was caried to prifon halfe dead and more, the bloud gufhing out of her mouth amayne, and in fo greate aboundaunce, that

it

it could not be otherwise, but that somewhat was broken
within her body: but after .viii. dayes God deliuered her frõ
these rauening Lyons, and set her with himselfe in euerlasting rest & peace. The bruit of which fact the Inquisitours
laboured ernestly to suppresse, lest it shold be noised abroad
among the cõmon people, that they had so villanously torne
in péces this tender Lady vppon the racke: but the behol-
ders of this their tiranny could not hold it in. Now surely,
if she had ben a witch, or a traytor to her husband, or a murderer of her owne childzen, and the temporall Magistrate
had dealt so with her to make her confesse these horrible
factes, what time he were to geue vp his accomptes (as the
maner is) he should pay for it ful dearely, if so be that he had
thus cruelly, and without all reason entreated any person
whatsoeuer. Yet the holy House is not to yelde accompt of
any such matters, but may racke to death euen such, whom
they themselues after more precise & exact proofe, do acquite
for innocents, & eschape scotfrée therfore, as it came to passe
in the example of this vertuous lady. For being one of such
estate, & of so good name and fame that they must necessarily
yelde some accompt of her case vnto the common people,
and were destitute of proufes sufficiét (though they had left
no deuise or policy vnpractised, that they could imagine) seing the matter so apparaunt to all the world, that by no
means it could be dissembled: therefore, the very first day of
theyr next Triumph, they caused their senténce which they
had geuen vpon her to be openly red there vnto the people
on this wise: Forasmuch as this Lady died in prison (with
out shewing how or by what meanes I warraunt you) and
vppon diligent hearing and consideration of her cause is
found innocét: therefore, the holy house doth wholy acquite
and discharge her of all sutes and quarels commenced a-
gaynst her by the Fiscal, and doth restore her to her former
estate of estimatiõ and honour, absoluing her clearely from
all guilt and crime: and therupon doe commaund, that re-
stitution be made of all such goodes as were seised into the

Sequester

Sequestre vnto ý hands of such persons as haue right & title therunto. &c. Thus, after that they had most beastly murdered her on the racke, they made her this goodly amends to denounce her not guilty. God will one day (no doubt) aske an accompte of this theyr beastly and barbarous tyranny, sith they maintayne it by the same power and authority in earth, which he hath ordeyned, for the reuenge of these and such lik iniuries.

Notwithstanding, in the yeare of our Lord God. 1563. it happened that the holy house was aduised and fully bent to lay theyr baytes and spread theyr nettes in certayne quarters there : but if they had not vppon better aduisement afterward, wound them vp agayne, they them selues vnawares had geuen Rome such a gird, as I beleue all the Lutherans hetherto haue not geuen it a greater. And thus it was. There were certayne persons that were more busy a great deale, then I beleue they had thanke for, which found great fault with a foule company of Monkes and other religious men, for abusing theyr Auricular confession, vnder the colour therof, masking with honest matrons and maydens that resorted vnto thē, making it a meanes to breake theyr sutes by, and to compasse theyr purposes. The which thing the holy house thought in dæde worthy of consideration and redresse. But forasmuch as it was a hard matter to know who were these twoers and brokers, where none was appeached specially and by name (as it hapeneth in a matter wherin a multitude offendeth) they caused proclamation to be made throughout all the churches within the prouince of Siuil very solemnly, that whosoeuer knew of theyr own certayne knowledge, or had heard by reporte of others, of any Monkes or other religious or spirituall persons (as they call them) that had abused theyr holy sacrament of Confession, to any such abominable actes or enterprises, or that any other gostly father had dealt in any such like sort with any of his shriste children, that euery such

person

person and persons priuy to any such matters, should come
in within 30. dayes and signify it to ý holy House of Inquisition, enioyning moreouer very great penalties for such
as should refuse or contemne to come in accordingly, and
to make declaration, what they were able to say: The proclamation was no sooner made & published, but there came
such a number of woomen, onely inhabitatuntes within
the city of Siuil to complayne of theyr ghostly fathers, that
xx. Notaries, and as many Innquisitours would not haue
suffised to take the names of such as came in and entred
theyr complaynts: wherfore, the Inquisitours, hauing more
to doo then well they could dispatch, gaue them other 30.
dayes to come in and doo the like. But because so litle tyme
would not serue (they came in so thicke) they gaue them so
much more respite agayne the third time: and after that the
fourth, and there they were enforced to lay a straw . For
very many honest matrones and of good calling, partly of a
foolish feare and superstition, lest they should be excommu-
nicated, and partly in respect of theyrs husbandes whome
they were loth to offend and bring into a Iealousie or suspition of theyr honesties, kept them selues at home, thinking
to espy out some better opportunity to speake with ý Inquisitours apart. Wherupō they attired thē selues with bailes
or mufflers after the maner of theyr countrey and went to
the holy house as priuily as they could . Notwithstanding
theyr husbands did so narowly watch them during all the
time of this appeaching, that they could not possibly passe so
priuely but diuers of them were espied, wherby they occasioned theyr husbands vehemently to suspect theyr honesties.
On the other side it was a ioly sport to see the Monkes and
friers and priestes go vp and downe hanging downe theyr
heads, all in dumpe and a melancholy, by meanes of theyr
guilty consciences, quaking and trembling, and looking e-
uery hower when some of the Familiars should take them
by the sleue, and call them Coram for these matters. In so

much that a number feared leſt as great a plague were
come among them, as the perſecution that was ſo hote a-
bout that time againſt the Lutherans. But ẙ Inquiſitours
perceiuing that theſe matters thus purpoſed, would redoûd
not onely to the great hinderaunce of them ſelues, but alſo
turne to the decay of the whole Church of Rome, and that
this onely enterpriſe of theyrs, if it ſhould goe on and take
effect, would be enough to bring al their ſpiritualty into vtter hatred and obloquy, but ſpecially tend to the diſcredit of
their auricular confeſsion, which began already to be but of
ſmall accompt (although it was a matter that otherwiſe
deſerued both ſtraitly to be examined , ẙ ſeuerely to be puniſhed)yet did they in time take it vp, and made a ſtay therin, contrary to all mens expectations : winding vp all theſe
matters wherof the Court was now orderly and lawfully
ſeiſed. And as the report was, the Monkes and prieſtes
made a common purſe, and with a good round ſumme grea-
ſed the Pope in the hand, ſo that he was content to graunt
a generall pardon to all the whole company of Confeſſors
of his fatherly loue and affection towards them, remitting
al offences done or committed by them, and commaunding
the Inquiſitours to ſurceaſe from proceeding any further,
but wholy to ſuppreſſe ſuch things as were paſſed already,
not ſuffring them in any caſe to come to light. Howbeit
thoſe that are priuy to the Inquiſitours dealings, ſay it is
an vnlikely matter, affirming, that if ẙ Pope ſhould make
any ſuche graunt, yet is the holy Inquiſition of ſuche pree-
minence, that if they take in hand any matter of weight,
they will not ſurceaſe vppon the Popes inhibition or
countermaunding, and that it is oftener ſene, that their au-
thoritye preuayleth againſte the Popes, then his agaynſt e
them, as by thys enſample following may more plainely
appeare.

Not paſſing two yeares before this, the biſhop of Rome
had by a like foliſh part and vnawares cut the Inquiſitours

combes

tombes, by publiſhing a generall Iubilie whiche they call a generall charter of pardon, for the ſafety of all Chriſtendome, becauſe Chriſt by like did not ſufficiētly prouide ther fore : beſides a number of other pardons and indulgences for ſuch as were ſuſpected to be Lutherans : ſo cunningly can thys fellowe make a gaine of the Goſpell to hymſelfe. And wheras he cannot auoid the dart that Chriſt hath ſent into ẏ world to plague him withal, but that he muſt be ſtriken therewith, he ceaſeth not to turne it ſome way to hys owne aduauntage. The wordes of the pardon were theſe: That who ſo in time paſt had bene a Lutheran and would forſake that ſect, might be abſolued therof by his ghoſtly father. An olde deuiſe of the deuill, that in as much as there aroſe about the ſame time great trouble of Spain, but ſpecially in Siuil the chiefe City therof, and that a number offended therein, and beganne nowe to ſhrinke from them, they might the more quietly and with leſſe daunger kéepe them in obedience, going about to winne them by a kynd of clemency and mercy though fained and counterfait, rather then by dealyng with them ſtraitly or ſeuerely. Howbeit, here was nothing found fault withall ſaue onely the preiudicing of the holy Houſe, wherof, as it ſemed, the Pope had no great regard. Wherupon, they of the Inquiſition beyng ſomewhat moued, by reaſon that that one onely clauſe had loſt them a good boutẏ contemned the Popes pardon and reſiſted it with might and mayne, commaunding peremptorily that no ſuch pardon ſhould be publiſhed, as ſhoulde turne the holy houſe to any preiudice : by meanes whereof neither was it receaued ne proclaymed . Loe here may a man ſée Sathā deuided againſt himſelfe, and perceiue therby, that this denying of ẏ Popes abſolute authority, which theſe good gentlemen puniſh in others with fire and ſword as being a neceſſary article of our beliefe, is but a noſe of waxe, whiche they turne what way they liſt, ſo that it ſerueth them rather in ſtede of a trap to entangle vs withall,

R.iiii.   then

then accompted of, as any article of our faith, in the obſer-
uation wherof conſiſteth our ſaluation.

The property of euery tyrant is, ſpecially to hate both
mercy and truth, and to vſe all cruelty and extremity that
may be: or els to ſeke vtterly to be hated, when he ſeeth there
is none other meanes to vphold him. As it was ſayd ſome-
tyme by one: Whom men feare, they do but hate. And truely, if a man be diſpoſed to marke them well, he ſhall eaſely
perceiue, that there hath ben hetherto no tyraunt, that hath
more duely obſerued theſe lawes, nor executed them more
cruelly, then this holy Houſe hath done, deuiſing to doo all
iniury and extremity that poſſibly they can, onely to bring
men in feare and awe of them: ſo that they ſeeme to deſire
nothing ſo much as this, that all men may feare them, hate
them who dare, for as much as they puniſhe trifling toyes
& matters of no importaunce, yea ſuch as are ſcarce blame-
worthy, moſt ſeuerely and beyond all meaſure, as by the
enſamples here enſuing may appeare moſt manifeſtly.

At what time their church was in ſo good & quiet eſtate,
that the Inquiſitours had leyſure enough to take their ple-
ſure abroad, it chanced that the biſhop of Tarracon high cō-
miſſioner in the Inquiſitiō at Siuil of whoſe reuered father-
hood, I haue made mencion before, walked in a ſōmers day
for his recreatiō by the ſwete gardens ẙ ſtand by the Riuer
Guadalqueuir, accompanied with al his train & in his ruffe
as he was wont at diuers other tymes to doo. Hard vppon
the banke of a certaine ponde that was in the ſame garden,
where my Lord Biſhop at that tyme was recreating hymſelfe, by chance there ſate a litle child playing, that was the
gardiners ſonne, not paſſyng two or thre yeares of age, out
whoſe handes one of the Inquiſitours pages happened to
ſnatch a rede wherwith ẙ child was making himſelf ſport,
as childjen are wonte to do, by meanes wherof the chylde
cryed after his rede. The father hearing the child cry, came
ſtraight way to know the cauſe, and vnderſtāding it, was
ſome-

somewhat offended therewithall, and prayed the Bishops page to geue the litle child his rœde agayne: but because he made little accompt of the gardiners wordes, proudly scorning and disdainyng the poore man, he offered to snatche it from hym, and by reason that he held somewhat hard, a shiuer of the rœde raced the Pages hande. It was no deathes woûd Iwis, nor any great mayhme, such as should deserue any great punishment, but onely a small scratch, lyke as a broken rœde could make, I wot not well what to make of it, nor how to describe it, such a thing as ÿ very child would haue made no mone for. The page yet goeth to his lord that walked not farre of to make complaynt of this bloudshed. Whose lordship commaunded, that the Gardiner should be taken immediatly and caried to Triana where he was ladē with yrons, and there continued by the space of 9. monthes and in the end lost that little that he had, which was not much, God wots, and yet a hard thing for the poore man to recouer and get before hand agayne, his wife and children perhaps staruing in the meane time. And all this was only because he had no speciall regard to the bishops page, in forbearing him as a member of the holy house, but after the 9, monthes he released him, making him beleue: that he had dealt with him in much more gentle and mylde sort, then his case deserued.

There was also in Siuil a certaine poore man, that laboured for his owne liuing, and for his whole families ful duely and truely, with the sweat of his browes, whose wyfe a certayne churchman kept agaynst his will, and neyther the holy Inquisition, nor any other Courte would punishe this villany. This poore man on a tyme beyng among hys companions, where one of the company ministred talke about purgatory, and happened to take his tale by the end, of mere simplicity, rather then of any malice, and to say, that he had purgatory enough for his share in that a bile knaue kept his wife from him perforce, &c. The which talke comming

S.i.

ming to the good priestes eare, gaue him matter enough to
worke vppon, and to procure the poore man a double displeasure. Whereupon he accused him to the holy House, as
one holding an euill opiniõ of purgatory. And they thought
this a great deale more heynous offence, then the wicked
facte of the priest. For the poore soule for this only offence,
was taken and thrust into prison, where he remayned two
whole yeares together, and at the length was brought vppon the stage, and had iudgement to weare the Sambenite,
by the space of 3. yeares more, in some priuate place of imprisonment, & after that time expired, to be dismissed or fur
ther retained as the Inquisitors should thinke good. Nether
did they leaue him any one grote of all his poore substance,
as they did let the priest alone with his harlot, but notwithstanding his long imprisonmẽt, did likewise confiscate that
litle that was remayning. Behold, this is the Spanish Inquisition, which so stoutly maintaineth the christian fayth,
purgeth religion of heresies, and persecuteth the teachers
thereof.

Moreouer there was in Saint Lucars a certayne straunger, howbe it such one as had remayned in Spaine by the
space of. 20. yeares, who of a very blinde superstition dwelt
in a wildernes within a chappel: where hearing it reported
on a time, that a great number of Lutherãs were daily apprehended at Siuil by the Inquisitours, & that they had made
proclamation, wherby commaundement was geuen vnder
paine of excõmunication that euery man should repayre to
the holy House with all speede, & declare to the holy Inquisition whatsoeuer he knew either by himself, or by any other
concerning any of these aforesaid matters (for the Inquisitours ment speciall fauoure to suche as voluntarily would
come in and accuse them selues) this doltishe Yeremite
came to Siuil, went to the holy House, and accused him selfe
before the Inquisitours, The matter was, for that he being sometime at Geneua, about. 20. yeares agoe, had heard
a certaine

a certayne Frier dispute of such matters, namely of Iustification by fayth in Christ, of purgatory, and such other like, and liked therof very well, though afterward since that time he gaue no great heede to them, nor greatly remembred them, and therfore came now to confesse his fault, and to pray theyr pardon. But as soone as the Inquisitours had heard his confessiō (perhaps to fil vp some empty roume in their iayle, or to make vp theyr tale wanting an odde man) they sent the heremit to prison, where after he had remayned a space, they brought him out vpon the stage, and there gaue sentence vppon him to weare the Sambenite, and to suffer 3. moneths imprisonment, and to forsayt al his goods. So shameles (Loe) are these shauelings, that they can play such prety prankes openly, and so seuerely punish these trifles euen in theyr owne dearlinges.

There issued also in the selfe same Triumph a certayne honest man a Citizē of Siuil without eyther cappe or cloke, hauing a taper in his hand, of whō they exacted, after he had bene imprisoned a whole yeare together, a hundred ducates towards the charges of the Inquisition. The cause of hys trouble was, for saying that these outragious expenses bestowed in the erecting of those curious monumēts (as they vnproperly terme them) made of paper and wickers on holy thursday to Christ that is in heauen, as also the other, that are spent on Corpus Christi day (as they of Siuil ar meruelous excessiue that way) should be more acceptable in the sight of God, if they were bestowed vpō the pore in almes, or in the bestowing of pore and fatherles maydens in mariage. For the which wordes the party was both punished in this sort, and as one suspected for a Lutherane, abiured de vehementi.

Also at the selfe same time, and in the very same Triumph there was a certayne pore man brought before the people, who on a time as there chaunced a quarel to arise betwixt him & a priest of Eciia Citia in Granata, hapened to

ſay of the pꝛieſt in pꝛeſence of other, that he could not be per
ſuaded, that euer God would come downe into the handes
of that moſt abominable adulterer. Foꝛ ẏ which ſaying, the
Oꝛdinaries deputy had puniſhed this pooꝛe man, howbeit
ẏ pꝛieſt held not him ſelfe content therwithal, but did afterwardes befoꝛe the Inquiſitours lay blaſphemy to his charge
who notwithſtanding his foꝛmer puniſhmente, commaunded him to be ſhut vp cloſe foꝛ a yeare, ⅋ at the end therof,
cauſed him to be bꝛought out befoꝛe the people in theyꝛ ſolemne Triumph with out either cloke oꝛ cap, with a taper in hys hand, hauing a barnacle clapped vppon hys tong,
to reuenge the blaſphemy that he had vttered and ſo was
abiured de Leui.

Among the reſt, there were alſo two bꝛought into the
ſtage at the ſame time, both young men, and ſtudents: The
one foꝛ wꝛiting in his tables certayne verſes, the authoꝛ
wherof was vnknowne which were ſo cunningly contri-
ued, that they ſéemed to ſoūd both wayes, either to the great
pꝛayſe oꝛ diſpꝛaiſe of Luther, as it pleaſed the reader to conſtrue them : foꝛ the which onely cauſe he endured a whole
yeares impꝛiſonment, and was afterwardes bꝛought vppon
the ſcaffold in his hoſe and dublet, bare headed, with a waxe
taper in his hand, and baniſhed Siuil and the ſuburbes therof foꝛ 3. yeares ſpace, and abiured, de Leui. The other onely
foꝛ taking a copy of thoſe verſes liking them well foꝛ the deuiſe ſake and pꝛetie iuention, had the like iudgement, ſaue
onely that in ſtéede of baniſhment, he payd 100. ducates towardes the charges of the holy Houſe.

With ſuch examples as theſe be, a man might eaſely
fill whole volumes, but that I ſuppoſe theſe to be ſufficient
which are al redy repoꝛted, to occupy mens eares withall,
that they may vnderſtād and ſe a great ſoꝛt of moꝛe ſtrange
parts then theſe, which the Holy houſe playeth daily, wherby appeareth moſt manifeſtly by what ſpirite they are guy-
ded and gouerned in all their doings, and what their intent
is

is, and how good their title is wherby they claime and challenge to the place it self the name of the holy House, to themselues the titles of holy Fathers and Patrones of the Faith:
wherewith they haue bleared mens eyes hetherto, so that
it is easy for euery man to iudge whether christian Godlines and the true knowledge and worshipping of God, with
the kingdome of Christ (the perfect comfort of all good men)
be by these meanes encreased & enlarged, or rather not destroyed, scattered, and subuerted, and Sathans kingdome,
that is built vpon lies, compassed by craft and subtiltye, vp-
holden and maintained by cruelty, robbery, and murther
of many good and Godly men, whether I say it be not hereby
more amplified and enlarged.

¶ Certaine speciall treatsies vppon diuers Godly martyres of
Christ, who dying very constantly like good christians for
the profession of the gospel, yet the Inquisitours notwith-
standing deuised to defame and sclaunder them
with apostacy and reuolting.

THe Inquisitours thinke it not sufficient to execute such
by most cruel death, as cotemning all their tiranny remaine firm & constant in ý profession of the gospel of Christ
before theyr faces, & in open Court, but seke by all meanes
possible as much as lieth in them, vtterly to extinguishe in
them ý life of their souls, which is Christ Iesus dwelling in
theyr harts by fayth, of whom they haue declared théselues
to be faythful confessours, as well at theyr death as in their
life: For when they sée all their policies to be void & to haue
none effect, because Christ taketh into his mighty protectio
& safegard al his seruaunts, so that no mã is able to take thé
out of his handes (as he sayeth him selfe) then deuise they
meanes to robbe them as much as in them lieth of theyr
name and renoume of constancy, by scattering abroad false
tales and misreportes of them after their deathes, yea
sometimes ere they be dead, as they stand vppon the stage

clap-

clapping their engines vppon their tongues, becauſe they ſhould not côtrary them, repozting by them, that they haue foz ſaken they2 fozmer fayth and returned to the Romiſhe religion.

And this is a double deuiſe of the deuils owne b2ayne, foz two ſpeciall conſiderations, whiche do euidently p2oue that they are aſſiſted by his wicked ſpirite. Foz hereby they doo not only robbe the Party2s themſelues of their due deſer⸗ ued p2ayſe foz their conſtancy and perſeueraunce: but alſo the church of Ch2iſt is ſpoiled of thoſe examples, wherin ſhe ſhould otherwiſe reioyce, in making her reckoning. Ther⸗ foze ſith that in diuers Actes of fayth (as they terme them) they haue dealt in this ſozt with diuers, of whoſe conſtancy God hath many waies aſſured vs, it wilbe expediêt that vn to this fozmer treatiſe I do alſo adde theſe ſeuerall & parti⸗ cular hiſtozies, to the intent that the honour and eſtimatiô that is due to good and godly Martirs, may be yelded vnto thê accozdingly, and the church likewiſe reioyce as ſhe hath good cauſe: laſtly that the memozy of thê may be p2eſerued and kept, both to the glozy of God, the increaſe of his church and the vtter ſhame and côfuſion of this their holy houſe.

Iohn Pontio de Leon.

IN the firſt ſeſſion holden at Siuil againſt the p2ofeſſours of Ch2iſtes religion (whom they call Lutherans) whiche was the 24. of September, in the yeare of our Lo2d God 1559 there was b2ought fozth in the triumphe at the ſame tyme one Don Iuan Ponce de Leon, ſonne to Don Rodrigo Pô⸗ ce de Leon Earle of Balen bozne of a noble houſe, and a ve⸗ ry good goſpeller, as well foz his learning and knowledge, as foz the p2actiſe thereof, with the continuaunce of manye yeares, as I my ſelfe am able to make repozt foz the great familiarity and acquaintaunce that I had with hym a long ſeaſon, and therfoze (if néde were) could geue a true and a fayth⸗

faithfull testimony thereof (before God I speake it) but that all that euer knewe him, or that had occasion to marke hys conuersation, will with one consent (I dare say) testify the same. Among other vertues that appeared to be in him vnfaynedly and without hipocrisie, he was singular in one thing, namely for his exceding loue and compassion towardes his poore and nedy brethren : in so much that being left very welthy by his father, hable to continue that port y his ancestours kept, fell by such meanes almost into starke beggery : howbeit such as was to him neither noysome nor græuous. Notwithstanding, diuers haue geuen their blind and foolish verdites of him therfore, attributing that to folly and prodigality, which he did of a rare & singular vertue. But sithens he liued so well that none could iustly so much as suspecte any euill example of life to be in hym, and many were in their extremities relieued by his goodnes : besides this, accepted in so good part his poore and hard estate, as by all mens iudgementes he did very paciently, and in such sort as a great deale meaner men would scarce haue taken a farre better estate then he was in, these thinges must nedes be euident proofes of a singular grace of God to be in him and such a perfect kind of vertue, as was voyd of all hypocrisie. Yet in recompence of that singular pitye and compassió which he shewed in this world towardes others, he was apprehended by the Inquisitours for professing the Gospell, and after he had manfully maintained his quarell against their malicious falsehoodes during the tyme of his imprisonment (which was the space of .ii.or.iii. monethes) whether it were the very extremity of their torments that enforced hym, or theyr fayre and flattering promises of safety and deliueraunce that allured hym, but he shrunke at the length and yelded, where erst he was inuincible, stouping and submitting him selfe to the obedience of the Romishe church. The first that euer entised him so shamefully to reuolt was one of these stinging and venemous flies,

S.iiii.   whom

whom they had cast into prison with him, in maner as hath
bene already declared: who being a man very welllearned
and besides that a deepe dissembler, dyd rather by hys conning enchantmēts bewitch him, thē by any force of reasons
dissuade or seduce hym. Howbeit though God suffered him
so to fall for a while, that he might somewhat vnderstande
the frailty of man and sensibly feele it in hymselfe, yet still
remembring his owne worde and promise, that none shall
take any of his flocke from vnder his handes, dyd not long
tyme thus leaue him to himselfe, but raysing him vp again
most mightely, restored vnto him double the strengthe that
he had before. For the verye night immediately before hys
execution he did most manfully defend the truth against his
Cōfessour in the hearing of diuers as well prisoners, as also ý Officers of the holy House (for at such times, their confession is not mere auricular) in so muche that beyng demaunded by the priest, whether he would be shriuen or no,
where before the tyme of his apprehension and imprisonment he vsed commonly to go to shrifte, he now refused, rebuking the priest for his labour. And beyng vrged with his
former doings, aunswered, that he did it to serue the weaknes of his brethren & for feare of offence to thē, that as yet
were not proceded so farre, and yet made his choyce of hys
ghostly father so, as his shrift was more like a godly colla-
tion, then a popishe confession: Mary now (sayth he) as the
case standeth there needeth no such yelding. The next day
when sentence was pronounced vppon hym, were openly
read these articles amōg others, for the which he was chiefly and principally condemned. First that he should say, that
from the bottom of his hart he abhorred the Idolatry that
was committed in the adoration of the bread, and therefore so oft as it was hys chaunce to meete it, being caried a-
broad to sicke persons, he eyther turned some other by way
and auoyded it, or els hasted so that he forewent it, because
he should otherwise haue bene enforced to doo vnto it some
kind

kind of worſhip oꝛ honoure, and at many times chauncing
to be in the high Quier, would turne his backe becauſe he
would not behold the Leuation, and foꝛ the moſt part vſed
to go to the place where execution was accuſtomably done,
(like as was Smithfield here in London) and there woulde
walke a good ſoꝛt of turnes, to the ende that by continuall
meditation of the martirdome, but ſpecially of that faith-
ful and gloꝛious confeſſion, which the wicked of this woꝛld
by foꝛce and tyꝛanny cauſed the godly there to make vnto
Chꝛiſt (by thus acquainting himſelfe with the place) he
might be the moꝛe emboldened, looking one day to be called
thether, and ſo ſhould in the meane tyme pꝛepare himſelfe,
patiently to take it when it came. Likewiſe, at ſuche tymes
as by oꝛder he ſhould receaue his Maker (as they ſay) he v-
ſed to remoue his houſhold, and to ſend them to ſome other
place, making thē beleue at theyꝛ returne ẏ he had ſo done:
becauſe they ſhould not be offended to ſee him take ſuch liberty. But ẏ effect of his confeſſion moꝛeouer was thys: that
the iuſtiſication of a Chꝛiſtian man reſteth only in the merites of Ieſus Chriſt thꝛough only faith in him, ⁊ that other
purgatoꝛy there was none. As foꝛ the Popes pardons ⁊ indulgences, they were but mere parchment ⁊ lead, ⁊ he very
Antichꝛiſt. ⁊c. concerning my ſelfe (ſayth he) I am not only
willing but deſirous to die, ⁊ ready to ſuffer any other puniſhment foꝛ this truth which I haue confeſſed, eſteming of
this woꝛld and the treaſures thereof in none other reſpect,
then to ſerue my neceſſitye, and the reſt to beſtowe in the
mayntenaunce and ſetting foꝛwarde of the ſame doctrine
which I haue of late pꝛofeſſed, and therefoꝛe I beſeche God
dayly vppon my knees, both foꝛ my wife and childꝛen, that
they may all continue in this quarel to the very death. Notwithſtāding the holy Houſe laboꝛed earneſtly by al means
to depꝛaue him, ⁊ therwithal, to depꝛiue him of the due commendation foꝛ ẏ notable confeſſion made by him, ſpꝛeading
abꝛoad falſe tales, of his fall and departure from his late

T.j.   pꝛofeſſion

profession, most spightfully and malitiously. Howbeit I am able in fewe wordes to confute them, euen by this one argument, that in the exemplifications which they caused to be made of such matters as were done & passed in the act or session, being not very circuspect, they haue vnawares told the plain truth themselues, going about to set out the offences and punishmentes of this good man conteined in these wordes, which are extant vnto this day: Don Iuan Ponçe de Leon was burned as an Obstinate Lutherane heretike. The which word of it selfe, to such as doubt of the parties constancie, is occasion sufficient to suspect the Inquisitours crafty and deceitfull dealing. But as for vs, his good conuersation whereof diuers can beare witnes, hath credite and persuasion enough of it selfe.

Iuan Gonçales a preacher.

There was executed likewise, at the same time and Triumphe a certayne preacher that sometyme had bene a priest, but at that tyme no great clarke: yet afterwardes a man of very godly lyfe and conuersation, and one that became very well learned in the scriptures, whence onely he learned true Godlines geuing ouer all that Sophisticall & Dunsicall diuinity, wherein he had spent a great deale of tyme very idely. In all his sermons he bent his whole force to beate into mens myndes, the true way and meanes of our iustification to consist in Christ alone, and in steofast fayth in hym, all the merites of man quite abandoned and set apart. His name was Iuan Gonçales. But of such profession, there could ensue none other effect thē did. As for his confession, by the Inquisitours own reportes it was all one with the former that Don Iuan Ponçe made, so that it fell out accordingly, ȳ as before times they wer ioyned together in familiarity and frendshhip, they should also now be linked together in like profession, & make the like endes. Howbeit

the

The night before hys death, preparing him selfe to dye, he susteyned a great conflict with his Confessours, whom notwithstanding after much a doe on both sides, he sent away with shame enough. And at his departure out of the Castle Triana, towardes the scaffold, accompanied with two of his own sisters that went to the same feast that he did, leauing also behind him two of his brethern, wherof the one and his mother were in like case executed at the next Act, yet did he shew himselfe to be of a notable courage and constancy. For at the very first step issuing out of the castle gate, and standing in the full view of all the people, which had heard hym at diuers times make very many godly sermons; he began with a loud voyce to recite the. 106. Psalme. Deus Laudem meam ne tacueris. &c. cursing and condemning al hipocrits as the worst sort of people that were. Neyther chaunged he his countenaunce any thing at all after he was mounted vppon the stage, albeit they had stocked his toung, because he began somewhat to comfort one of his sisters, whome he knew to be tender of nature, exhorting her to constancy and perseueraunce. Also when his sentence was in reading he gaue very good eare vnto it, being nothing therewithall dismayed, eyther at the degradation, whereunto they setled themselues after their maner very solemnely, or at the putting on of such ornaments & ensignes, as were appoynted for him & his likes. The which thinges, though they seemed in the eyes of the world very odious, and much sounding to his rebuke and infamy, yet in the sight of God and his Aungels, were beautiful (no doubt) and glorious. To wit: they dispoyled him of those vile and wicked Massing robes, and arayed him with a Sambenite, a rope, and a paper hatte. But nighte drawing on, and such as should suffer being come into the place of execution, they were all commaunded to say they Credo, the which ech of them did seuerally: and when they came to that article: I bileue the holy Catholike church, they were also commaunded to adde thereunto

X.y.   the

the church of Rome. But there they stayed all at once. They were the Monkes and Friers in hand with Iuan Gonçales sisters, and other womē then presently to be executed, that they would adde it in their beliefe, and in that article put in the church of Rome. Who aunswered that they would doe as Iuan Gonçales did, not because they depended vpō him, or were doubtful either what to say themselues, or els what he would do, but to the intent that his tonge might by that meanes be losed, that he might declare his mind as wel cōcerning that article, as the rest of his whole beliefe. Whervpon hauing his toung at liberty, like a good & godly scholemaster he comforted them, willing them to be of good chere and told them there was no more to be added. Immediatly after this confession thus by them made, they broke theyr necks with a trice, ere the fire were kindled, and forthwith began to noyse abroad, that they had added those wordes of the Romish church in that article of their beliefe, accordingly as they were willed to do, & so departed, acknowledging and confessing the church of Rome to be the true and catholicke church.

Of foure women of Siuil.

IN the congregation at Siuil which the Inquisitours had well nigh consumed by fire, among those that had bene a long time professors of the truth, there were 4. womē most notable and famous aboue the rest, for their good and godly conuersation. That is to say, Isabel de Vaena, Maria de Virues, Maria de Corneto, & Maria de Bohorques yongest of the 4. for she was scarcely 21. yeres of age, & yet for vertuous conuersation comparable to her other fellowes: but in þ knowledge of holy scriptures, which she had gotten by continuall reading, and studying, and conference with godlye and learned men (whereof there was in Siuil a great number at that tyme) she became so singuler, that she dyd not

onely

onely farre excéede and surpasse her fellowes, but many of
our Masters ý are taken foz great learned Clerkes, whome
in the time of her impzisonment, she dziue oftentimes to the
wall, by their owne confession, and made them ashamed of
themselues. But Vacna the firste woman was a Matrone
foz maners, and her house a Schoole of vertue, & a place of
resozt, where the congregation assembled to sing Psalmes
and hymmes to god both day and night. Nothing was there
pzophaned, nothing done of hipocrisy and dissimulation, all
was pure and perfea religion. At the last, the time beyng
come that God had appoynted foz them, to be made ready
and ripe foz him, and so to be both apt, and able pzofessours
of his name and truth, the Inquisitours sent foz the, and at
one dzaught caught these 4. w diuers other of theyz neighbours. The first thyng that occasioned this Bohorques to
such earnest studye of the scriptures, was a litle skil which
she had in the Latin tounge, wherin it was lawful to read
the scriptures, both as often, and as long as she listed, beyng
restrayned and fozbidden, that in no case the common people should read them in their owne tonge. Yea her scholema
ster D. Aegidio, a man whom she did specially chuse foz his
singular integrity of life, as wel as foz his excellét lerning,
was wont to geue this testimony of her, that he neuer came
into her company but he learned somwhat, and so departed
thence alwayes better learned then he came. During the
tyme of her impzisonment, the Monkes and Dominicanes
had great disputations with her, merueiling as much at the
passing excellency of her wit in aunswering all their subtil
and sophistical obieaions, and (as it were) cutting them so
quickly with the swozd of Gods wozde, as also at the wonderfull memozy which she had in citing the holy scriptures
so readely: in so much that after they haue done disputing &
reasonyng with her, they gaue very good testimonies of her
constancie & sober behauionr, albeit they termed it by the
names of wilfulnes & obstinacy. After they had kept her a

long

long time in that darke dungeon, & there caused her to endure all the cruell and extreme tormentes that might be (by
meanes wherof they forced her to confesse of her own sister
that she was also one of the same religion: which was the
occasion first of her sisters imprisonment, & so consequently
of her death, being murthered most cruelly among those vil
lains by extreme torments) they brought her forth vppon
the scaffold, with diuers other godly men & womē, wherof I
made mencion before. Howbeit she came in such sort as one
making a semblaunce of ioy and mirth and conquest ouer
the holy Inquisition, rather then otherwyse. The which
straunge countenaunce of mirth, fo asmuche as it was
rare to see in her, and vnaccustomed, vttred by singing
Psalmes to God, the Inquisitours of spite and malice,
sought to alter into an other tune, by setting a Barnacle
on her toung in the way as she went, which notwithstanding ere they came to the scaffolde they did vndoe agayne.
When they had read theyr sentence vpon her openly, and
geuen iudgment of death, the Inquisitours asked her whether she would recant yea or no, acknowledging her heresies which heretofore she had most wilfully mayntayned.
Whereunto she answered them roundly, that neyther she
would, nor truely could confesse so much. And so from thēce
she passed with her other companions to the place of execution, accompanied with these hypocrites still calling vppon
her & her fellowes by the way to adde the church of Rome
in the article of theyr crede; but she among the rest moste
stoutly withstode them. Notwithstanding the abominable villians, to the intent to blemish their good name and renowne by theyr most villanous trecheries, strangled them
with halters, as though they had at their last houres, returned to the Romish church: in consideration whereof, the Inquisitours taking pity on them, would not suffer them (say
they) to be burned quicke. Moreouer, theyr tyranny did also
extend to the very walles, where these holy assemblies, and
con-

congregations were kept. For there was special commaundement geuen, that the house wherin Væna dwelt, should be raced to the earth, from the very foundation, and conuerted to a perpetuall waste ground, in the middest of the plat an inscription to be set in marble, for the wicked and Idolatrous generation, a monument of many misdædes: but to the Godly, a perpetuall memoriall of the true seruauntes of God, in whome Christ did most truely and perfectly dwell.

Hernando de Saint Iuan.

This man likewise, was one of the chiefe and most worthy members of the same congregation. I meane for the true feare of God that was in him, his singular honesty, his feruent and exceding zeale of doing good to his neighbours without any regard of his owne commodity, not in respect of his parsonage, or any curiosity about his body, or otherwise in his behauiour or spech. A young man in dæde, yet for integrity of life, very notable and famous, President of ÿ Hou e of learning (as they terme it) ϯ chosen therúto by the iudgements of many godly men that were first founders therof, to instruct ϯ teach ÿ youth in ÿ Colledge called the Colledge of children. In the which office after he had remayned by the space of ɕ yeares, to his great commendation, he was perceaued to be a Lutheran, that is to say a man conformed to the very paterne of true ϯ perfect piety: whereunto also (as his duety required) he had wrought hys schollers, as muche as lay in him to do in a tyme of so great persecution ϯ tyranny. But his reward for his paynes, if we respect mans recompencyng, was much like vnto that which the common sort of thankles people yeld a man for his good desertes: but respecting fayth, such as Christ foretold his disciples that they should find among men. For being most terribly tormented vpon the Ieobit or ÿ Trough ϯ so shaken in euery ioynt, that when he was taken downe thence, he was not of ſtrength able to moue any part of his body: not withſtāding thoſe villians the tormenters toke & drue him by the heeles in this plight all a long to his priſon, as it had bene a dung-ſacke or any carraine. The occaſion why the Inquiſitours dealt ſo extremely with him, was for anſwering thē ſomewhat roundly & homely, without relenting or yelding vnto them one iote. Yet during the time of this ſtrayt impriſonment, God vſed him as a meane to comfort and to confirme a certayne yonge man called Morzillo, a Monke of the cloiſter of S. Iſidore, laid in for profeſſing the goſpell openly, who by meanes of the Inquiſitours fair and flattering promiſes, had a litle before relented and yelded ſomwhat in religion. The which thing (no doubt) was the ordinaunce of God, that theſe two ſhuld be matched together in one priſō. For this Hernando perceauing the yong Nouice to faynt in courage, rebuked him ſharpely, accuſed him of cowardiſe before God, & driuing him therby to repentance, confirmed, and ſtrengthned him at the length. So that within few dayes Morzilo prayed to come to his aunſwere, and before the Inquiſitours, then and there, ſolemnely renounced that recantation whiche he had latelye made, deſiringe that hys former confeſſion mighte ſtande, the whiche he toke to be very chriſtianlike. Yet was he ſtrangled at the very ſame time and afterward burned: Mary whether he dyed in Gods fauour or the Inquiſitours, ȳ knoweth God alone. But to returne to Fernando. After ſentence was geuen, the Inquiſitours demaunded of him, whether he were determined ſtill to continue the ſame man, and to affirme the ſame hereſies. Whereunto he aunſwered them verye roundlye and bluntlye (after hys faſhion) in the hearing of all the people, that he had vttered nothing but the very pure and perfeſt Goſpell, and the true beliefe of a chriſtian man, and therefore was farre from accompting them here-

ſes

ces. Wherupon immediatelp they toke away from hym a
croſſe of wood which they had thꝛuſt betwixt his fingers and
the coꝛde that bound his handes,and therwithall clapped a
Barnacle vpon his tong,which remayned there vntill the
fire had conſumed it,and thus was he burned quicke.

Iulian Fernandes.

IT is a wonderſull thing J aſſure you foꝛ a man to conſi-
der, that in ſo wcariſhe a thing as this Iuliano was and
ſo pooꝛe,that a man would think he had nothyng lefte but
ſkinne and bone,there ſhould be ſo great courage and ſtout
nes of ſtomacke:but that the holy pꝛophet ſayth, and daply
experience beſides confirmeth, that God hath oftentymes
choſen the weakelings of the woꝛld to confound the ſtrong
and mighty.Foꝛ this ſame Iulian Peguenne(as commonly
he was called foꝛ the ſmalenes of his ſtature)being in Germany without all the Inquiſitours reache, and there con-
uerſaunt with many learned men,among whome he came
to the knowledge of true and perfect godlines, by the aſſi-
ſtaunce of the holy ghoſt,rather then by any mans perſwa-
ſion oꝛ counſell,tooke in hand a very waighty and a dangerous chterpꝛiſe:to wit,the tranſpoꝛting into Spain of two
great dꝛyfattes full of Bibles pꝛinted in the Spaniſh tong,
ſuch was the feruency of his zeale to publiſh ẜ ſet abꝛoad ẜ
light of the Goſpell in his owne countrey. In the which at-
tempt ẜ enterpꝛiſe,there was as great cauſe of feare, as if
be had vndertaken to bꝛing in carte loades of Scorpions oꝛ
other moꝛe venemous beaſtes,the hipocrites had ſo ſtopped
all ventes and made a reſtraint in euery poꝛt, becauſe no
maner of light oꝛ vnderſtãding ſhould by any means come
vnto them. Notwithſtanding all this,God vnder his mighty pꝛotection,and by his own ſafe conduct,bꝛought that holy burthen thether,and that whiche was moſt miraculous
of all,ſo pꝛouided, that it was both landed and diſcharged
within the walles of Siuil, where were ſuch buſy ſearchers

and catchpolles prying in euerye corner, that a man myght with a great deale more eaſe haue deceaued Argus for all his eyes, of the cowe which he had in charge to kéepe. The which dew of Gods grace ſent vnto them ſo ſeaſonably, that Paradiſe of the Lords, did moſt ioyfully and thankfully receaue, whereby the fruit (no doubt) grew to ripenes, and became more plentiful againſt the time of harueſt and reaping. For at the laſt this matter broke out, and came to the Inquiſitours knowledge: firſt by meanes of a fooliſh fellow, more fearefull a great deale then nede was, and afterwards by an vnfaithfull brother, pretending to profeſſe the Goſpell, wherein he ſéemed to haue profited reaſonably well, but ſhortly after ſhewed him ſelf to be a Iudas, and a champion for the Inquiſition, cloking and colouring his malicious purpoſe, with that counterfait pretence of religion, and by that meanes betrayed the whole congregation. Then the Inquiſitours well noſed like the deuil, & finding a little, followed on ſo farre til at the length they ſprang the whole couie, found the neaſt, tooke both yong and old, and ſo made hauoke of all. And this was the firſt rouſing they had, which broke that holy heard, that was ſo great in number that the huters themſelues at the firſt were afraid of them, and the ſpoyle of them ſuch afterwards, that they filled al their larders, and were enforced further to ſéeke for other cellers to beſtow them in, and to cauſe ſo many ouens to be heated, that they were almoſt quéched with ſuit of the Deare. For there were taken at Siuil at that one tyme. 800. and. 20. of them or thereaboutes, roſted at one fire. Among the which, this Iuliano was one of the firſt that was apprehended and ſent to priſon, where he lay continually, ſolitary and without any company, laden with yrons aboue. 3. whole yeares. By meanes whereof, there were dayly, diuers and ſundry ſights to be ſene. And yet the conſtancy of this man was ſo great and ſo wonderfull, that the tormenters themſelues, were ſoner wearied, then he vnpaciét for all his torments,

                                                            yea

yea notwithstãding hys weake and wearish body, yet he al
wayes remayned of sufficient strength in mynd to abide all
their tyranny, in so much that he neuer departed from the
racke with worse chere or lesse courage, then he was of at
his entraunce: so that all their tormentes, all their threat
nings, and all extremity which they could do or pra se vp
pon hym, did not make him yelde or shrinke one iote, but
that returning from the racke, or rather drawn thence tho
rough other of his fellows prisoners, he would signifie vnto
thē, how he had conquered and confounded his enemies, sin
ging on this sort : Vencidos van los frayles, vencidos van:
Corridos van los lobos: Corridos van, as much to say in en
glish as thus. The Monkes depart vanquished, they depart
vãquished: ŷ wolues do flie to shame, they flie to shame. But
long before this time came, he was much troubled in ŷ first
dayes of hearing with the Monkes and other such maintei
ners of iniquity as they are, by whom the Inquisitours be
ing vtterly vnlearned thēselues, vse to controlle & ouerrule
heretikes. From whome so oft as he returned, he delyghted
alwayes to sing that song, in token of triumph ouer his ad
uersaries. And on the great & solempne day of their Doome,
being brought out of his priso into the court of ŷ Castle Tri
ana, to be apparelled with such trinkets, as are apointed for
persons condemned (like as other of his companions were)
the report is that with a meruailous good courage & counte
naunce he began to exhort them in this wise.

My brethren be of good cheare, this is the hower wher
in we must be faythfull witnesses to God and hys truthe
before men, lyke as it becommeth the true seruauntes
and souldioures of Christe, and within this litle whyle we
shall haue him ready to witnesse with vs agayne, and shall
within fewe howers triumph with him in heauē for euer.
But immediatly as he was making this good and godly ex
hortation, the villaynes set a Barnacle on his tong, and so
he went to his execution. Howbeit standing vpon the step

U.ij.   wher

whereon they that are to be executed vse to stand, being not able in wordes to vtter the courage and constancy of his mynd in the pacient sufferaunce of all these tormentes for the Gospels sake and the profession thereof, he expressed no lesse in gestures and behauiour. First, kneling downe, and kissing the steppe whereupon he stode: and afterwardes being tyed to the stake and couered vp to heade and eares with fagots, did diuers and sundry times shrinke hys head in the middest of them, as one most willing to receiue hys death, and desirous to hasten the same: whereby like a good souldiour of Christ, he did very well foresee and prouide to haue his confessiō notified, and the infirmity and weaknes of his feeble brethren (if any such there were among them,) holpen and remedied, encouraging them by these signes & tokens which he gaue them, both stedfastly to stand to the truth, and lightly to esteme of the punishment. There was also present with him at his death one D. Hernand Rodrigues a false apostle, whose importunitye being not able any thing to remoue him from his profession, caused it to appeare in the eyes of men, so much the more glorious: who supposing that the terrours of death would somewhat haue dismayed him, obtained leaue of the chiefe officer, that hys tong might be losed, vpon hope that he would signifie hys conuersion to the common people by worde of mouth. But it fell out quite contrarye. For immediatly after that his tong was at libertye, this Iulian made as playne and solemne a protestatiō of his faith, as euer he did at any other tyme in all his life. As for his frende and acquaintaunce that gaue him so euill counsell, speaking flatlye againste his owne conscience (as he knew full well) he gaue him such an Item, and so toke him vp for stumbling, that the villain hauing not a word to answere him for very shame, to the end to be euen with him some other way, fel into this outcry and exclamation. O that Spayne the conquerer and dame ouer so many countries should be thus troubled with

such

such a caytife. Kill hym: Kill hym. And J warrant you there
were butchers enow ready to do as he badde them , and to
geue hym hys deaths wound. The rumour also was spzed
of thys man, that he had likewise recanted during the tyme
of his being in pzison : but God be thanked it fell out in the
end farre otherwise.

Iuan de Leon *a Monke of Saint Isidors cloyster.*

THis man at the first was but a tayler in Mexico that
famous Citie in the West Indies called Noua Hispa-
nia, and at his returne thence to Siuil agayne, felt in hys
conscience (as many good men do) a certayne feare of God,
though blind and not pzoceding of knowledge, whereby he
was moued to become a monke. Yet his hap was such by
Gods good meanes, who did so pzouide for his desperate at-
tempt, that he entred into Saint Isidozs cloyster in Siuil,
wherein the greater part of the couent at that tyme was
well affected in religion. But after he had bene schoeled ther
by the space of two oz thzee yeares, and conuersaunt among
them , he beganne to be weary of this monkish and soli-
tary kind of life , seeking meanes to forsake his ozder , as he
did in deede : colouring the matter with his continuall disposition to sicknes, and yet being once out, had such a desire
to talke with his former schoolemasters, that had instructed
him in the true and perfect religion, that he returned thether agayne, for conference sake and for their company. But
all in vayne. For in the tyme of his absence all they for
whose respect, he entred into that ilfauoured ozder once a-
gayne, had left their coules and were fled into Germany.
Whereupon he, perceauing that there was no place of a-
bead for him, determined to alter his purpose so soone as he
could certaynly learne what was become of his old companions, and whether they were gone . But here perhaps
some euill disposed persons will call him a double Apostata, in forsaking his ozder twise . Mary the wiser sozt wyll

U.iiij   geue

geue hym double honour therefore, and accompt hym the
godlier man two to one. Therfore trudgyng after his fellowes ℞ (as it were) tracing them, he met with them at the
length at Franckford with much a doo, both for the painfulles
nes of his iorney and the perils of passage: and from thence
went with them to Geneua, to meete with the rest of hys
acquayntaunce that were setled there. About the same time
by meanes of Queene Maries suddaine death, and that the
crowne of England descended vppon the most gracious La
dy Queene Elizabeth, they of the Englishe congregation,
that by occasiō of the late tyranny were dispersed here and
there in Germany, were by gods good grace called home a-
gayne into their owne countrey: wherupon diuers Spani-
ards that soiourned at Geneua, thinking England a meter
place for their congregation, did accompany the Englishe-
men, that returned homewardes into England, & for theyr
more safety deuided themselues into seuerall companyes.
For the Inquisitours tooke the departure of the Monkes in
so euill part, aswell in respect of forsaking their order, as re
nouncing their religion, that albeit they were but fewe in
number, yea but a handfull (to speake of) in respecte of the
worlde, yet they determined to plague them surely, if they
could come by them: and thereuppon sent out their spyes to
lye in wayt for them euery where as they should passe, speciallye at Colyne, Franckforde, Antwarpe, and all the
high wayes that lay from Geneua that way: and in lyke
case all the wayes on the other syde from Geneua to Mil-
layne. The charges whereof were allowed oute of the
kinges treasory largely enough, both of the kinges owne liberality, & of the desire which ÿ Inquisitours had to catche
them. And God wots much a do there was, sparing neither
for labour nor coste to finde halfe a dosen dogges to do thys
feat, and to hunt them out: besides other great priuiledges
and immunities that were promises to such as woulde vn-
dertake to bring them agayne. A straunge thyng to consider
how

how the Inquisitours detest and abhorre the light of the gospell, that they persecute it to the very death. This fellowe
therefore had gotten him a companion, one Iuan Fernandes
of Valladolit, a very godly man, and purposing to passe together into England thorough Germany, were layd for at
Argentyne, by meanes wherof they were dogged, and take
in a certaine port in zelland, as they were taking shippe to
crosse ouer into England. And being apprehended, this Iuan
de Leon toke the arrest with so good a courage, that he neuer chaunged countenaunce at it, but so sone as the messen-
gers had sayd that theyr errant was to him, he made them
answere straight way. Well (quod he) let vs goe in Gods
name, for he (no doubt wilbe with vs. Wherupō they were
both brought backe into the towne, and there racked most
pitifully to the entent to make them confesse of their other
companions, and within a few dayes after were shipped and
caried into Spaine : ech of them during the tyme that they
were in ÿ ship, hauing a certaine Iron chaine wrought like
a nette, that couered both heade and face, within the which
ther was also an other engine of Iron made like to a mans
tongue, which being thrust into their mouthes, toke away
the vse of their tongues. And in these continuall paines and
torments, besides other ginnes and fetters of Iron wherewith they were bound both hand and fote, they were brought into Spayne, and there deliuered into the Inquisitours
prisons : Iuan de Leon to the Inquisitours prisone at Siuil,
and his fellowe to Valladolit, where he was afterwardes
in defence of Gods quarell executed by fire quicke. As was
also one Doctour Caccalia a companion of hys, but a little
before him, whose brother or sisters daughter this man
had maryed. Howbeit Iuan de Leon remayned a great
while in prison, where he tasted the Inquisitours tyranny,
suffering both hunger and colde, as also endured all theyr
torments ech after other: and at the last was brought forth
in their solemne shew, arayed in like sort, as the other that

W.iiij. had

had continued and perseuered as he had done. It was a pi-
tiful thing to behold and (no doubt) would haue made many
a man afraid to sée so grisely a sight, and such a ghste as he
was: his face so ouergrowen with heare, his body so leane
as any rake, haue nothing left to couer his bones saue only the very skinne, and to the encrease of his payne, theyr
Barnacle was set vpon his tonge, that it was lothsome to
sée the long streames of fleume come out of hys stomacke
and hang roping from his mouth to the ground, as he stode
vpright. But when sentence of death was pronounced vpō
him, hauing then his tong released and set at liberty, to the
intent that he might abiure and recant (as they supposed he
would haue done) he made such a confession, wyth suche a
countenaunce, so quietly, without any apparaunt motion
or affection, though in few wordes, yet so effectually, as if he
had bene in his best estate & most liberty that euer he was
in. At the very last houre of his death, there was assigned
vnto him a certaine Monke to dispute with him, one of the
same cloyster that he himselfe had once bene on, and whose
nouice he was the first yere after that he entred that vnluc
ky order, that he might record vnto him the principles of his
old popery and supersticion. Howbeit the moe meanes that
they vsed to assault him withall, the stronger he grew and
the more hable to resist them: for Christ (doubtles) lyke a
good captaine defended his souldiour. In the end, he was executed as cruelly, as in his life time tofore he had bene tormented miserably, but with as quiet and patient minde as
might be. For so it was alwaies likely that so good a mā as
he, should make so good an ende.

Francisca de Chaues.

TOwards the furnishing of the same shew there was also one Francisca de Chaues a modest virgin and one of a
perfect profession, a Nonne of ÿ cloyster of Saint Elizabeth.

A

A wonderful thing to consider how the perfect knowledge
of Christe coulde come to her thorough suche Irons dores
and grates, notwithstandyng all the froward superstition
wherin she was almost drowned. But the election of God
in his sonne Christ is a matter of suche force and efficacy,
that nothing can withstad it at the tyme apointed. Besides
this, her hap was so good otherwyse to haue vnto her schole-
maister one D. Aegidio, of who we haue to speake hereafter. Truly the shining light of Gods gospell could not long
time be hid vnder that bushel, but whe the time was come,
it would appeare and shine to the ioy and comforte of the
whole church of God, and to the abolishyng of darknes and
iniquity. Well, the conclusion was, that coming before the
Inquisitours and entreated as others had bene before her,
at the legth she was brought out vnto the stage or scaffold:
where she (albeit that in all her life tyme she had had no
great conference with me) yet many times by her manlike
aunswers, did put the Inquisitours to a foule foyle: and did
moreouer, not onely most constantly affirme the truth, but
also most sharpely rebuked those good Fathers, calling the
dombe Dogges & the generation of Vipers. But of all the
rest, the small regarde which she had eyther of death or the
paynes therof, and specially the chereful coutenance which
she kept still cue to the very fire, was most worthy the sight
of all that beheld it.

Christoual de Losada a Phisition.

This man in like case was scholer to D. Aegidio taught
and trained vp by him in the principles of true religion.
Among whose other good gifts and blessings of God wherwithall he was indued, thys one thyng was in him moste
worthy of admiration, that whomesoeuer he toke in hand
to teache and instructe in vertue and godlines, he did therwithall (as it were) kindle a certayne feruent zeale in their

harts, wherby the yſwer enflamed to al the exerciſes of loue
and charity both inwardly and outwardly, and beſides this
meruelouſly animates and encouraged to patience at the
very houre of theyr deaths. Wherby he gaue an euident te-
ſtimony to ſuch as were lightned wyth Gods ſpirit, that
Chriſt was always preſet with him to make perfect his mi-
niſtery, writyng ω his holy ſpirit in theyr harts inwardly
ẏ ſame effect that he in words pronounced outwardly. And
beſides the good hap that this man had to light vpon ſo good
a ſchoolemaiſter, it was alſo his chaunce to meete wyth no
woꝛſe a father in law, a man ſo zealous and well affected in
Gods religion, that this Lolada being a ſuter to his daughter, although he were a fayꝛe condicioned man, handſom-
ly learned, and better ſene in his faculty thē a great ſoꝛt of
practiſers be, yet would he not graunt vnto him his good
wil foꝛ hauing his daughter to wife, til he were foꝛ a while
become ſcholer to Doct. Aegidio, and learned of hym ſome
godly and vertuous inſtructions. A very hard condition ſur-
ly, foꝛ a learned man, and one that thought himſelfe ſuffici-
ently cathechiſed, to ſubmit himſelfe to an other mans inſtruction, but ſpecially to Doct. Aegidio that was commōly
ſuſpected in religion at that tyme. Howbeit at the length
he condeſcended therunto, whether foꝛ vertues ſake, as deſirous of better inſtruction, oꝛ foꝛ his ſuities, I wot not. But
howſoeuer it were, oꝛ in what reſpect ſo euer he did it at the
firſt, he applied it ſo earneſtly, that notwithſtanding he loſt
his maiſter ere he could well haue ſpared hym, yet after his
maiſters death he declared how much he had profited vnder
hym: in ſo much that as wel foꝛ his ſingular learnyng and
ſkill in ſcripture, as foꝛ his vertuous and godly conuerſation, he was thought ẏ hableſt & woꝛthieſt perſon tobe Su-
perintendent ouer ẏ whole congregation, which was great
in number, though here and there diſperſed in coꝛners. As
in deede he tooke it vpon hym, and dyd very wel diſcharge
ẏ office of a preacher among thē, ſo far as he might in ſuche
aduerſity

aduerſity. Afterwardes by meanes of thoſe bookes of Iulian Pequenno he was apprehended by the Inquiſitours being a thing almoſt impoſſible that ſuch a faithfull paſtor ſhould hide him ſelfe when his flocke was diſperſed) before whom he made a playne proteſtation of his fayth, for the which he endured, firſt hard & ſharpe impriſonment with moſt cruel tormentes, and the open infamy of their ſolemne ſhewe, and laſtly was committed to the fire. Where he, ſtåding at the ſtake, diſputed very notably of true religion agaynſt thoſe importunate hypocrites, who vppon a falſe perſuaſion that they had to conuert him, gaue him ý liberty of his tonge, to the intent he might haue anſwered theyr expectation. And whereas they of policy fell out of theyr Spaniſh into Latin becauſe the common people ſhould not vnderſtande them. Loſada alſo (not greatly marking theyr meaning herein) began to talke in Latin ſo copiouſly and eloquently that it was a ſtraunge thing to heare a man almoſt dead to thys world, to haue his wits ſo freſh & his tong ſo ready, as euer they were at any time in all his life.

Chriſtoual de Arellano.

CHriſtoual Arellano a Monke of the clopſter of Saint Iſidore in *Siuil*, was by the confeſſion of ý Inquiſitours themſelues ſimply the beſt learned of all that came before them, and was betrayed by his owne frends, ſuch I meane, as had receaued a great deale more commodity and honour by him, thē euer they had done by any, & yet by their means was brought wythin the Inquiſition. The cauſe why he was ſo highly eſtéemed and accompted of for learning, was becauſe of his great reading & ſtudy in the ſchoole doctoures, as they terme them. That is to ſay, Aquinus, Scotus, Lombardus and ſuche like, that whatſoeuer had eſcaped them in all theyr workes, making for the maintenaunce of the truth with a very good iudgment and a paſſing memorie, next aſ-

X.y.   ter

ter the Scriptures, and the sounder sort of the Fathers and
doctours of the church, he did both redely vouch, and applied
them to his purpose very directlye, and so brought to passe,
that all his aduersaries, with whom the authorityc of suche
trifling writers weigheth more then the holy scryptures of
God were confounded with theyr owne doctours. Notwithstanding all this, he was condemned to the fire. For with
these manie tyrants fire and fagotts is aboue learning and
truth, and hable to controll and ouerrule them bothe. But
ere he came so farre, he was first brought solemnely and set
vpon the scaffolde to haue sentence pronounced vpon hym,
where there was a shameful matter most impudently layd
to his charge. That he should affirme, y the blessed and pure
virgin Mary, the mother of Christ was no more a maid then
he him selfe was. A seemely speach for these good Fathers to
publishe and proclaime in suche an open audience, if it had
bene so that any were so beastly or so wicked to saye it. Yet
such meanes they vse to bring them into hatred among the
common people, whom they know many men to haue good
opinion and estimation of, for theyr singular and approued
vertue. Yowbeit when Arellano heard that horrible blasphemie, hauing the vse of his tong as God would haue it)
he cryed out in the hearing of all the people, that it was a
most impudent and sclaunderous lie, saying that as well at
this present, as also at all other times heretofore, he did e-
uer firmely hold, and beleue the contrary, being thereunto
persuaded by diuers and sundry places of scripture, which
he could presently alledge if neede were. Also for a further
vexation, there stode of purpose one of the Monkes of the
same house, that had bene his gretest enemy, laughing and
reioycing at his misery, thinking it by like, not sufficient to
cause so godly a man, so excellently well learned, and a verye innocent besides, to be brought into so pitifull a case,
but to amend the matter withall, seemed to tryumph ouer
him in this extremity. The suddeine sight wherof, did some
what

what moue this good man:yet like a good chriſtian he put it
vp quietly and pacified him ſelfe, geuing a good example of
pacience to all that beheld it. Finally,ſtanding at the very
ſtake he comforted and encouraged a certayne monke of the
ſame houſe called Iuan Chriſoſtome that ſometime had ben
his ſcoler, and now become his fellow:and ſo partaker as
wel of his death as his doctrine.But foraſmuch as I certainly know not the very true cauſe why this Monke was executed,I haue therefore not annexed him here vnto the reſt.
Yet thus much I can truely ſay of him.A preacher he was,
both reaſonably well learned and of good conuerſation & liuing,for any thing that euer was obiected to the contrary.
And therefore thoſe hogges that minded nothing but theyr
bellies,did not greatly like of him.

Garſias Arias commonly called Maeſtro Blanco.

The wonderful prouidēce of God toward his elect which
contrary to common courſe,doth mightely ſaue and defend many that depely were drowned and lay a long ſeaſon
ſouſed in ſuperſticion and blindnes, fanſying it of will and
withſtanding the knowne truth agaynſt theyr owne con
ſciences(which ſinne the holy ſcriptures call the ſin againſt
the holy ghoſt,declaring vnto vs that the prayers of the con
gregation ſhall not auayle ſuch perſons as are ſpotted therwith) this prouidence I ſay, did moſt meruelouſly appeare
by this one mans example to be of ſuch force,that the deeper
that men are drowned in deſperation, the higher it afterwardes aduaunceth them in honoure. This Arias whom
they commonly called Maeſtro Blanco,becauſe of his white
heares and fayre ſkinne,had a very ſharpe wit, and for hys
time was well ſtudied in diuinitye : Marye therewythall
ſomwhat crafty and ſubtile with a little ſpice of inconſtancy:which vices alſo he did ſo couer with a counterfait cloke
of religion,that he was hable to deceaue hym that thought

him self the wisest man, yea, and did deceaue a great sort in déede. It hapned in his time that there were two sortes of preachers in Siuil and either of them had a great nomber of auditours disposed to heare ech part, as they best fansied the one or ŷ other. The one of them concerning doctrine & precepts, came nigher to the discipline of Epictetus the Stoick, then to the rule of holy scripture. But herein they were inferiour to Epictetus, that all his sayings & doings were one, but in these there was some oddes: for they neuer ceased calling and crying vpon the people to moue them to often fasting, to mortification, to denying of them selues, to continue in prayer at all times, lowly to thinke of themselues, which they called humility, & to shew ŷ same aswel in apparel, countenance, behauiour & speach, as in al ŷ rest of their life. But if you had stripped these fellowes out of theyr side coats Well, I wil not say al, but ye should wel haue perceiued them to be men. In summe, al their religion, both top & taile (as they say) rested in workes and outward exercises of ŷ body, quite contrary to the other sect, & therfore they wold séeme to be doers in any case. Wherupon they left the true exercises of a Christian man, I meane iustice, mercye, and fayth, the only meanes to attayne true righteousnes, and ranne by heapes to Masses, to hallowed places, to shrift (as they call it) and many other such like toyes which the scripture calleth spiders webbes that wil neuer proue good cloth, hoping by these and such like meanes to be purged and clésed from their sinnes. Moreouer they vrged pouertye, with sole and single life, euen vnto such as were already coupled in matrimony, but especially the vow of obedience, as doe the foolish Friers, to the intent to get them auditours. And this (say they) is the true denying of our selues, and therefore extolled it as much as the obedience that is due to God himself. Further, to the entent to képe them in blindnes & ignorance still, they disswaded men frō the reading of bookes written of diuinity, specially from Erasmus workes, by the

which

which they should learne nothing but a little pride in their owne knowledge, referryng them rather to Henricus Hopius, and Bonauentures workes, the A. B. C. and the scaling of Mount Sion, and suche others, wherin they should learne humility and obedience towards al but specially towards their elders & superiours. Among others they also cited vnto them, Masius, Cauallus, Guerta, Petrus Cordebensis, and many other moe then I can well call to mynd: For whome perhaps it had bene farre better, neuer to haue ben borne, then to leaue such monuments behind them. Of the which sort of preachers there were diuers, I confesse, in some respects very honest and godly men, but yet none, that vnderstanding the iugling and trecheries of their maisters would forsake them and take a better way. For sundry of them by their vnseasonable kind of fastyng, and their curious searchyng of high and secret misteries of Diuinity, fell into a Phzenesie, or els proceedng in their foolish enterprise, grewe euery day worse and worse, that is to say, of honest men, became very wycked Pharasyes, enemies and crucifiers of Christ, and in the ende twise so euill as their maisters were whom they followed. The other sorte did deale more sincerely with the holy Scriptures, declaring out of them what was true iustice and perfect godlinesse by meanes wherof they brought to passe, that that City bare the name aboue all other in Spayne for their iuste and true dealing, by the space of a dosen yeares together, so that it appeared that they had fruitfully and effectually hearde that piece of Scripture that treateth of true and perfect iustice. For hereupon came all that plentifull Haruest that hath bene inning these 8. or 10. yeares, of those good seedes of the Gospell, which the were by them so painfully sowen. The brightnes wherof, accordyng to the nature of light, dyd so playnly discouer al that counterfait holines, and Pharisaicall deuotiō, that it could not be but that nædes there must ensue thereafter, first hatred and then persecution. The

F.iiii, chief

chief laboꝛers in this harueſt, were Conſtantiño, Aegidio and Vargas, Doctoures all, and men both ſober, wiſe, and learned: whoſe trauayles in ſetting foꝛward the Goſpell in ſo great miſſes of ignoꝛaunce, and the woꝛthy endes which they made at their departures out of this life, as they bee woꝛthy of eternall memoꝛy, ſo will we ſhield thē that they ſhall not be foꝛgotten. But yet of all the other aduerſaries vnto the truth, this Arias was moſt ſpiteful, and moꝛe malicious thē any of the reſt (perhaps becauſe the other erred of ſimple ignoꝛaunce, but he contrary to his owne conſcience kicked agàinſt the knowen truth) foꝛ that ẙ other had bene moꝛe generally receaued, was moꝛe ſightly in ſhew, & moꝛe beneficiall to them that followed after it . Howbeit he would not gloſe ſo opēly as other of the ſame ſoꝛt would, foꝛ feare of diſcredityng himſelfe with diuers men of good reputation, and well affected in religion, wyth whome he was growen into ſome fauour and good opinion, by reaſon of that vertuous and godly diſpoſition which they ſawe in him in apparaunce: but in ſuch ſoꝛt behaued himſelfe and ſo cunningly conueyed his matters, that though ſuch as had tryed him knew what was in him, yet others tooke him foꝛ a deare frend of theirs, and eſteemed of him as if he had bene their kinſman oꝛ bꝛother. But as touching his ſubtilties & diſſimulatiō, he ſhewed it moſt at one tyme ſpecially aboue all others, at what time cōplaint was made to the Inquiſitours by a ſoꝛt of hipocrites, perſecutours of ẙ truth, of one Gregorio Ruiz a man (as the repoꝛte went of hym) verye well learned, foꝛ a certayne thing vttered by him openly in a Diuinitie Lecture in the Cathedꝛall churche of Siuil touchyng the controuerſies in religion, and concernyng ſpecially a mans iuſtification. Foꝛ where the Inquiſitours had aſſigned him a day of hearyng, two dayes befoꝛe the day of hys appearaunce, it was hys chaunce to mæte wyth thys maiſter Arias, with whom he had ſome acquaintaunce, by reaſon that they pꝛofeſſed one kind of ſtudy, but chiefly foꝛ
the

the report of vertue that was spoken of him though vnwor
thely. Wherupon amongſt other that were aſſigned, thys
Arias alſo was charged to be there at that day, and to pre
pare himſelfe to diſpute againſt Ruiz, who like a crafty a
poſtle ſo vndermined this Ruiz, that he gat of him all the
reaſons and argumentes which he had deuiſed agaynſt the
day of diſputation for the maintenaunce of his ſide. For
Ruiz (God wots) taking no great hæde thereof, nor ſuſ
pecting him of any ſuch trechery more then he did his ghoſt
ly father, communicated the ſame vnto him. Which after A
rias had obteyned, he gaue him a frendly farwell, and ſo left
him. At the day of diſputation when both parts were aſſem
bled, this Arias was alſo preſent, & ioyned himſelfe to the o
ther ſide that were aduerſaries to Ruiz. The which when
Ruiz beheld, he was ſomwhat aſtonied therewithall, and
perceaued at the length hys Legierdemaine ſeing hym ſo
readely cut of his arguments, which he had made hym
priuy vnto two dayes before, and to aunſwere them ſo ful
ly and exactly that he had nothing to reply agayne: where
vpon the ſelg ſeule being thus circumuented, and ſpoyled
of all hys weapons, yelded hym ſelfe, leauing to Arias the
honour of the field which he moſt like a Judas had gotten
by treaſon and trechery. The like honeſt part alſo for all
the world he played with D. Aegidio. For whereas he mea
ning nothing but well (as the moſt conſtant bruit is) had
referred the matter concerning the opinion of hys know
ledge and learning to this mans iudgement, becauſe he
knewe him to be hable to iudge as a great ſorte of others,
he gaue ſuch a verdit, as it had ben ſomwhat reaſonable for
him to haue geuen in a matter of vntruth. Notwithſtāding
he was the firſt in al Saint Iſidors houſe in Siuil, that ſtar
ted out of that dead ſlæpe of ſuperſtition and ignoraunce,
wherein they were all dead and drowned, and by meanes
of a few ſparkes which this man had ſet on fire, a great part
of the houſe beganne to ſhake of their drowſines and to ſee

a glimmering of the truth a farre of appeare like the dawe-
nyng of the day, and to defire that the vayle mighte bee
drawne, to the ende that they mighte the moze eafelye fée
the fhining beames of true religion. Foz the whole fcope of
all his fermons, foz the which there was a fpace appoynted,
as it fell out moft conueniently, fometime by night, from
two of the clocke in the mozning, til 4. was wholy to ouerthzow all their pzofeffion: howbeit not openly, but couertly and as it were a farre of. Firft he taught them that fin-
ging and faying of their pzayers all the day and night, was
no feruice, noz pzayer vnto God: that the exercifes of a
true Chziftian man were other then the common people
tooke them to be: that the holy fcriptures were to be reade
and ftudied with diligence, whence alone the true knowledge & feruice of God and of his holy will, of true religion,
and fuch as was moft allowable in his fight was to be had
& learned, to the obtayning whereof, we muft (qued he) vfe
pzayer as a meane, pzoceding afwel of the fence and féeling
of our owne infirmities and neceffities, as grounded vppon
perfect truft and confidence in God. Thus, by laying thefe
and fuch like foundations of Chziftian religion, hée made
them to loth that ftale ftuffe of their old and fozwozne religion, and wzought in them an earneft defire of the better,
but fpecially moued them to the ftudy of holy Scriptures.
Mozeouer, beffdes his fermons he read daily a lecture vpon
Salomons pzouerbes very learnedly and made application
thereof with good iudgement and difcretion, and had pzi-
uate and familiar conference with diuers, fuch as he was
dayly conuerfant withall and vfed to accompany, onely to
the fame end and purpofe. And foz this one thing hys happe
was alwayes very good, to haue fuche fchollers as were
tractable and foone wzoughte, and (which was wonderfull to confider) fuch as were not greatly wedded to theyz
monkifh fuperftitions though they were bowed, wherby he
had leffe to do with them, and might with moze eafe geue
the

the aſſault, and in ſhort time batter down this forced Ram-
pyre of ſuperſtitiõ,with the perfect ſhot of Gods word. How
beit his head was ſo full of toyes and new deuiſes, that after all theſe wholeſome preparatiues, wherewith he had ſo
wrought in thẽ ÿ the reſt of their ſuperſtitious dregs might
more commodiouſly be expelled, and that they were halfe
wonne to his doctrine, he made them fall to vnſeaſonable
faſtings and watchinges before ÿ Sacrament: whence they
ſhould looke for I wot not what inſpiratiõs, he cauſed thẽ to
remoue al their ſtuffe, bookes & beds,out of their cells, & to
lye vpon the bare earth, or els to ſlepe ſtanding, to weare a
heare cloth in ſtead of their ſhirtes,and a hoope of Iron next
to their ſkinne, with a number of ſuch toyes mo,as though
thoſe ſtinking weedes would not haue taken roote faſt e-
nough of themſelues,except the earth had firſt ben eared vp
with the coulter of Gods word,as was before declared. For
after that he had weeded the old ſuperſticion, he did nothing
els but ſow a like ſeede agayne, more corrupt and perilous
then the other that grew before. By meanes whereof many of hys auditours got ſuch good as is like to enſew of ſo
daungerous a doctrine. In ſo much that many of them fell
ſtarke madd, ſome ſo conſumed with melancholy, that they
were halfe frantike: ſome caught vncurable diſeaſes and
paines in the head, & became almoſt brainel/eſſe, ÿ they were
not able to ſerue any turne thereafter: but they ÿ had ſtron-
ger bodyes, and better ſtomackes to beare it out withall,
had ſuche a phariſaicall pride and glory in themſelues by
meanes of that vaine perſuaſion of holynes and perfectnes,
that no wiſe man will accompt them in muche better caſe
then other of their fellowes. And yet perhaps were *Arias*
excuſable herein from this ſo greuous guilt,either for want
of better knowledge, or by deſtiny if it were ſo, firſt to take
vpon him that office,and then ſo meanely to execute it,but
that I am right wel aſſured that his conſcience did cõdemne
al ÿ traſh,which he had plãted in place of truth. For at ÿ be-

ry same time being among his companions, he would take great pleasure in remēbꝛing the folly of such men, ẏ wer so foꝛward to runne any way that he would pꝛescribe and a-poynt them. Notwithstanding such is the foꝛce and might of Gods election, that these few good seedes sowne among those fitches, fructified in the end to the great increase of godlines merueloussy In so muche, that diuers and sundꝛy of them, hauing their consciences cleared and purged of their old hi-pocrisie, and scarcely well stayed oꝛ quieted with these new deuises, sought further by occasion hereof, foꝛ some better instructions, and vnawares happened vpon the other soꝛte of pꝛeachers, that taught the truth with moꝛe sincerity. Of whome (after they had entred some acquaintaunce wyth them) they learned the pꝛinciples of pure and perfect reli-gion, leauing by litle and litle that euill opinion which they had generally conceiued agaynst the Lutherans. After-wardes beyng persuaded that they could by no meanes at-taine the perfect knowledge of the truth, except they would somtime peruse their wꝛitings, God did likewise meruay-loussye pꝛouide foꝛ them herein, that they had not onelye such bookes bꝛought vnto them by a miraculous meanes, as they had a long tyme desired, euen at such tyme as they se-curely slept and sought foꝛ no such thinges: but also all o-ther soꝛtes of bookes that were extant at that tyme eyther in Geneua, oꝛ any parte of Germany: so that hauing suche stoꝛe both of bookes and maisters to instruct them, they be-ganne to nosell theyꝛ whole couent, in so much, that where at the first there were onely two, that durste geue the at-tempt in so dangerous an enterpꝛise, there were very few in the whole cloyster (which at that tyme was very well furnished) but they had some taste of true religion and god-lynes thereby, and none repyned agaynst it. Theyꝛ tyme that erst was spent in mumbling their mattens and pꝛime, was now bestowed vpon lectures of diuinity: their diriges either cut of altogether oꝛ curtalled very shoꝛt: theyꝛ char-

ters

ters of pardons graunted by Popes in auncient time wher
vnto al that crue leaned before, was now accōpted for ſtale
ſtuffe. As for images, they had a ſmal deale of worſhip done
vnto them or none at all. Layne faſting was turned into
ſemely ſobriety: neither was any taught to be monkiſh, but
to be ſincerely and truly religious, nor any mention made
of proceding in theyr former ceremonies, but much talk rather in deriſion therof, and to haue them abolished. Neyther
did they put this light vnder a buſhel, impriſoning it within
theyr owne walles but ſent it abroad into the Citie and the
townes and villages adioyning, aſwell by publiſhing of
bookes as by other priuate conference. Then all thinges being brought to ſo good paſſe, that nothing was left in vſe
ſaue only their ſtout idoll of their maſſe, and their monkiſh
profeſſion that reſted in their coule and their crown, which
could neither with good conſcience be longer ſuffred, nor attempted without preſent perill, and yet no great good like
to enſew thereof, they began to deuiſe firſt, and afterwardes
determined with them ſelues to forſake theyr neaſt and to
flie into Germanie, where they might liue wyth a great
deale more ſafetye of theyr liues, and freedome of theyr con-
ſciences. A very bolde enterpriſe (doubtles) and as ſome
thought both raſh and deſperate. For neyther was there a-
ny great poſſibility or likelyhoode, that not one or two, but
ſo many at once, and ſuch as were not onely the ſoueraigns
of the whole houſe and fellowſhippe, but famous ouer the
whole Citye for their excellent learning, ſhould forſake
ſuch a cloyſter, as the like was not in all the territorye of
Granata, leauing it in a manner deſolate, & eſcape in ſafety
from the furtheſt part of Spayne into Germany. And if
they ſhould ſteale away in ſeuerall companies, and at ſundry times, then were they like to be in euill caſe that ſhould
tary hindmoſt. For ŷ Inquiſitours ŷ had bene quiet a great
while, hauing intelligence hereof by ſome rancared knaue
or other, would beſtyrre themſelues of all handes. There-

fore they concluded briefly, that eyther all which were priuy to this coūsell, must depart speedely together, or els looke
to be apprehended shortly after. But God seing them in this
distresse shewed them a meanes how vnder an honest pretence a dosen of them might take occasion to depart within
one mouth, t ech betake him selfe a seuerall way towardes
Geneua, where they determined to make theyr aboad, and
purposed to mete altogether within one tweluemonth. As
for the rest being as yet but yong nouices in religion which
remayned behind because they did not greatly like of going
away, they within a while after aboad the brunt of the hurly burly whē it came. For at the very same time there were
3. burned out of that cloyster, and diuers of the rest diuersly
punished. In so much, that from that day till this, there was
neuer any examination of matters touching fayth in Siuil,
but that house hath alwayes made out a man, or two. And
very likely it is, that the truth sowne t planted there, hath
taken so deepe roote, that it stickcth to the hard stone wals,
so that whilest any one stone standeth vpcn an other it will
yearely yeld them one or two Luthcrans.

I haue by occasion entred into this discourse somewhat
largely partly in respect of Christes church, towardes the
which I should scarce behaue my selfe vprightly, if I should
robbe these mē of theyr renowne due vnto them, in regard
of the ouerthrow which they haue geuen to Idolatry and
superstition behauing them selues as couragiously, as they
aduentured daungerously, preferring vertue and godlynes
before authority and power, voluntarily refusing theyr present estates wherein they liued with some worship and in
much pleasure, and in steede thereof contenting them selues
to be poore and disdayned, banished from theyr owne countrey, to suffer shame and ignominye: finallye, to be euery
houre in danger of theyr liues which they led notwithstanding in very great misery. Of the which good and prosperous
successe, a great part next vnto God we do owe vnto thys

Arias

Arias, of whom our purpose is presently to entreate, forasmuch as all this great fire, that hath enflamed to Gods glory, not onely that house, but diuers places in ye citie abroad, besides a number of other without ye citie which we meane not to touch, bred of those few sparkes which this man kindled at the first. Who by reason of his vnconstant and fickell nature, being halfe suspected of his friendes, and hated of straungers, was diuers and sundry times complayned vpõ to the Inquisitours, conuented before them, answered the matter, & so discharged. At the last it came to passe, in that troublesome time wherein euery man almost was apprehended for religion, that Arias also went to the pot with his fellowes in deede, though he had diuers times shifted it of before. The which ende was foretold him two or. iii. yeares before by Constantino, and that with a behemēt affirmation. On a time whē Constantino bad this Arias to hys house to diner, where where present at the same time Aegidio and Vargas, to the intent to take him vp somewhat roundly for his halting, forasmuch as gentle admonitions vsed before would nothing preuaile. But in processe of talke as they were rebuking him most earnestly, he start out in a brauery, and sayd that he feared greatly lest he should shortly see bulles set forth in open shew, prophesying somewhat plainly of ye Inquisitours Theatre. Wherunto Constãtino made him this answere. Behold Arias, before God I tell it thée, that thou shalt not sit mounted aloft, as thou supposest to see & behold other, but shalt stãd below & be cõdemned thy selfe. As in déede it came to passe by Gods secret and diuine prouidence, that notwithstanding he had ben in time tofore a faythles fellow, yet his last apprehēsion turned not to hys vndoing, but wrought in him effectually, and contrary to hope brought forth in him the fruites of true repentaunce. For he did so earnestly and déepely lament and bewayle hys former estate, that whereas before times he had ben as fearfull as euer was Hare of hound or Ape of whipe, now being vppon the racke, with a meruelous cōstancy (which argued in him a wonderfull eschaunge) he withstood the enemies of Gods truth, and toke vp the Inquisitours sharply, that sat in their seats of maiesty like Demigods, saying ŷ they were meter to driue packs, and that such an office were more fit for them, then to sit where they do in seate of iudgement, & take vppon them the determination of causes in religion, wherin they were as blind and yet as bold as Bayard, declaring moreouer vnto them, that for his owne part he was harrely sory, and did most earnestly repent him and would do while he had a day to liue, for that he had wittingly and willingly in theyr presence impugned the truth agaynst the godly defendants of the same, wherof he him selfe was now become a defender. Many other sharpe rebukes so oft as he came to his auswere, the Inquisitours receaued at his hands. But in the end he was brought forth after their guile & accustomed maner of pompe, arayed with all their robes, honourable (no doubt) in the sight of God, though in mans iudgement reprochfull and ignominious: a man to be reuerenced for hys age, but specially for the harty repentaunce of his former life, and for that notable confession of ŷ truth which he made, leaning vppon hys staffe: and so departing from the stage to the stake with a mery and cherefull countenance, he made satisfactiō to ŷ church of God by this notable example of repentance at his death, for all the mischiefe that he had done therto by his vnfaythfull and hipocriticall dealing in the rest of his life time before. O man most happy of all other, worthy to be shryned, and to haue a seuerall place among the chiefe champiōs of Gods truth here in this world, that hast forsaken such wickednes and follie, and returned to make the like protestation of Gods truth that other Martyres and Confessours haue done before thee. Paul, that chosen and elect vessell of God, placeth hym selfe among the first sort of sinners, because he had bene a persecuter of the church of God, though of a good zeale, yet not

grounded

grounded vpō knowledge. In what place thē or what degrē shall we set this Arias of ours among the sinfull sort, who wittingly and willingly, secretly not openly, behaued hym selfe like an enemy & persecuted the same? Paul referreth it to the secret purpose of almighty God, that he might obteyne the more mercy, whereof he had made him selfe vnworthy so many wayes, saying it was to this end, ý Christ in him might poure out all the aboundance of his mercy and graces, for an example to all them that should truly beleue in him. How much then & how plentifully hath Christ opened his cofers, & bestowed his mercies (the treasures of his goodnes) vpon this newe Paul, if we may so terme hym? How sure and certayne a token doth he geue hereby, of hys excceding great mercy, grace, and loue towards all sinners? Therfore by this one example, this lesson may we learne as by the true mirrour of Gods goodnes, to kepe our selues from rash iudgements and speches, towards such as we sée in the most desperate estate that can be, forasmuch as we can not certaynly tell what God hath determined concerning them, but ought rather to follow the counsell of Paul, that is, to hope the best.

D. Iuan Ægidio *a Canon and preacher in the Cathedrall church in* Siuil.

Thys Doctour Aegidio, albeit he was a man both apt to attayne learnyng and painefull besides, yet hauing bestowed hys tyme in vnprofitable studies, notwythstanding that he had runne hys ful race & attained the highest degrées in Schooles, and professed diuinitie a long tyme, (such was the state of learnyng in those dayes) that he had scarcely his Latin tong. Besides this his small skill either in the tongues or any other good learnyng, he was a wicked contēner and blasphemer agaynst the holy Scriptures. Yea I haue heard him self bewayle the euill successe of learning

Aa.i.   ning

ning and ſtudy in his time , and the ignoraunce of that age confeſſing it to be ſuch, that whoſoeuer had any wayes medled with ẏ holy ſcriptures in the vniuerſitie of Alcala, where he him ſelfe ſtudied , was ſo farre of from being accompted of among the learned , that many would ſcornefully and in great deriſion terme him a good Bible, preferring Lombardus, Scotus, Gregorius Arithmeticus, and ſuche other Dunſes before the expreſſe word of God, for profoundnes of wiſdome and déepe diuinitie. Afterwardes being publike reader of diuinitie at Siguence, he was ſent for to Siuil, by one Alexander that was his predeceſſour there , to the intent he might be their preacher in the cathedrall Church in Siuil, where he was ſo highly commended, both for his vertue and learning, that he was made Subdeane of the Church , contrary to their orders , hauing neuer bene examined by the Doctors, as the cuſtome is . And truely for ſuch ſchole diuinitie, as was generally and vniuerſally receaued all chriſtendome ouer, he was very famous, and of great credite, marie he neuer had attempted to preache openly , nor once opened the Bible , to read or ſtudy the Scriptures . And therefore the very firſt time that he came into the pulpit, contrary to all mens expectations, he was founde altogether ſo vnfit for ſuche a function, that he began to be greatly out of conceit with him ſelfe , and to growe in contempt of others: by the daily encreaſe wherof on bothe partes , they fell ſo to repent them , the one for admitting him ſo vnaduiſedly, the other for taking vpon him that office ſo arrogantly, being vnable to diſcharge it , that both they minded to remoue him , and he him ſelfe determined to forſake the. But in proceſſe of time, after he had thus paſſed ẏ pikes by ẏ ſpace of a yeare or two, it was his chaunce to mete with one that gaue him ſuch inſtructiõs (or rather it was ẏ ordinance of God, ẏ prouided ſo wel, both for him ⁊ for the whole citie) that within a few houres conference, he learned by that parties meanes the ready way for a preacher to trauail in, and

what

what the office and duty of a preacher was: to the obteyning
wherof it was told him ÿ he must vse other meanes, other
books, and other maisters, then hetherto he had done. Wher
at D. Aegidio was somwhat astonied at ÿ first, hearing him
make such a sermon vnto him, but especially meruailed
to se his boldnes, that being but a plaine fellow and as a
mã would say a very Russet cote, besides that, one takē not
to be very well in his wittes, would presume so boldly, to
teach such a Doctour as he was, being neither familiarely
acquainted with him, nor knowing him to his thinking.
Yet D. Aegidio being of a gētile disposition by nature, and
hearing him discourse so largely of the duty of a preacher,
wherin he acknowledged his owne infirmitie, did the more
easely bridle him selfe, and gaue him the hearing quietly.
The force of whose persuasions (being a man indued wyth
Gods spirite) was so great, that from that day forward D.
Aegidio was quite altered and become a new mã, thinking
all his former life and labour euill spent, and therfore began
a new to trade an other path which should lead hym vnto
perfect wisedom and learning, wherof as then he knew not
one steppe. Furthermore, perceauing his counseller to stãd
so long vpon that poynt which concerned the duty of a good
preacher, he toke it to be a sufficient calling for him to that
vocation, whereof he knewe he shoulde neyther reape
commodity nor estimation in this world. Perhaps many
wil maruel to heare the party named that was the occasion
of so suddeyn a chaunge and alteration of such a man in so
short space, taking vpopn him to teach him the true way to
perfect wisdome. Truely I must nedes disclose it to the end
that the wonderfull misteries of Gods election may be ma-
nifested and reuerēced, who by the foolish of this world con-
foundeth the wisedome of man. His name was Rodrigo de
valer. a man 26. yeares ago condemned at Siuil by the Inquisitours for a false Apostle, a conterfayt Prophet, and a
wicked deceiuer of the people, and therupõ banished, and in

Aa.y. his

his exile suffred for the profession of the truth . Whose
wonderful kind of calling to the true knowledge of Christ,
sithens I am occasioned to make mencion of the person, it
shall neyther be greatly impertinent briefely to speake of,
nor tedious to such as be godly disposed . This Rodrigo de
Valei (a citizen of Librixa, a famous town as any is in al the
precinct of Granata, both for y antiquity therof, and chiefely
for the fame of one Antonio de Librixa a notable Clarke
as any was , and one that first restored the purity of the latin tong in Spaine in these our dayes) was discended of
a good house & of sufficient ability to maintaine the worship
therof:howbeit he employed his wealth,not to vertue , but
as commoly such men of ability do,which thinke al their ho
nor to consist in the maintenaunce of a good stable , and the
furniture therof,in games,in costly & excessiue apparell, in
hunting and other such like pastimes & exercises. For in all
these qualities he was singular aboue al the yong gentlemẽ
of the whole Citie: in so much that he sought not onely to
match such as were his equalles in degrée and habilitie, but
also to excéede them farre.In the middest of these vaine fantasies,a certaine motion came into his mind (by what occasion , or through whose persuasion , or otherwise by what
meanes God knoweth) but he suddenly left all his olde de-
lights,contẽning the spech of the people (which was a hard
thing for a man to do) and bent him selfe wholy both body &
soule to the exercise of vertue & godlines, that a man would
scarcely iudge him to be a man of this world. Moreouer the
wonderfull chaunge that appeared to be in him otherwise,
aswel in his speche and behauior,as in his apparel that was
fine and sutable before, gorgious as might be , and now
quite altered into simple stuffe and playnest fashion, was
well liked of some , but on the other side a great number
thought it meare madnes or starke folly . But as the like
false verdites geuen of the holy Apostles that were indued
with the holy ghost, were attainted by the effectes of the

same

same spirite, so the perfect feare of God with the bewayling
of his former vanities, the ernest desire of righteousnes, &
his whole talke tending to these ends and concerning these
matters, alwayes framed according to the prescript rule of
Gods word, was a sufficient proofe and euidence to men of
perfecter vnderstanding, that the spirite of God most certainely possessed him. In his youth time he had gotten a little smacke in the Latine, by the helpe whereof he was conuersaunt in the holy scriptures both day and night, so that
by continuall study thereof, he had a great part of them by
hart, and could make application therof to his purpose sensibly and meruailous redely. He had also daily conflicts with
he spirituall men (as they call them) the priests & monkes,
which were the causes (sayth he) that not only the estate of
the clergy, but also all Christendome was so fouly corrupted, that they were almost hopelesse of remedy: for which
causes he did also diuers and sundry times sharpely rebuke
them. Whereat this Pharisaicall generation much mar-
ueiling, inquired of him how he atteined so suddenly to all
this skill in holy scriptures: How he durst presume so arrogantly to inueigh against the very supporters and lights of
the Church: For in deede he spared none, but would tell the
proudest of them his minde, being but a lay man, voyde of
all good learning, and one that had spent the greater part
of hys tyme in vayne and vnprofitable studies. Likewyse
they examined hym, by force of what commission he did it:
who sent hym : how he was called : and by what tokens he
declared the same. Alas for them good men, when they can
not deny their abhominations, nor longer hold out the light
which discouereth theyr darkenes, euen now as in all other
ages from time to time, they are driuen to these shifts. How
beit Rodrigo de Valer answered them truelye and with a
bolde courage to euery demaunde : that he had not fished for
that wisdom and caught it in their most filthy puddels, and
muddy ditches, but had it by the only goodnes of the holy

Aa.iij.   ghost

ghost, who poureth whole clouds of grace into the hartes of true beleuers most aboundantly. As for his boldnes he told them, that both the goodnes of his quarel, & he that sent him gaue him the encouragement, and that the spirite of God which is bound to no estate or degrée, be it in name neuer so spirituall, specially if it be corrupt, hath heretofore chosen very idiots and fishermen, and placed them in the rowme of Apostles, to controle the Sinagoge of the learned touching the law, to appeach them of ignorance, and to cal the whole world to the knowledge of their owne saluation: & that the same Christ had sent him, whose name and authority he had for his warrant: but as for any signe to declare the same, he sayd it was the token of a bastardly generation, and of the braunches degenerate from the true stocke of the children of God to aske for any signes in the time of such light, when al thinges shine therewith, yea very darknes it selfe as cleare as noone day. At the length for these and suche like matters he was called to his answere before the Inquisitours, wher he disputed very earnestly of the true Church of Christ, and which were the markes to know it by, how man was iustified in the sight of God, and of such other pointes of religion: the knowledge whereof, he confessed that he had attayned vnto by no meanes or helpe of man, but by the onely handy worke of God, and his wonderful reuelation. Howbeit his madnes and phrenesie, wherewith the Inquisitours supposed hym to be troubled, excused him for this time, yet to the end that he might the soner come to him selfe againe, they condemned him in the losse of all hys substance and sent him packing as poore as Job: but he neuer repented himselfe thereof, or became other man, in so much that within a yeare or two after, he was sent for agayne about the same matters and then driuen to make recantatiō: mary in consideration that they tooke him to be lunatike still, they spared hym hys life, adiudging him neuerthelesse to

wears

weare the Sambenite, and to suffer perpetuall impzison=
ment during life, saue only that on sondayes they bzought
him fozth, with many other mo of his companions, and
caried them to Saint Saluatozs church to heare seruice.
Wheras diuers and sundzy times he arose out of his place,
and in the hearing of all the people controlled the pzeacher
when he taught them amisse. At what tyme it so chaunced
that the Jnquisitours were not halfe so bad as other that
had bene befoze them, so that his fact was wound vp quietly
and excused by madnes and folly. Afterwardes, he was re=
moued out of pzison to Saint Lucars into a certayne house
of religion, where he dyed, being a man aboue. 50. yeares
of age, a very wonder to the wozld at that time, sent to a=
wake men out of their deade sleepe of wickednes and igno=
raunce wherein they lay snozing and snozting so long. And
fozasmuch as those articles whereof he was moste vniustly
condemned, were straunge and not heard of in Siuil at those
dayes, he had a Sambenu appoynted to weare, such a one as
was of the largest sise that any were in hys tyme, the which
at this day is to be sene foz a speciall monumêt of a notable
heretike in the vestry of the chiefe church in Siuil in a place
where euery man may easily see it, wyth this inscription
wzought in capitall lettters. Rodrigo de Valer Citizen
of Lebrixa an Apostata, & a false Apostle of Siuil, that sayd
he vvas sent from God. By this mans aduertisement as J
shewed befoze, was this Doctoz Aegidio first awaked, and
by his instructions, came to the first knowledge of the true
Gospell of Chzist, which lay buried a long season befoze so
that neither maister noz scoller once heard so much as one
wozd therof. Therfoze so oft as his matter came in hearing
befoze the Jnquisitours, this Doctoz Aegidio dyd alwayes
stand his good frende as much as in him lay, thzough whose
meanes it was thought that he foūd the moze fauour at the
Jnquisitours hands in the mitigation of their sentence vp=
pon hym being a relaps as theyz terme is. But in the ende

Aa.iiij.   Doctoz

Doctor Aegidio himself bought full dearely that litle curtesie that was shewed to this man at his mediation. For their
by he purchased himselfe, bothe much hatred, and grewe
daily into great suspicion with all that packe of Phariseys
that could not well away with his perfect and vertous sincerity. Besides these good instructions, this Aegidio was also
familliarlay acquainted & conuersant with Constantino de
la fuente, a man excellently well learned, by whose dayly
conference, he profited meruailously in study, fell to the reading of good authours, and so grew to profounde knowledge
in the holy scriptures: but specially concerning such matters
wherof he would preach to edify the people withall, he both
learned them perfectly by conference with other wise and
learned men, and partly by his own reading and experience:
at the length, began to preach as learnedly, godly, and zea-
lously, as he had before times done coldly, foolishly, and vn-
skilfully. Then began the hearers to feele the meruailous
force of that doctrine which these 3. men of great credite and
estimation, Ægidio, Constantino, & el grande vargas, taught
with one consent, in so much that the more they grew in knowledge from their old ignorance and blindnes, the more wer
these men had in reputation among them, and the old hipocrites despised, that had taught them other doctrine to the
great perill of their soules. Whereuppon there were dayly diuers complaints brought to the Inquisitours eares of
these men: but specially of Doct. Aegidio, who of meere simplicity, and by reason that he was in some more authority
then the rest, did more openly inueigh agaynst the aduersaries of the truth, whome they began chiefly to enuie at such
time as the Emperour in respect of his singular learning &
integrity of lyfe, elected him to the bishopricke of Dortoys.
For then those hypocrites began to bestirre the of all hands
and to lay all their heads together to geue him a lift, thinking that if he were once consecrated bishop there, he would
keepe a foule coyle in their kingdome. Therefore they cited

ſed him to come befoze the holy Houſe wher plaint was en
tred againſt him by ſuch as were their crafts maiſters, able
to wozke him miſchief, and to bzing it about cloſely, ſo that
by their meanes he was caſt into pziſon, and thereuppon
examined. The firſt matter was concerning the iuſtification of a Chziſtian man, ꝉ diuers other that depend theron,
as of mans merites, of purgatozy, of the meanes of ſatiſfaction foz ſinnes deuiſed by mans bzayne, of the number of
Mediatours, and whether there were any moe then Chziſt
alone, alſo concerning the aſſuraunce of faith in ſuch as are
iuſtified ꝛc. Beſides theſe there wer alſo other matters that
fell out by occaſion of an abhominable Idoll of the bleſſed
virgin Mary, wzought very artificially by Ferdinando the
king (as the repozte goeth) the which Image, vppon diuers
feaſtes of the bleſſed virgin is ſet vp and ſhewed to the people wyth great pompe: whereuppon Idolatry oz the woz
ſhipping of Images came in queſtion. Alſo by like occaſion
of a certaine chip of wood that is very ſuperſtitiouſly honou
red in the ſame Church as a péece of the Croſſe whereon
Chziſt was crucified, the whiche relique Doctoz Aegdio
wiſhed to be burned, ꝑ ſame matter likewiſe came in talke.
Mozeouer, cōcerning inuocation ꝛ pzayers to dead ſaintes,
and the baniſhing out of pulpits the deuiſes of mans bzain,
and of placing therein the perfect and expzeſſe wozd of God
and other ſuch neceſſary matters of like impoztaunce, and
therwithal to ſet him fozward, he was charged to be an carneſt fauourer of Rodrigo de Valer, &c. Wherunto Doctoz
Aegidio made aunſwer particularly, but chiefly touchyng
the firſt poynt. Wherof he made ſo perfect and abſolute a
deféce, ſo learnedly, ſo Godly, and ſo abſolutely, as any hath
bene hetherto heard oz ſéene in the which aunſwer he gaue
his aduerſaries twenty wayes to take aduauntage of hym,
and thereuppon to inferre diuers other ſuch hereſies. But
at that tyme the Inquiſitours were not growne ſo bold, as
ſince then they haue bene, noz in déede durſt not burne ſuch

a man as he was for these quarels, albeit they were vrged
and called vpon on euery side very earnestly so to do. Therfore seing that they could in no wise make him chaunge or
alter hys mynde, they begā to deuise which way they might
saue his life, because the Emperour who lately had elected
him to so great a bishoppricke, as also the whole Chapiter
of the Cathedrall Church in Siuil were become very ernest
suters in his behalfe. There was also one of the Inquisitours named El licenciado Anthonio del Corro a good and
a fatherly old man, who for that assuraunce which he had by
his owne knowledge of the good cōuersatiō of Doctor, Aegidio, and of the frowardnes of his accusers, stood his very good
frend, though his wicked associate Pedro diaz was sore a-
gainst him, who like a proud Apostata forsooke the truth,
wherin the same Rodrigo de valer had instructed him in his
priuate lectures vppon Pauls Epistle to the Romaines, for
the which he gaue him at that time most harty thanks, and
yet notwithstanding was now become a turncote. When
Vargas was dead and Constantino in the low countries
with the Emperour being his chaplaine & confessour, there
were certayne arbitratours apoynted on both partes concerning this religion that was newly come into Spayne.
And Doctor Aegidio for his part among others named one
Bartolome de Zamora, a Mōnke of the order of Saynte
Dominike, a man very well learned and one that knewe
the truth. Who afterwards by the Emperours meanes
was preferred to the Archbishopricke of Toledo whence he
was shortly after deposed for religion, or as it is more pro-
bably coniectured, vpō some priuy grudge, which the Archbishop of Siuil, high commissioner in the Inquisition, bare
vnto him, and so, after many conflicts with y Inquisitours,
at the length dyed. But at that tyme he could not be present
at this triall by reason that he was attendaunt vppon the
Emperour. So that Arias who was commonly called Ma-
estro Blanco, was iudge at that tyme. But what his verdite
was

was, is already partly reported in the speciall history that I
haue written of hym, and perhaps the same may come forth
to light hereafter particularly ioyned with the aunswere
that Doctor Aegidio made thereunto. But whether Arias
were thereto nominated by the Inquisitours themselues,
or by Doct. Aegidio, as yet it is not certainly knowne: so that
some being absent, and some fearefull to speake their mindes
for feare of afterclaps, the determination thereof was referred to on called Fray Domingo de Soto, a sophister of great
fame in the vniuersity of Salamancke, and one other frier
of the order of Saint Dominicke, who after great expectation of his comming, at the last came from Salamank to Siuil, and there entred disputatio with D. Aegidio y was but
a playne dealing man and a small foresight, more crafe-
tely and subtilly then other had dealt before him. First, pretending much good will towardes him and perceauing that
by dealing with him openly, he coulde in no case remoue
hym from his opinion, he fained himselfe to be iumpe with
hym in the same: mary he aduised him, that forasmuch as
those articles that presently were called in question were
somewhat odious in most mens eares, to the end to qualifie
the same, he would make and publish some apt declaration and exposition thereof, the which he offred to prescribe
vnto him in the best sort that he could, that he might vse it
if it liked hym, or els they two to conferre about it, and set
it forth to the better discharge of their consciences, furtheraunce of the truth, & contentation of the hearers. Where-
vpõ de Soto prescribed such a president: both of them conferred about it, and in y end agreed without any controuersie.
There was a solemne day of hearing appointed by the Inquisitours for that purpose, and two pulpits set in the Cathedral church, the one for D. Aegidio, the other for de Soto
and al the people were assembled thether. De Soto began his
sermõ and proceded accordingly. Immediatly after the end
thereof he drew forth of his bosome a declaration quite con-

trary to that, whereupon they were agréed. For in the former there was nothing but that which was confonãt to the
truth and his owne conscience: in this, no such matter, but
only a plain recantation of all those things whereof he was
accused, and had bene a maintayner of tofore by the space of
two whole yeares, and lately also during the tyme of hys
impꝛisonment. But the pulpits were such a distance a sun-
der, that by meanes therof partly, and partly with the mur-
mure of the common people whiles euery mã gaue his verdit therof, there was such a noyse, that D. Aegidio could not
well vnderstand what de Soto sayd: but yet foꝛ the good opinion which he had of him, gaue him suche credite that at the
end of euery article, when de Soto craftely asked his consent
thereto, willing hym to speake aloud that the people might
heare him, oꝛ els to signifie so much by some countenaunce
oꝛ gesture he did so, confessing that he did agrée to all those
things which de Soto had read vnto them. Whereupon he
was presently condēned to suffer impꝛisonmēt foꝛ.3. yeares.
Moꝛeouer this crafty Monke pꝛocured a pꝛohibitiõ against
him foꝛ pꝛeaching, reading oꝛ wꝛyting by the space of.10.
yeres after, enioyning him during that time, not to depart
Spaine. Whereat D. Aegidio meruelling much, hearing ÿ
his punishment was no greater, knowing nothing hereof,
noꝛ vnderstanding after what soꝛte he was circumuented,
til the time that he was bꝛought to pꝛison againe, whether
diuers of his frends resoꝛting to visite him, began to rebuke
him foꝛ denying the truthe. The which thinges we neuer
came to haue any notice of, but of his owne mouthe in the
time of his impꝛisonment, During which time it was hys
chaūce to heare of the death of.3. of his most deadly enemies
Esbarroia, a sophistre and a frier of the oꝛder of S. Dominik,
Pedro Mexia one that tooke vpon him very arrogantly, the
title of a Philosopher without any maner of good learning,
and Pedro Diaz the Inquisitour that played the Apostata,
and foꝛsoke the truth most wickedly as was befoꝛe declared.

Neither

Neither is it to be otherwise thought then to be the secrete iudgement of God that.iii.of the greatest enemies that the truth had,and sorest aduersaries to this innocēt man should dye all within one yeare,eche after other,while D. Aegidio was in prison,and his matters in examination,and(as it is reported)that some of them should depart scarce quietly. Howbeit he liued foure or fiue yeares after that retractation which was compassed of him by such deceitfull meanes, and was neuertheles estemed of all that godly congregatiō, and did as much good to other afterwardes, as at any other time being at his most liberty.In the which time by reason of an embassie which he was sent in,he visited his brethren that somtimes had bene schollers to D. Cacalia at Valladolit professing the gospel vnder him,and renouncing al wickednes and impiety.Whome after he had comforted & confirmed,in his way homeward as he returned to Siuil being sore shaken in that long iourney, by reason that he had not bene acquainted with trauaile of a greate while before, he sickned,and thereupon within a fewe dayes after departed this troublesome life,and went to euerlasting rest.

He left behinde him certaine commentaries vppon Genesis, and Paules Epistle to the Colossions, vppon certayne of the Psalmes, and Cantica Canticorum, written by hym in the Spanish tong very learnedly, and like one plentifully indued with the holy ghost,the which are reserued in the custodye of diuers men of trust and credite as iewells and tresures to the behofe of the church.The which allbeit they were both learned and godlye, yet other thinges whych he wrote in prison, doe so farre exceede them for the speciall affections moued (no doubt) by the spirite of God and expressed therein,that a man may easelye see the force of affliction and tribulation,how muche it auayleth the godly for deepe iudgement in matters of diuinitie. But wythin two or thrēe yeares after his death the new Inquisitours thinking that the other who had the examination of him,had delt a

trary to that, whereupon they were agréed. For in the for
mer there was nothing but that which was consonãt to the
truth and his owne conscience : in this, no such matter, but
only a plain recantation of all those things whereof he was
accused, and had bene a maintayner of tofore by the space of
two whole yeares, and lately also during the tyme of hys
impꝛisonment. But the pulpits were such a distance a sun-
der, that by meanes therof partly, and partly with the mur-
mure of the common people whiles euery mã gaue his verdit therof, there was such a noyse, that D. Aegidio could not
well vnderstand what de Soto sayd: but yet foꝛ the good opinion which he had of him, gaue him suche credite that at the
end of euery article, when de Soto craftely asked his cõsent
thereto, willing hym to speake aloud that the people might
heare him, oꝛ els to signifie so much by some countenaunce
oꝛ gesture he did so, confessing that he did agrée to all those
things which de Soto had read vnto them. Whereupon he
was pꝛesently condéned to suffer impꝛisonmét foꝛ.3. yeares.
Moꝛeouer this crafty Monke pꝛocured a pꝛohibitiõ against
him foꝛ pꝛeaching, reading oꝛ wꝛyting by the space of.10.
yeres after, enioyning him during that time, not to depart
Spaine. Whereat D. Aegidio meruelling much, hearing ꝭ
his punishment was no greater, knowing nothing hereof,
noꝛ vnderstanding after what soꝛte he was circumuented,
til the time that he was bꝛought to pꝛison againe, whether
diuers of his frends resoꝛting to visite him, began to rebuke
him foꝛ denying the truthe. The which thinges we neuer
came to haue any notice of, but of his owne mouthe in the
time of his impꝛisonment, During which time it was hys
chaũce to heare of the death of.3. of his most deadly enemies
Esbarroia, a sophistre and a frier of the oꝛder of S. Dominik,
Pedro Mexia one that tooke vpon him very arrogantly, the
title of a Philosopher without any maner of good learning,
and Pedro Diaz the Inquisitour that played the Apostata,
and foꝛsoke the truth most wickedly as was befoꝛe declared.
Neither

Neither is it to be otherwise thought then to be the secrete iudgement of God that.iii.of the greatest enemies that the truth had,and sorest aduersaries to this innocēt man should dye all within one yeare,eche after other,while D.Aegidio was in prison,and his matters in examination,and(as it is reported) that some of them should depart scarce quietly. Howbeit he liued foure or fiue yeares after that retractation which was compassed of him by such deceitfull meanes, and was neuertheles esteemed of all that godly congregatiō, and did as much good to other afterwardes, as at any other time being at his most liberty.In the which time by reason of an embassie which he was sent in,he visited his brethern that somtimes had bene schollers to D.Cacalla at Vallado= lit professing the gospel vnder him,and renouncing al wic= kednes and vnpiety.Whome after he had comforted & con= firmed,in his way homeward as he returned to Siuil being sore shaken in that long iourney, by reason that he had not bene acquainted with trauaile of a greate while before, he sickned,and thereupon within a fewe dayes after departed this troublesome life,and went to euerlasting rest.

He left behinde him certaine commentaries vppon Ge= nesis, and Paules Epistle to the Colossions, vppon certayne of the Psalmes, and Cantica Canticorum, written by hym in the Spanish tong very learnedly, and like one plentiful= ly indued with the holy ghost,the which are reserued in the custodye of diuers men of trust and credite as iewells and tresures to the behoofe of the church.The which allbeit they were both learned and godlye, yet other thinges whych he wrote in prison, doe so farre exceede them for the speciall af= fections moued (no doubt) by the spirite of God and expres= sed therein,that a man may easelye see the force of affliction and tribulation,how muche it auayleth the godly for deepe iudgement in matters of diuinitie. But wythin two or three yeares after his death the new Inquisitours thinking that the other who had the examination of him,had delt a great deale moze easely with him thē became Inquisitours, seing that they could not cite his spirite to apeare befoze thē which was in quietnes and rest , therfoze they determined to shew theyz spite towardes his carcas & dzy bones. Wherbpon they digged him out of his graue, & buried in his place and bnder his name a puppit of straw, bzought his cozps bppon the scaffold, and bsed it in such sozt as they would haue done him selfe that sitteth in heauen with Chziste on the right hand of hys father, if they could haue caught hym here in earth . But God that dwelleth one high , laugheth at these theyz follies.

Doctor Constantino de la fuente *a canon and preacher in the Cathedrall church in* Siuil.

IT was the singuler good hap of the church (sauing that it heaped condemnation bppon it the moze)that Constantino should come in place after so godly a man as D. Ægidio was : by whose meanes Constantino in very shozte space merueloussy increased and pzofited in bertue and sound religion. And therfoze,fozasmuch as the wozthines of this mā was so great , I am iustsy occasioned somewhat largesy to discourse of him in this histozy . Wherin I feare it greatsy, lest I shall not be able sufficientsy to set out the commendation of that man accozdingsy as his wozthines deserueth: Foz how can I deuise to sound thy pzaypses sufficientsy , being y most famous diuine of any y hath liued in our daypes, & one whome God of his aboundant gracious goodnes, dyd indue so plētifully with so rare qualities, as hardsy are to be sene together agayne in one man, so that well they may be wondered at,but neuer balued to their wozke.It is a strāge matter, and almost incredible, and yet true that I will repozt of him , foz I am able to iustifie it : that of many thousands of men that haue bewed this mans qualities thozousy,there was neuer any, but eyther loued him passingsy, oz els hated him spitefully. Therefoze as he was ozdeyned to be both beloued & hated so extremity : so had he many malicious

cious enemies, & as many earnest frends & fauourers. And
here I comprehend not vnder the name of frends, such as he
himselfe bare good will vnto, more then I accompt those
men among the number of his foes to whome he wished e-
uill: but onely such as he knew not, and yet they with all
their harts both loued and honoured him. For those that he
bare speciall affection vnto (forasmuch as he knew the vn-
constancie of this world) were onely one or two in all hys
life time. Notwithstanding, such as he thought woorthy
to be beloued in respect of their vertue, he woulde pleasure any way that possible he could. His youth, in comparison of other young men that be studious, perhaps he bestowed not so praysably: yet so, as it was no hinderaunce to him
in his age afterwards, but that he passed it with great commendation. For being a man of a meruailous pleasaunt
wit, and in matters of disport pleasauntly disposed (otherwise very faire condicioned) he diminished his credit and
estimatiō somwhat after he was grown in yeares, by vsing
himself ouer much to iesting. Howbeit, that was only with
his aduersaries, who notwithstanding would as greatly
haue disliked him on the other side if he had bene as sage
and graue as eyther Curius or Cato. And in deede there are
a great sort of his sayinges in many mens mouthes, which
being well weighed and considered are more woorthy to be
called wise Apothegmes, then pleasaunt tauntes: but they
are such as cannot aptly be expressed, & retayne their garce
in any other language. Neyther did he so commonly vse to
iest at any or so finely, as at those hypocrites the Monkes
and priestes that had a certayne pride in themselues, of a foo
lish pharisaicall opinion of holines, being but in mere toyes
and trifles. But most of all he vsed to girde the folish preachers, wherof there was neuer any age so full, whome the
holy scriptures accompt to be the vilest sort of people that
are, comparing them to salt that hath lost his sauour, and
wil serue to no vse. Neyther can any man sufficiently mer-

uell

uell at hys passing wit that being in a barbarous age, whe
al good learning was almost lost, and forgotten among men
in this vniuersall time of ignoraunce, he did either only at-
teine to grounded knowledge, or had very few his equalles.
And in the toungues to wit, the Latin, Greeke, and Hebrue
became so notable without any teacher, that he alone had
bene sufficiently able to restore them vnto vs of hym selfe.
As for all other kind of learnyng that serued to the furnishing of a perfect oratour he attained not only a superficiall
sight therin but a perfect & absolute knowledge. With these
helpes he fel to ye study of holy scriptures, wherin he became
so wel learned euen in his youth, ye whensoeuer he was occasioned to shew his opinion concernyng any matters, or
the significatiõ of any termes therin, he left nothing vntouched that any might doubt of, except such as were blynd but
sardes and could see nothing. Moreouer, he was so eloquent
in his own tong, that all his auditours were brought into a
great admiration therof. Being thus furnished with these
good giftes, he fel to preaching, and without comparisõ passed all thē of this age or of the age before him. Besides these
good qualities, he had a singular good discretion and iudgmēt
in all his doinges, the whiche he had atteined vnto, partly
by great study, partely by long practise and experience, but
specially by great search and profound knowledge in holy
scriptures, wherin he plainely saw, as it had bene from the
top of a high tower, whatsoeuer all the world did. At such
tymes as he preached (which commonly was about eight of
the clocke) there was so great resort to his Sermon that after 4.of the clocke in the morning, and many times from 3.
it was hard to get a good place in all the church where a mã
might conueniently heare hym. Notwithstanding all thys
fauour and affection which al the people bare vnto hym (except the malicious hypocrites) besides his meat and drinke
for his reasonable sustenaunce, and his library which was
but meanely furnished, he gathered together no other great
sub-

substance: for he was a man farre from those 2. plagues that haue alwayes infected the church of Christ, couetousnes and ambitiō. In so much that being offered a good Canonship in the church of Toledo which many a mā of his order would thinke him selfe in happy case if he might attaine vnto, he was so farre from the greedy desire thereof, that he contemned it rather, caring not for it, but after his accustomed maner iested at it merely. For immediatly after the death of ȳ bishop of Vtica that was preacher in the Cathedral church, the whole Chapiter with one consent offred him that place which they commonly call the opposition, and sent for him thether very honorably. Whereunto he made them answere without any great deliberation, that he had great cause to yeld thē many thankes for their good opinions conceaued of him, in that they thought him worthy of so great a dignity, saying ȳ he would do the best he coulde to requite their curtesies. Howbeit, forasmuch as his fathers and his grandfathers bones buried many yeares agoe were now in rest and quiet, he would in no case doo any thing wherby the rest that they wer in might be interrupted. And this (I suppose) was the summe of his answere & the very wordes which he spake. For about ȳ time there grew hote quarells, betwixt the Archbishop surnamed Siliceus (a mā of famous memory forsooth) & the Chapiter of the same church. The Archbishop was hated of the chiefe men of the chapiter, because he had openly and in opprobrious maner reported them to be descended of the line of the Iewes: and they on the other side being mē in good estate & not able to beare these reproches thought to be euen with this foolish bishop that came from cart and plough, and by good hap (as a mā may say) without al respect of learning or honesty, was preferred to ȳ highest dignitie in all Spaine next vnder ȳ king, & because he was a troubler of common quiet they purposed to worke him all the spight that might be: by meanes wherof none were spared that had bene buried by the space of a hundreth yeares

but

but ẙ this good archbishop vnder pretence of religion made inquiry of the Canons fathers, grandfathers, & great grãd-fathers, driuing them to deriue their petegræ out of theyr graues. The which foolish and vngodly controuersies Con-stantino tooke occasion to quippe them for, at such time as he was set for to supply that place. In like sort not long before he refused a Cannõship in ẙ church of Quenca both rich to the purse and worshipfull besides for estimation, situate in his owne natiue soyle. Moreouer, being the first man that brought the knowledge of true religion into Siuil, he did so plainely set it forth and so sincerely, so sharpely rebuked those pedlers that solde all their packs of pardons and other fansies for pence, laying such things so sore to theyr charge, that notwithstanding they saw full well ẙ he would proue a plague both to them and their whole generatiõ, yet could they not find any iust cause to accuse him of but to theyr own shame, & yet ceased they not to hate him deadly. How-beit he tooke away theyr stings so clene, that they could ne-uer come conueniently to poyson him: neyther did he slacke for all that to set forth the truth, notwithstanding that he knew they lay in wayt for him priuely. And surely it was the singular prouidence of God which so blessed that citie, that there should be in that church at once thrée such notable men and so excellently learned, Constantino, Aegidio, and Vargas, which before times were students together in diuinity, and now furtherers of vertue and good religion with one consent, and with like zeale. For Vargas did read vppon the Gospell after Mathew, in the Cathedrall church, and that being done, did afterwards take in hand to expoũd ẙ Psalter. Aegidio preached dayly: Constantino not so oftē as Aegilio, but to as great fruit and edifying, continuing all together, ech man in his rowme, till afterwards, that God sent stormy tempestes, to the ende to try ech mans building, that Vargas in the middest of this hurly burly, while he and his aduersaries were bickering together, died

Con

Cõstantino was set foz by ý Emperour & his sonne Phillip and fozced to fozsake Siul. So that D. Aegidio was left alone like a lambe among a fozt of wolues to minister matter foz a tragedy: the which is already declared in his histozy. After whose death Constantino left the Emperours Court, where he had gotten both wisedome and learning and returned to Siul agayne to set fozward the light of the gospel that had bene stopped foz a while. The which thing he did with as much zeale as euer he did befoze time: so that both he himselfe was very well esteemed, and his sermons liked of all the people exceedingly. It was also hys chaunce by reason of a certayne ozder taken by the whole chapiter, to be appoynted the next lent after his comming to pzeach euery other day in the Cathedzall church. The which when he refused to take vpõ him because of his late sicknes, being scarcely well recouered, he was cõpelled to doo it perfozce, notwithstanding that he was so weake a creature that he was sometime caried thether, and foz faintnes once oz twise in a sermon cõpelled to dzinke a dzaught of wine to refresh himself wall, & to make him able to hold out til ý end of hys houre. The which (doubtles) was a very straunge sight to behold: & yet such fauour euery mã bare towards him, ý he was dispensed withall to vse that liberty. Afterwardes being restozed to his health, he deuised a ready way to set fozward his purpose, and such as none had trodẽ in befoze him. Foz by his meanes one Doctoz Escobar a famous man in Siul, both foz life and learning, to whom the Senate of the City by common consent had committed the charge and ouersight of the Colledge of childzen (commonly called the house of learning) conferring with Constantino about the matter, translated the reuenue that some dzonken chaplein would haue deuoutly dzonke foz hys soule, into a yearely stipened, towards the maintenance of a Diuinity lecture in the same colledge, whereof this Constantino was chosen reader. Who both happely toke in hãd & effectually pursued

Cr.y. that

that profitable exercise : beginning first wyth Salomons Prouerbs, the booke of the preacher, and Cantica canticorū. Which after he had passed through very lernedly, he proceded into Job, and expounded it more then halfe. All which works are extant at this day in written hand, gathered very painfully by one of his auditours named Bab. Wherin it shal appeare hereafter, as I can haue leasure to publish thē, how farre he hath exceded all that euer haue written vppon these bookes hetherto, and how excellently well learned he was. But some euill spirit enuying the good successe of that Citie, vnder the pretence of feruēt zeale, caused hym to forsake that course wherin he ranne before, and afterward incombred him so many wayes, that he was neuer cleare quit of all till his dying day. About what tyme welneare it happened that ý chief Canonship (which was first founded for a preacher) fell voyd in the Church of Siuil by reason of Doctor Aegidios death. Wherunto the whole Chapiter woulde willingly haue chosen Constantino as one whome they thought of desert worthy the place, for the notable gifts that both they and all the whole Citie saw in hym of a long tyme while he continued preacher there, but that it would not stād with ý rules of their house to admit hym thereunto without oppositions. For vppon their last errour in chusing D. Aegidio, immediatly after, they entred an order, that none thenceforth should be admitted to enioy that place without their accustomed kind of oppositions biuall in all Churches. Whereas Constantino on the other side had alwayes scorned & derided those ceremonies, as toyes not much vnlike the contentions of iugglers and minstrels for the best games. Moreouer one Valdesio byshop of Sui & a courtier, owing Constātino a priuy grudge from the first tyme that he preached before the Emperour and grew into his fauour, was very earnestly in hand with the Chapiter, pressyng them with their owne decrœ, after he vnderstood ý they were about to vndoe it againe. Whervpon

vpon there was a day apointed fo2 the oppoſition, and publiſhed in the moſt famous Cityes in Spayne, ſo that diuers
came flocking, as it had bene a ſo2te of crowes about a cary-
an. But the wiſer ſo2t kept themſelues away from encoun-
tring wyth hym, fo2 the great fauoure and eſtimation that
he was in,ſo that there were but onely two that aboade the
b2unt:the one called Maiuelo a Cannon of Alcala the other
a Cannon of Malaga, hoping by like to get ſome great booty
thereby. Howbeit the firſt vppon better aduiſement returned home againe ſho2tly after to Alcaia : the other Cannon
of Malaga bolſtered by the Archbiſhop to ſpight Conſtantino withall,wilfully continued the ſkirmiſh. At the length,
Conſtantino being ouercome th2ough the great entreatye
and perſuaſion of the Chapiter,but eſpecially moued by the
impo2tunate ſute of a frend of his, to whom I wiſh he had
not yeloed ſo muche in this (fo2 then perhaps he had bene a-
liue at this time) reſolued himſelfe to ſtande fo2 the Canon-
ſhip,and to diſpute after the accuſtomed o2der:and ſo by ful-
filling that ceremony, he of Malaga was ſent to ſhake hys
eares,& the Chapiter p2euailed againſt the biſhop. There
was alſo at the ſame time a little 3eale which blinded Conſtantino, leſt perhaps ſome p2ater ſhuld haue ſtept in place
that would alwayes be barking againſt good and godly doctrine,whereas by his accepting of the ſame place there was
a certaine likelihoode and hope,y the doctrine thereby ſhould
haue the mo2e free paſſage. In reſpecte whereof, he was the
mo2e willing,rather then fo2 any greedy o2 couetous deſire
of attaining any welth thereby, the which vice he alwayes
contemned with a manly courage.Wheruppon,his aduer-
ſarye that ſtode againſte hym perceauing himſelfe vnable
to weigh with hym, eyther fo2 learning, countenaunte, o2
fauour which he found at the Chapiters hand,bent hymſelf
wholy to take exceptions to his perſon and to diſable him y
way. Firſt he beganne to obiect againſt him all hys youth-

ly toyes, namely mariage, ψ which was before he entred into orders, charging him that neither he was rightly priested, nor came by his degrée of Doctorship orderly. On the other side a meruelous rable of ψ hipocrites that had ben of his old acquaintaunce began to be galled a fresh seing hym so highly preferred, in so much that they fell to reuiue olde matters concerning diuers points of religion, vrging them more ernestly then they had done before tyme, and that in the Court of the Inquisitours, wherein Valdesio his aduersary sat as iudge. Notwithstanding in the middest of these broyles, Constantino hoping vpō the good wils of the Chapiter, was installed, and whiles ψ controuersies were at the hotest, there was much busines in that Church by meanes of certayne bookes of Iulian Pequenno, wherof I made mētiō before. In the which stormes what place was there wherein Constantino might shroud his head? And yet being brought before ψ Inquisitours, albeit he had thorowly displeased all his aduersaries in ψ former braules before, yet notwithstanding he auoided all their quarels piked agaynst him by his quicke & ready answers (after his accustomed maner) so casely, that they could in no case get him to make any open protestation of his fayth, by the which theyr hope was to compasse and circumuent him. And in very déede he had escaped at the length, but that God of his wonderfull prouidence compelled hym sore agaynst hys will, briefly and plainly to confesse his truth. For, nigh about the same time there was a very honest and a substanciall wydow, named Isabel Martinez apprehended, in whose house Constantino had hidde certayne speciall bookes for feare of the Inquisitours, which he might not auow the kéeping of in Spaine without presente perill. Whose goodes beinge sequestred accordinge to the custome of the Inquisition, her sonne one Francisco Beltran had conueighed diuers Chestes of the best stuffe that hys mother had, because he would saue somewhat, so that these Cormorauntes should

not

not deuout all. The which thing comming to the Inquisitours eares, by meanes of his vntrusty seruaunt who disclosed it, was the occasion that they sent immediatly one Don Luys Sotelo their Alguazil to demaund those Chests. Who resorted vnto hym accordingly & as he begā to say his message soberly, Beltran forgetting the Chests and supposing that the cause of his comming had bene for Constantinos bookes, tooke the tale out of his mouth and sayd vnto him: Don Luys, I know whereabout you come, and therefore if you will promise me on your honesty quietly to depart vppon the receit thereof, I will shew you them. The Alguazil meaning the Chestes (as for the bookes he neither came for them, nor knew of any such before) promised hym so to do. Whereupon Beltran caried him forthwith into a secret place farre within the house, and plucking forth a stone or two in the wale, shewed him Constantinos iewels of paper in dœde, but farre more precious then gold or pearle. Whereat the Alguazil being somwhat astonied, to find that which he looked not for, told him that he came to demaund no such maner of thing, but certayne Chestes of his mothers gœds, which he had purloyned from the Sequester. As for his promise made vnto him for his quiet departure, he sayd he was not bound thereby otherwise, but that he must nedes cary both him and his bookes to the Inquisitours. Thus by these meanes came all Constantinos writings out of corners to light, and to ý Inquisitonrs handes, contrary both to his owne expectatiō and his aduersaries, which would haue geuen a great pece of money to haue come by them before. And among other of his writinges there was one great volume found writtē throughout with his owne hand, wherein (as the Inquisitours them selues reported in their sentence which they gaue vppon him afterwards standing vppon ý scaffold) he did openly and playnely in maner, as it were for his owne satisfactiō, handle these speciall poyntes, that is to say: the state of the church. The true church and the Popes church, whome he called very Antichrist: the sacrament of the Lords supper: the inuention of the Masse, wherein he sayd that the whole world was deceiued and abused through ignoraunce of the holy scriptures the iustification of a Christian man: Purgatory which he termed the Wolues head, saying that it was a deuise of the monkes to fade their owne bellies: also Bulles and Popish pardons, mans merites, Christ, and other articles of Christian religion. The which tooke so soone as it came to the Inquisitours hands, they demaunded of hym if he knew his owne hand: howbeit he shifted the of frō theyr purpose a good while, and droue them of from day to day, til at the last vnderstāding the will of God, who had now takē away all euasions from hym, he acknowledged hys owne hand, and confessed it to be his owne writyng, protesting openly, that all thinges therein conteyned were ful of truth and sincerity. Therfore (said he) take ye no further paynes in seking witnesses to testifie against me, sithe you haue so plaine and perfect a confession of my opinion & beliefe, but do and deale with me as it shall please you. After the which examination and aunswere, he remayned in prison by the space of two whole yeares: where partly by occasion of hys corrupt and naughty diet (though he were not a man greatly curious or dainty therin before tyme) but chiefely, of very sorow cōsuming him to see so much labour, both of his owne and others his fellowes spent in vayne vppon that good church, which now was so miserably sacked, he fell first to be a litle crased, and afterwardes being not able to abyde the exceding heate of the Sunne which made his prison like a hothouse vnto him, was fayne to strip himselfe into hys bare shirt and so to continue both day and night. By occasiō whereof he fell sicke of the bloudy flixe and within 15. dayes after dyed amiddes ỹ filth and soyle of the prison, rendring vp his sweete soule to Christ, for the promotion of whose glory he had oftentimes before aduentured it most maniful-

ly

ly. And in this tyme of his sickenes as well as at the houre of his death, there was present with hym a certayne young man, a Monke of S. Isidors cloister both vertuous and well disposed, who also was prisoner there for religion at the same time and put in the same prison with him to kepe hym company. This Monkes name was Fernandez. Perhappes in the eyes of foolish worldlings this Constantino semed to dye, but in very dæde he resteth in peace. As for the cruell tortures, which other haue accustomably bene tormented withall, the truth is, he neuer tasted any, not for any regard that these cruell termagantes had of such a man as he was (whose displeasure he had earnestly procured agaynst hym by his sharpe and quicke aunswers while he was prisoner) but ether, for that they determined to differre his punishmēt, meaning to deteine him in prison a longer space, to the intent to discourage him and to kæpe other that fauoured his doctrine any way, or were entred in that religion in continuall awe: or els, because they thought not that he should haue bene taken forth of their hands so suddenly. Wherupon, the Inquisitours bruted a rumour abroad to the same end & purpose, to daunt such as had bene his schollers, that they might come tremblyng into the Court, and accuse themselues before they were sent for, vppon hope of the Inquisitours mercy: causing it to be noysed, that he in his life beyng vpon the racke had confessed vnto them of diuers that were his auditours and scholers. To the whiche ende and purpose, diuers of the nexte pryson adioynyng to his, were subornd to affirme that they heard the cries & shrikes which he made at the tyme of his tormēting. Therfore now after his death, seing him to be taken out of theyr hands by Gods good meanes, so that now they had hym no more aliue among them to extend their cruelty vpon, they determined notwithstādīg to worke him such poore spight as they could, in derogating from the good estimation and report which he had of all men, spreadyng false and slaunderous

rous tales vpõ him that he should strike himselfe in a vaine with a péece of a broken glasse, to auoyd both shame & paine. There were also openly in the streates ouer all the City diuers filthy and sclaunderous ditties song by boyes, in hys dispraysle: but whether they were published by procurement of the Inquisitours, or some of their parasites, or of mere malice deuised and set out by the foolish and variable people, God knoweth, but the other is the more likely. Al so against the day of their solemne triumph, his corps was taken out of the graue, & in place thereof a puppit of straw put, & afterwardes set vp in a pulpit so artificially, resting the one hand vppon the pulpit, and holding the other vpright, that it resembled Constantino very liuely in such sort as he was wont to preach. And no doubt but that dumbe Image did preach as effectually in many mens harts at that instant as euer he him selfe had done being a liue, in derission of whome this puppit was made. Then, at what time sentence was to be geuen vppon him (to the hearing whereof diuers came from places farre distant from Siui.) the Inquisitours cõmaunded that it should not be pronounced out of the pulpit where other iudgemēts were accustomably read, but caused the Image to be brought into their holy Courte, and there to haue sentence published: which place was so high that the people could not well vnderstand what was read. Whereupon Calderon the temporall Magistrate thinking it not conuenient, and that some other subtelty was ment thereby, moued the Inquisitours in open audience that iudgement might be geuen in the accustomed place, or els read in such sort that ÿ people might vnderstand vpon what occasions they had condemned him. Whereunto when the Inquisitours gaue no great eare but proceded as before, there began to be a great tumulte among the people, forasmuch as they could not well brooke that iniury, nor indéede would not haue put it vp as it séemed, but that they saw Calderon somewhat more quicke

with

with the Inquifitours, ꝫ to tel thē their duties once againe: so that they commaunded the Image to be caried into the accuſtomed place, and ſentence to be pronounced aloud to ſatiſfie the people withall. The reading whereof, occupyed about an howꝛe and an halfe: and the chiefe matter contayned therein , was that which J haue recited befoꝛe out of Conſtantinos booke. Marie the Inquiſitours added moꝛeouer that of purpoſe and vpon good conſideration they had omitted many things that were ſo hoꝛrible , ſo wicked, and ſo ſtraunge, that it was ſoꝛe againſt Gods foꝛbod, to vtter them in common audience. There be diuers of this mans woꝛks extant that haue paſſed ỹ pꝛint. Firſt a bꝛiefe ſumme of Chꝛiſtian religion. Alſo one other diſcourſe in the ſame argument moꝛe at large, but ſomwhat imperfect oꝛ rather ſcarcely halfe finiſhed: foꝛ he purpoſed to haue compꝛehended the whole body of Chꝛiſtian religion, in two tomes. In the foꝛmer he treated of fayth: In the other he thought to haue handled the ſacraments,and to haue ſpoken of woꝛkes ꝫ generally of the duety of a Chꝛiſtian man.As foꝛ ỹ foꝛmer part , it was already publiſhed two oꝛ thꝛee yeares agone: whereby he pꝛocured to him ſelfe ſome diſpleaſure and ſuſpicion of hereſie among the common ſoꝛt of learned men, foꝛaſmuch as entreating of faith he did not plainly inueigh againſt the Lutherans, noꝛ attributed any pꝛeeminence to the biſhop of Rome, but had wꝛitten rather in derogation of pardons , of purgatoꝛy, of mans merits, ꝫ ſuch other like trifles, then in the auauncement thereof,vpon ỹ which ſuſpicions being examined, he would anſwere thē that ſuch matters as they wanted in his woꝛke were moꝛe pertinent to his ſecond tome,wherein he purpoſed to diſcourſe of them moꝛe at large . But this other volume neuer came to light, except perhaps it were that which was hidden in the widowes Houſe ꝫ came to the Inquiſitours hands,the ſpeciall points whereof they publiſhed, as J haue befoꝛe declared . Moꝛeouer he ſet foꝛth a Catechiſme , which perhaps

in other places els where of more fredome and liberty was
not greatly accompted of, but yet in these places of darknes
and ignorounce, and vnder such tiranny, it gaue much lyght
to many. There be also extant v. sermons which he made
vppon. vj of the first verses of the first Psalme. Wherin the
learned may see, aswell the profound learning that was in
him, as also his singular art for conueyaunce. But of all
his workes, which surely were as learnedly written, and as
godly as any that euer were read in Spayne, the confession of a sinner not passing two or three shetes long, exceded
all the rest, both for the zeale, learning, and eloquence vttered therein, most liuely expressing the affections of a Christian man, incident to such an argument. First he bryngeth
in a man before the iudgement seat of God, making him to
see, and liuely to lament his owne filthines and abbomina-
tion, to cast of all whatsoeuer these Phariseys flattering
themselues with theyr owne righteousnes were wont to
couer our nakednes withall, being either deuised or established by man, and therein he peruseth all the x. Commaundements orderly, confessing him guilty of the breach therof,
and therewithall maketh so plaine and so absolute an exposition of the whole lawe, in that short summarye, that in
suche a breuiat (be it spoken without offence to any) I haue
not hetherto sene any so lightsome. In the ende he clotheth
them with the wedding garment of Christes righteousnes
by fayth, wherewith alonely he encourageth and embolde-
neth man before the face of God, as muche as he discomfor-
ted him before whe as he brought him to the perfecte knowledge of himselfe and the consideration of his owne case and
estate. Finally, there is no one iot that concerneth Christian religion, but he hath touched it, referring it to some purpose in that briefe table: nor any affection that can be in a
man, from the very first letter of the law till the last end of
the Gospel, and the fruition of the heauenly habitation, but
he hath most liuely expressed it. Neither had he bene euera-

ble

ble to deuise such a péece of worke, notwithstāding his passing giftes of nature and helps of art, except he had first lear
ned them by often experiēce in himselfe. All ý which bookes
of his writing, worthy (no doubt) to be reserued for euer, albeit the Inquisitours had a litle before vnawares allowed,
yet at this time they cōdemned thē: not for any thing found
in them worthy of condemnation (as they themselues testified in their sentence vpon him) but because there shoulp
be nothing extant that might remaine as a monument or a
memoriall sounding any wayes to the cōmendation of him
whom they had holden accursed. Lastly, they shewed their
poore spight vpon that good mans dry bones, which they dig
ged out of the earth, & vpon that counterfait Image made
to his likenes. Howbeit he himselfe being exalted aboue
the clouds and taken out of their chaines, and deliuered frō
their vniust iudgements (besides the losse of these notable &
worthy monuments mencioned before) hath caused a great
number of his familiar frends and acquaintaunce comfort-
lesse to sit, lamenting and bewayling the misse of such
a man. O detestable tyranny that deseruest a thousand curses, seing thou canst not restore them a-
gain, what amends wilt thou be able to make
to the world for the death of so many godly
men as thou hast most shamefully
slayne and murdered?

FINIS.

A Register of such persons as were burned at Siuil in the yeare of our Lord.
1559.

DOn Iuan Ponce de Leon *sonne to* Don Rodrigo de Leon, *Earle of* Baylen.

Iuan Gonçales *a preacher borne at* Palma.

Catalina de Herera,
Maria Gonçales. } *Sisters to the same preacher.*

Hernando de Sant Iuan *borne at* Malaga.

Francisco Foxio Morzillo *a Monke of S. Isidors cloyster in* Siuil *brother to* Sebastiano Foxio Morzillo, *the late writer in Philosophy. Of this* Morzillo *mention is made, Folio.* 71.

Miguel Valenciano *a monke of the same cloyster.*

Medel de Espinosa *an embroderer condemned onely for receyuing into his house certayne of* Luthers *woorkes that were brought out of* Germany.

Luys de Abrego *a man that was wont to get his liuing by writing of Missals and such other Churchbookes.*

Iuan de Cafra *father to him that escaped out of prison, wherof mention is made Fol.* 4. *whose picture notwithstanding was burned at the same tyme.*

Francisca Lopez de Texeda de Mançanilla *wyfe vnto the same partie that so escaped.*

Carlos de Brusas *a Flemming.*

Anthonio de Bulderec *a Frencheman.*

Maria Bohorques
Maria Virues
Isabel de Vaena,
Maria de Corneso } *Of these mention is made in the history more at large, Fol.* 66.

Diego Ortiz *otherwise called* Iuan Christiano.

¶ In the yeare of our Lord God 1560. The 2. of December were burned these that followe.

Vlian Hernandes *borne at* Valuerda. *This mã was a corrector to the printe of suche bookes as were printed at* Geneua *in the Spanish tonge, and afterwardes for the zeale he had to set forward the Gospell, returned into* Spayne, *where after he had continued certayne yeares distributing Testamentes and other godly bookes that were in the Spanishe tounge to diuers men and in sundry places, he returned into* Flaunders, *and by occasion of a certaine booke which he had gẽe a Smith who shewed the same secretly to a priest, that complayned therof further to the Inquisitours, this* Iulian *was sought for, and apprehended by certayne Familiars that hunted after him in his way goyng to a city called* Palmia, *and by them was cast in prison, afterwardes condemned by the Inquisitours and died most constantly for the profession of the Gospell of* Christ, *hauing great disputations duryng the tyme of his imprisonmẽt with a learned Clarke and a famous Diuine one* D. Hernand Kodriguez.

Iuan de Leon *borne at* Pallentia *a monke of S.* Isidors *cloyster the same that was apprehended in* Zeland *as he was taking shippe to go into* England *at the departyng of the Englishmen from* Geneua *after the death of* Queene *Mary*,

Guiliermo Brocemolez *a Mariner*,

Nicholas Burton *an Englishman of whome mention is made in the booke of* Martires.

Francisca de Chauez *a nonne of the cloyster of S. Elizabeth in a citie called* Gibraleon.

Bartolome Fabricio de Bayena *a Frenchman.*

Anna de Ribera *wyfe to* Hernando *de Sant Iuan*,

Francisca Ruiz *the wyfe of one* Francisco Duran *of Siuil.*

Leonor Gomez *the wyfe of one* D. Hernando Nunnez *a phisition in the citie of* Gibraleon.

Eluira Nunnez *daughter to the same* D. Hernando *by hys former wyfe.*

Lucia Gomez *daughter to the sayd* Leonor Gomez *by her former husband.*

Dd.iiij. Leonor

Leonor Gomez *wife to an other* Hernando Nuhnez *an Apothecarie in the citie of* Lepe.

Iuana de Maçuelos *one of* Siuil.

Melchior de Salto *a citizen of* Granata.

In this acte also were burned the bones & picture of D. Ægidio *and the bones and picture of* D. Constantino de la fuente, *of whome mencion is made in the bookes more at large in their seuerall histories.*

At the same tyme likewise was red the sentence of the Inquisitours geuen vpon that noble woman Donna Iuana de Bohorgues *which dyed amiddes the tormentors handes, wherin she was declared and pronounced to be guiltlesse, and innocent, as is also described before more at large in the history. Diuers and sundry others both men & women aswell of nobilitie as of worship were at the same tyme condemned to perpetuall imprisonment and their goodes confiscated.*

In the yeare of our Lord God, 1563,

the 10. of Iuly, did suffer these that followe.

BArtolome Kebret *a Frenchman.*

Roberto Filippo *borne at* Trigueros en el condado.

Iorge Cohinchlo *of* Brudges *a Flemmyng.*

Francisco de Mone *one of* Zeland.

Gulicrmo de Vtrecte *a Hollander.*

Henrico del Opilbo *a Hosier.*

In the same Acte there was brought into the scaffolde one called Fray Domingo de Guzman *a Dominicane Fryer and a Preacher one of the cloyster of* S. Paule *in* Siuil *who hauyng brought diuers Lutherane bookes (as they commonly terme the in* Spayne*) lent the same to diuers in* Siuil *and beganne to professe the gospell and to preache it to others, wheruppon he was apprehended and comited. But forasmuch as he was bastarde brother to the* Duke de Medina Sidonia*, and in hope of preferment to some Archbishoprike, he openly recanted. How beit the Inquisitours fearyng to suffer any that had bene at any tyme enclined towardes like religion to be preferred to*

any

any such place of authoritie and countenaunce, did first commaund that all his bookes which were aboue 1000 volumes should be burnt before his face, and his recantation notwithstanding awarded him to perpetuall prison.

Diuers others haue bene burned since that tyme in the same Citie whose names the reporters hereof cannot come by as yet God graunt that in tyme they may likewise come to light.

A register of such as were executed

or otherwise punished by imprisonment and confiscation of their goods in Vallolet the 25. of May. 1559.

Juan Garsia *a goldsmith one that commonly vsed to geue the protestants intelligence of the sermons (which for the most part were by night) was most trayterously betrayed by his owne wife, who following her husband on a tyme priuily & finding the place of his resorte, detected the same to the Inquisitours.*

El Licenciado Herrera *borne at* Toro *chiefe customer in the borders of* Nauarre.

D. Caçalla *who before his going to the stake was first disgraded vppon the scaffold.*

Donna Katalina de Ortega *in common reputation a widow daughter to the* Fischal *the kings atturney in the court of* Inquisition, *and at that time a chiefe Councellour to the high Inquisitour, howbeit she was priuily contracted and maried to the same* Doct. Caçalla.

Francisco de Biuero *a priest brother to the same* D. Caçalla, *hauing his tong pinched betwixt a clefte sticke because he remayned most constant in the open profession of his fayth.*

Donna Beatrix *of the order of the Nonnes which be commonly called* Beate *sister to* Doct. Caçalla *a woman had in great estimation among the people for her vertue and godlilines, who was also secretly contracted and maried to a certayne Monke of great name and fame, called* Fray Domingo de Rosas, *that was afterward burned.*

E. j.   Kata-

Katalina de ſtrada. Both young women and borne at
Iſabell Romana.   Pedrozo.

Theſe were condemned onely for denying the authority of the
Pope and his doctrine of purgatory, and for affirming that the
communion myght be celebrated wyth any common bread.
They were moreouer charged with a certaine letter written
by them to ſome of their frends that were of the ſame Religion, the which letter was at the tyme of their execution openly
redde vppon the ſcaffold.

Beſides this, Iſabell Romana was charged further that ſhe
ſhould ſay that Martin Luther was a Prophet and an Apoſtle ſent by God, and that the ſtate and order of religious men
and women (as they terme them) was a mere deuiſe of mans
inuention, foraſmuch as all Chriſtians were religious, that is
to ſay in her vnderſtanding and conſtruction, conſecrated to
God.

Chriſtoual de Campo borne at Zamora.

Chriſtoual de Pauilla a Citizen of Zamora Scholemaiſter
to the Lady Marqueſſe de Alcanizas, and with hym alſo
another Scholemaſter borne at Pallentia, and a certayne
Prieſt of the ſame countrey named Maeſtro Perez, and an
Engliſhe boye page to Don Luys de Roſas Marques of
Poza.

El Bachiler Herrezuelo an aduocate in the Citie Toro, a man
of notable learninge and godly conuerſation, and of ſuch con-
ſtancie and pacience at the hower of his death, that he ſemed
in all mens iudgements to dye without feeling any force of the
flame: who being at the hower of his death by diuers monkes
vrged with great importunitie to recant, made them anſwere
in this wiſe, that there was neuer any thing in the world that
gaue him more cauſe of admiratiõ then this that the world
ſhould be ſo blind and ſenceleſſe as not to eſpye theſe theyr
groſſe and palpable miſtes of ignoraunce and ſuperſtition.

The bones & portrature of Leonor de Biuero mother to both
the aforeſayd D. Caçalla and Franciſco de Biuero were
likewiſe burned at the ſame time.

This acte continued 9 howers, from 6 in the morning, till 2 in
the afternoone with like pompe and ſolemnitie as is ſet out in
the

the table or figure hereto annexed, the Queene being present to see the execution and continuing there till the end.

¶ The Register of such as were at the same time condemned to perpetuall imprisonment with confiscation of their goods.

DOn Luys de Roſas Marques of Poza ſonne to Don Sancho de Roſas.

Dóna Maria de Roſas a Nonne of S. Katherins cloiſter ſiſter to the ſame Marqueſſe of Poza with another Nonne alſo of the ſame cloyſter. This Donna Maria was intirely beloued of king Phillips ſiſter the Queene of Portugall by whoſe meanes and procurement ſhe was releaſed for wearyng the Sambenite and reſtored immediately into her cloyſter agayne whereat the Inquiſitours greatly repyned.

Donna Iuana Enriquez daughter to the marques de Alcanizas the wife of one Don Iuan Alonſo Mexia.

Iuan de Biuero.

Donna Iuana de Silua wife to the ſame Iuan de Biuero.

Iuan de Vlloa a knight of the order of S. Iohn borne at Toro Don Pedro de Sarmiento.

Donna Mencia de Figueroa ſometime one of the maydes of honour to the Qeene of Boheme, afterwardes maried to the ſayd Don Pedro de Sarmiento.

Donna Franciſca de çuniga daughter to a Citizen of Vallolid called Anthonio de Baeça.

Donna Conſtança de Biuero a widow, ſiſter to D. Caçalla.

Diuers other women of meane eſtate to the number of 30. were likewiſe condemned to perpetuall priſon and loſſe of that tittle ſubſtaunce which they had whoſe names we know not.

¶ The Register of thoſe that were burned in Vallolet the 8. of october anno, 1559.

DOn Carlos de Seſo an Earle.

Fray Domingo de Roſas a Dominicane Fryer, ſonne to the aforeſayd Marques of Poza, who being brought vppon the ſtage and hauing obtayned licence of the king to ſpeake a fewe wordes in the hearing of the people, beganne to diſcourſe

E.ij.   of

oy tne poyntes and articles of Chriſtiã religion Whereupon the king being in preſence commaunded to remoue him, neuertheleſſe he procedeed till two of the garde tooke him & perforce ſet their engine of wodde vppon his tonge (Which in the treatiſe before is termed a Barnacle)and ſo carried him from the ſcaffold, accompanied with a number of monkes aboue a hundred, ſlocking about him, rayling and making exclamation agaynſt him, ſome of them vrging him to recant, but he notWithſtanding anſwered them With a bolde ſpirite that he Would neuer renounce the doctrine of Chriſt and ſo paſſed to the place of execution.

Pedro Caçalla *brother to* Doct. Caçalla.

Iuan Sanches *otherwiſe called* Iuan Fernandez, *ſometime ſeruant to* Doct. Caçalla, *the ſame partie that was taken in* Zeland *With* Iuan de Leon *as they were taking paſſage into* England, *whereof mention is made fol.*76.

El Licenciado Diego Sanches de Logronno *a Prieſt.*

Donna Eufraſina *a Nonne of the Cloyſter of* S. Clare.

Donna Catalina Reynoza *a Nonne of* Belen *of the order and profeſſion of the* Barnardines *daughter to* Ieronimo de Reynozo *baron of* Auzillo.

Donna Marina de Gueuara a Nonne *of the ſame houſe &* one diſcended of the chiefe of the nobilitie.

Donna Margarita de Santiſtiban, *a Nonne of the ſame cloyſter likewiſe.*

Katalina de Miranda, *of the ſame houſe.*

Pedro Sotelo *a Citizen of* Palo *in* Zamora.

Franciſco del Almarço *a towne in the Dioces of* Oſma.

The Register of ſuch as in the ſame Acte Were
condemned to perpetuall impriſonment with
the confiſcation of all their ſubſtaunce.

DOnna Iſabel de Caſtilla, *the Lady & Wife of* Don Carlos *Earle of* Seſo.

Donna Catalina de Caſtilla *Neeſe to* Don Diego de Caſtilla.

Donna Franciſca çunega.

Donna Filippa de Heredia, *a Nonne of the houſe of* Belen de de Medina de Ruiſeco.

Donna Catalina de Alcaras, *a Nōne of the ſame cloyſter.*

Madalena Fernandez, *of* Valuerda.

Anna de Medoça, *a widowe*

Anna de Caſtro.

Donna Tereza, *the wife of one* Anthonio de Torres.

Franciſco de Coca.

Leonor de Toro.

Iſabel de Pedroza, *the wife of one* Iuan de ſtrada.

Catalina de Herera del Pedrozo.

In the ſame ⁊Acte alſo were burned the bones ⁊and picture
of a certayne woman named Iuana Sanchez, *who dyed*
in priſon, and foraſmuch as in the tyme of her impri-
ſonment ſhe refuſed to ſhriue her ſelfe to a Prieſt,
they did ſhewe this poore ſpite vppon her car-
cas and bones after her death.

⁊⁊ The faultes eſcaped correcte
in this wiſe.

Fol.	Page.	Line.	Faultes.	Corrected.
3.	b.	16.	happening vnto him	happening vpon him
10.	a.	34.	matters of ſo great	matters of no great.
11.	a.	21.	plaine terme	plaine termes.
ibem.	b.	24.	vnto thow	vnto them.
16	a.	17.	ſufficeint	ſufficient.
22	a.	16b	mens eye	mens eyes.
25.	b.	3.	poze ſwzeth	poze ſwzetche.
28.	a.	2.	bgoly matrone	gobly matrone.
30.	a.	3.	good cherie	good cheare.
35.	a.	30.	euey bzother	euery bzother.
37.	b.	3.	many time	many tymes.
37.	b.	25.	Petro a Herrera	Pedro a Herrera.
50.	a.	32.	verbiliter	verbaliter.
33.	b.	27.	foz ſwont	foz ſwant.
83.	a.	36.	Eccia Citia	Eccia a Citie.
87.	a.	14.	auerſaries	abuerſaries.
86.	a.	3.	ſwhere a D. Aegidio	ſwhereat D. Aegidio,

A declaration by Alphabet of the particularities contayned in the figure following.

A.   THe Children of the hospitall with the Clarkes attending on them to kepe thē in order and aray, singing the Letanies with Ora pro illis, for the conuertes that haue recanted.

B.   The first sort of such as haue recanted, and for penaunce go in this solemne procession without clokes like slaues, with tapers in their hands vnlighted, ropes about their neckes, gagges in their mouthes and paper hats.

C.   The other that for penaunce in like sort weare a kinde of linnen garment made like a coate armour with a S. Andrewes crosse on the backe and brest, called a Sambenite.

D.   Those that are condemned to the fire accompanied with two monkes of the order of the Iesuites labouring them to recant, and two Familiars all armed to gard them.

E. Repre- ¶The vnder Shrieffes, called Algualziles.
F. senteth. The Constables of eche parishe, called Los Iurados.
G.   The Aldermen, called Los Veintiquatros.
H.   The two Shrieffes, called Los tenientes y assistente.
I.   The Mayor, called Alguazil Mayor de la Inquisition.
K.   The noble men and Courtiers.
L.   ¶The Clarkes, Vicars, and Parish Priestes.
M.   The Deane and Chapter.
N.   The Byshop or Ordinary to disgrade such as are condemned, being within orders.
O.   The Abbots and Conents of all the orders.
P.   The Kings atturney in the Court of Inquisition called the Fischal, hauing a flagge of Turkie worke embrodered, with the Popes armes, displayed in warlike fashion, and in the toppe of his standard a crosse of siluer and gilte.
Q.   The Inquisitours which are commonly 3. in Commission.
R.   The Familiars, Procters, & Promoters belonging to the courte of Inquisition.

All these are first marshalled in the court of the Castle Triana, & so issue forth in like order, to a place in the Citie appoynted for execution, where be erected two scaffoldes, the one for the Inquisitours, the other for the penitentes and those that are condemned to the fire, where sentences are red by the Clarke in open audience, and execution done accordingly. Also, if the court lie where any such executiō is done, the prince is vsually present in person, & hath a place of estate erected to beholde the sight.

✠Jmprinted at London by Iohn Daye
dwelling ouer Aldersgate beneath
S. Martyns.
⸿Cum gratia & Priuilegio Regiæ Maiestatis
per decennium.

Lightning Source UK Ltd.
Milton Keynes UK
UKHW03f1847160818
327307UK00032B/476/P